Accounting and
Performance Measurement

ISSUES IN THE PRIVATE
AND PUBLIC SECTORS

Paul Chapman Publishing Ltd
144 Liverpool Road
London
N1 1LA

British Library Cataloguing in Publication Data
Accounting and performance measurement:
issues in the private and public sectors
1. Accounting 2. Managerial accounting 3. Expenditures, Public
I. Lapsley, Irvine II. Mitchell, F.
657
ISBN 1–85396–324–0

Published in the USA and Canada by
Markus Wiener Publishers,
114 Jefferson Road, Princeton, NJ 08540
ISBN 1-55876-140-3

Typeset by Whitelaw & Palmer Ltd, Glasgow
Printed and bound in Great Britain

A B C D E F G H   9 8 7 6

Contents

Preface   v

Contributors   vii

Part I   **The Private Sector**   1

   1   The Accounting Challenge: Performance Measurement   3
      in the Private and Public Sectors
      Irvine Lapsley and Falconer Mitchell

   2   Financial Statements and Performance Measurement   7
      Geoffrey Whittington

   3   Regulating Change – The Role of the Conceptual   18
      Statement in Standard-Setting
      Sir David Tweedie

   4   Assets' Versus Firm's Value: What if the Parts Exceed 35
      the Whole?
      William T. Baxter

   5   On the Microeconomic Foundations of Financial Ratio   40
      Analysis
      Huw Rhys and Mark Tippett

   6   Directors' Perceptions of the Effects and Values of   52
      Share Option Rewards
      Don Egginton, Geoffrey Elliott, John Forker
      and Paul Grout

   7   The Measurement of Audit Quality   77
      David Hatherly and Tom Brown

   8   Activity Performance Measures and *Tableaux de Bord*   87
      John Innes

Contents

9   The Theory of Constraints and Performance   95
    Measurement
    Chris Salafatinos

Part II   The Public Sector   107

10   Reflections on Performance Measurement in the   109
     Public Sector
     Irvine Lapsley

11   Effectiveness – The Holy Grail of Accounting   129
     Measures of Performance
     John Small

12   Governance in the National Health Service   137
     Michael Mumford

13   Pragmatic Considerations and the Joint Cost Dilemma 153
     Falconer Mitchell

14   Performance Management in the Social Services: 166
     Its Meaning and Measurement
     Sue Llewellyn

15   Accounting for the Performance of Scottish Bus   181
     Companies, 1978–1993
     George Harte

16   The Rise and Fall of Value for Money Auditing   195
     Mary Bowerman

Index   213

Preface

We conceived this book to mark the 75th anniversary of the Department of Accounting and Business Method, University of Edinburgh, which occurred in 1994. The Department is the second oldest academic accounting department in the UK. A history of the first 75 years, *Towards a Viable Academic Department*, by Dr Stephen Walker (published by the Institute of Chartered Accountants of Scotland) can be obtained from the Department. At least one of the authors of each contribution has or has had a work association with the department. Together, the contributors represent distinguished but, in terms of their research interests, disparate groups. The theme of performance measurement as a general focus for all types of accounting activity has therefore been used as a unifying force underlying this broad-based collection. Our thanks are due to all those who have contributed to it and to the Royal Bank of Scotland whose generous sponsorship of an anniversary conference for current and former members of staff provided the foundation for this book.

Irvine Lapsley
Falconer Mitchell
Edinburgh, October 1995

Contributors

William T. Baxter
Professor Emeritus, London School of Economics; formerly Lecturer in Accounting, University of Edinburgh

Mary Bowerman
Lecturer in Accounting, Sheffield University Management School; Tom Robertson Memorial Lecturer, University of Edinburgh

Tom Brown
Lecturer in Accounting, University of Edinburgh

Don Egginton
Professor of Accounting, University of Bristol

Geoffrey Elliott
Senior Lecturer, South Bank University

John Forker
Professor of Accounting, Queens University, Belfast; formerly Lecturer in Accounting, University of Edinburgh

Paul Grout
Professor of Economics, University of Bristol

George Harte
Senior Lecturer in Accounting, University of Glasgow; formerly Lecturer in Accounting, University of Edinburgh

David Hatherly
Professor of Accounting, University of Edinburgh

John Innes
Professor of Accounting, University of Dundee; formerly Senior Lecturer in Accountancy, University of Edinburgh

Irvine Lapsley
Professor of Accountancy, University of Edinburgh

Sue Llewellyn
Senior Lecturer in Accounting, University of Edinburgh

Falconer Mitchell
Professor of Management Accounting, University of Edinburgh

Michael Mumford
Senior Lecturer in Accounting, University of Lancaster; formerly Lecturer in Accounting, University of Edinburgh

Huw Rhys
Lecturer in Accounting, University of Aberystwyth

Chris Salafatinos
Lecturer in Accounting, University of Edinburgh

John Small
Vice Principal and Professor of Accountancy, Heriot-Watt University; formerly Senior Lecturer in Accounting, University of Edinburgh

Mark Tippett
Professor of Accounting, University of Aberystwyth; formerly Lecturer in Accounting, University of Edinburgh

Sir David Tweedie
Chairman, Accounting Standards Board; formerly Lecturer in Accounting, University of Edinburgh

Geoffrey Whittington
Price Waterhouse Professor of Financial Accounting, University of Cambridge; formerly Professor of Accounting and Finance, University of Edinburgh

PART I

The Private Sector

1

The Accounting Challenge: Performance Measurement in the Private and Public Sectors

IRVINE LAPSLEY and FALCONER MITCHELL

In a business context responsibility is normally accompanied by accountability. In practice, this association is effected by establishing a system of performance measurement designed to report on the performance of those with responsibility to those with authority for the assessment of that performance. The public sector has long been dominated by considerations of its impact, in terms of social benefit and public interest. But now, in both the private and public sectors an economic motive is pervasive. Consequently, accounting information on financial performance constitutes a key component of the performance-measurement systems designed and used to support structures of accountability. This applies to information flows both inside the organisation (managerial accounting) and from the organisation to its shareholders and other interested external parties (financial accounting).

Performance, however, is a complex multidimensional concept. Accounting measures are but imperfect surrogates for the reality which underlies them. As such they suffer from a number of deficiencies. These include primarily their selectivity in representing performance, the frailties of the money-measurement unit and monetary valuations in the context of inflation and imperfect markets, their susceptibility to manipulation and restricted disclosure, their understandability and interpretability, their verifiability and the motivational effect which they have on their subjects, for example in promoting emphasis on the short-run, often at the expense of the long-run, performance. These issues, in combination, evidence the challenge facing accountants to produce reliable performance reports for stakeholders in a world which is increasingly dominated by considerations of cost consciousness, quality of service and value for money.

Part I of this book examines accounting performance measurement primarily in a private sector context. Chapters 2–3 address the above challenges in the context of financial accounting and related auditing. In Chapter 2 Whittington provides an overview of the difficulties facing the reporting accountant in attempting to translate reality into summary financial statements. Perhaps, as he suggests, the answer is to take a holistic view of performance measurement with the accounting statements being viewed as only one source of evidence on corporate performance. Moreover he suggests the 'roughness' of accounting measurements should not necessarily be viewed as a limitation but as a strength because this characteristic ensures that accounting will be viewed as a general guide to performance rather than the exclusive and definitive basis for measuring it. Chapter 3 by Tweedie is complementary to this analysis as it is concerned with the standardisation of financial accounting. As chairman of the UK Accounting Standards Board, the author is in a unique position to comment on standardisation. The process is designed to reduce the susceptibility of accounting to many of the above-mentioned frailties of practice. Standardisation also improves communication as the syntax of accounting is made formal and so is known more clearly by both the producer and user of information. Moreover, standardisation itself needs a foundation to guide the standard setter. This has been termed a 'conceptual framework' and it is central to the provision of a rationale for accounting practices. Without this normative base, justifications for a standard setter's actions may be problematic. The development of this framework raises many problems of its own, however, as Tweedie describes from his 'first-hand' experience. Chapter 4 completes the trio on issues associated with producing conventional financial statements. In this Baxter explores the dilemma of the net asset value of a firm falling below its value based on its earning capacity as a whole. In typical analytical style, he assesses the implications and appropriateness of asset write-downs and concludes with some wise counsel for practice in balance sheet construction.

The two subsequent chapters focus, respectively, on the use of financial statement information (to assess and interpret performance) and the use of executive share options to influence underlying financial performance in the longer run. Rhys and Tippett are concerned with financial ratios as a means of adding the comparability and analysis of financial statements. Historically, this is an area which has lacked a conceptual foundation to guide the derivation, selection and use of ratios. The authors contribute to the under-standing and explanation of ratio analysis by exploring, at the level of the firm, the nature of the financial variables which provide the basis for ratio compu-tation. Egginton *et al.* present the results of a survey of corporate directors of UK listed companies on their views on executive share options, a means of supplementary reward aimed at obtaining congruence between executive and shareholder interests. In this way executive share options can be viewed as one means of combating the short-termism which conventional financial accounting masks and fosters.

External financial reports are independently audited as a safeguard for their reliability. Thus the quality of auditing and the nature of the audit report are important factors impinging on the process of performance measurement and assessment. In Chapter 7 Hatherly and Brown argue the case for emphasising audit quality as a development issue by giving auditors incentives to compete on grounds of audit quality and requiring them to report in a manner which emphasises the quality of their work.

Managerial accounting, being internal to the firm, escapes the constraints of statutory and professional regulation and the disclosure restrictions caused by commercial confidentiality. In this context accounting performance measurement can be more varied and innovative. The final two chapters in Part I reflect recent developments of this type. In Chapter 8 Innes first reviews how activity-based costing techniques can improve performance measurement particularly at an operational level. The enhanced visibility which they can bring to the 'hidden factory' allows management to view how resources are being used within the business. Performance reporting is also enhanced by the availability of new sets of non-financial measures, the cost drivers. As Innes highlights, this information base sits well with the French '*tableaux de bord*' approach which mixes financial and non-financial performance measures in a manner to suit the relevant commercial situation. Complementing the activity-based costing development of the last decade has been the more recent emergence of the theory of constraints. As Salafatinos explains in Chapter 9, this focuses managerial attention on sales revenue, direct costs and the velocity of throughput. This prompts the business manager to 'make money' but it should also prompt the management accountant to develop performance measures which initiate and monitor this type of operational focus.

A public sector context provides a variety of additional and different challenges to the accountant concerned with performance measurement. To many interested observers, the public sector provides a leading edge on issues of performance measurement. There are a number of factors which support such an assertion. First, the long-standing nature of public sector bodies' involvement in issues of performance measurement, which, in recent times, is reflected in a variety of initiatives, particularly from the 1980s onwards, but which is preceded by the compilation and analysis of statistics in, for example, transport or health care for decades before this. There is also the manner in which performance measurement has surfaced within public sector annual reports and accounts, with financial and non-financial indicators routinely provided. There is also a hive of activity, with bodies such as the Audit Commission and the Accounts Commission promulgating performance indicators for local government and the National Health Service (NHS) and, of course, the development of the Citizens' Charter since 1991. More fundamentally, the activities of public sector bodies are subject to intense scrutiny, by the general public, users of such services, the media, oversight bodies and elected representatives – all of which creates a preoccupation with how well such bodies are performing their statutory duties.

This prominence of the performance-measurement issue in the public sector activity could be seen as a lot of activity – but does it yield results? There are a number of confounding issues, which mitigate against the effective use of performance measures in the public sector. At the heart of these difficulties lie measurement problems. Accounts of this issue as it affects different parts of the public sector are contained in the chapters in Part II – Lapsley on the railways and the NHS, Mitchell on blood transfusion and Llewellyn on the social services. This difficulty of constructing performance indicators is heightened by the influence of policy-makers on both substantive results of public service organisations and on such indicators. Small, who has had considerable experience at the head of a major oversight body, presents in Chapter 11 an eloquent case for the inclusion of matters of public policy themselves to be subject to audit.

Another dimension of the performance-measurement problematic within the public sector is the impact on the management of these services, particularly in the changing environment of quasi-markets for health and social care and the privatisation of former public corporations. In Chapter 12 Mumford addresses these issues in the context of the NHS. His thesis is that innovation is a central driving force in health-care activity. This presents the opportunity to focus on such innovation rather than mere conventional analysis of cost containment, transaction costs and the competing pressures of different power groups within the NHS, and in doing so presents a positive pathway for an exiting public service organisation. What of public corporations which have been privatised as part of the public sector reform of the 1980s? Harte in Chapter 15 presents an interesting analysis of this issue from the perspective of the performance of Scottish bus companies. Here we witness the disappearance of the story of performance indicators and operating statistics which were in the public domain when these organisations were in the public sector. With privatisation, this information was rendered invisible by managements, presumably on the grounds of commercial confidentiality.

Where will this accumulated effort of the past couple of decades end? That there is an abundance of performance indicators (of varying quality) within the public sector is not in dispute. There is evidence of the three Es of economy, efficiency and effectiveness, of 'value for money', becoming embedded in everyday discussion of matters affecting the public sector. This places this set of criteria (and accounting and auditing) at centre stage within the public sector. But will it continue? Bowerman in Chapter 16 offers an interesting critique based on the experiences, not just of the UK, but of other countries which have adopted the value for money trend, which suggests that its demise, if not certain, is at least beginning. This may appear to be a contradictory note in the face of the overwhelming effort of the 'productivity indicator industry' which stands astride the public sector, but it captures that dimension which has always accompanied performance measurement in the public sector – controversy.

Performance measurement and the issues surrounding it have, for long, provided fertile ground for the academic researcher. As the range of chapters in this book demonstrates, it is a complex and dynamic area encompassing technical accounting measurement issues, disclosures, constraints and behavioural considerations relating to preparation, audit and use of information whether for management, shareholders or in the public interest. Definitive solutions are rare and indeed inappropriate but improvements in existing practice are possible and can be guided and enhanced by the type of academic analysis evidenced in this collection.

2

Financial Statements and Performance Measurement

GEOFFREY WHITTINGTON

INTRODUCTION

Performance measurement is an implicit or explicit element in most of the conceivable uses of financial statements. The traditional role of financial statements is as a statement of stewardship by the directors. Although this is sometimes interpreted as requiring merely a factual account of how the directors have disbursed shareholders' funds, as a check on their honesty, good stewardship is also a matter of good management, as the biblical parable of the talents reminds us. In the past quarter of a century there has been increasing emphasis by standard-setters (e.g. following the Trueblood Report, 1973, in the USA and *The Corporate Report* (Accounting Standards Steering Committee, 1975) in the UK) and by academics (e.g. in the vast number of empirical studies of the impact of accounting information on share prices, following the classic work of Ball and Brown, 1968) on the importance of accounts as information for specific users and uses, defined more broadly than traditional stewardship. These uses typically contain an element of performance measurement.

USERS AND USES

There is a wide variety of possible users and associated users of financial statements. Traditionally, company financial reports have been addressed to shareholders, whose main interest is in the company's performance in generating a residual stream of earnings out of which dividends may be paid, although the quality (in terms of risk) as well as the quantity of earnings is relevant. Creditors will have a much stronger interest in minimising risk rather than maximising returns, and will be concerned only that their contractually fixed payments are met. They may have lending contracts with the firm which specify that specific accounting performance measures (such as gearing ratios) will be maintained at certain levels (Citron, 1992, provides evidence for the

UK). These bond covenants have been the subject of much academic study in the USA and UK as part of the 'contracting' literature, which sees accounting practice as driven largely by its use in contractual relationships. Another contractual relationship in which accounting performance measures may be used is the payment of directors, managers and other employees. Here again, the performance measures which are relevant may be somewhat different from those which are relevant to shareholders, e.g. it may be desirable to give management maximum incentives by rewarding them specifically for the element of performance over which they have control (see Egginton, Forker and Tippett, 1989, for a development of this theme in the context of executive stock options).

Among the wider range of users envisaged by *The Corporate Report* and the 1978 Green Paper is the wider community, which does not have a direct contractual stake in the company. The needs of this community might be better served by financial reports which break the traditional mould. For example, a value-added statement might be a clearer statement of the entity's contribution to national income than is the traditional profit and loss account. More recently, there has been increasing interest in environmental reporting, which also does not fit easily into the traditional mould, because it may encompass costs which are borne by the wider community rather than by the entity which incurs them.

For present purposes, in order to reduce the problems dealt with to manageable proportions, we shall ignore these important but difficult problems of reporting to the wider community. Instead, we shall follow the pattern adopted by many financial accounting standard-setting bodies, including the UK's Accounting Standards Board (ASB), by confining the discussion to the set of financial reporting information which is presented to shareholders and put on public record for the benefit of other users. This can be justified by assuming that most users of accounts will have at least some interest in the recent financial performance, current financial state and future financial prospects of the reporting entity. However, it cannot be claimed that what follows deals with the information needs of all users of accounting statements, or even the full information needs of any particular user. Instead, we consider the possible use of financial reports in presenting information which is of some use in assessing financial performance, not in providing complete measures for any particular user.

THE TIME PERSPECTIVE

Financial statements have traditionally sought to report information relating to past performance (typically a complete accounting year or, in the case of interim reports, a completed segment of an accounting year) and the current state of the business (as at the closing balance sheet date). This *ex post* perspective is often associated with the traditional stewardship role of accounting, in giving an 'after the event' account of management's stewardship rather than the *ex ante*, before the event, assessment of future prospects, which is associated with an economic decision-making perspective. On closer examination, however, this distinction is not quite so clear. The present provides a bridge between the past and the future, and the closing balance sheet, in *ex post* traditional accounts, is a statement of present position, and therefore the starting point for assessment of the future. It can be argued that a proper statement of the present position should contain current values rather than the more traditional historical costs. Stewardship which records only historical outlays cannot give a complete picture of how well management has discharged its obligations during a period, because it ignores the unrealised gains and losses which may have occurred in the value of the assets and liabilities of the business.

In practice, even accounts which purport to be on a historical cost basis do record important elements of current valuation, and these may contain a significant degree of valuation based on future expectations, e.g. in writing down fixed assets to reflect 'permanent diminutions' in value, and in making provisions for future losses arising from present commitments. Ironically, the Accounting Standards Board, which has sometimes been regarded as having an unhealthy proclivity towards current values, has recently been criticised for an over-restrictive attitude to provisions for future losses (in FRS 7). This illustrates the fact that even so-called historical cost accounting has always contained an element of judgement of future prospects: perhaps the most obvious example is the depreciation charge, which is necessarily based on expectations about the useful life and prospective scrap value of the asset.

Despite the fact that the closing balance sheet does necessarily provide a bridge between the past and the future, it would be unrealistic to hope that the recasting of the balance sheet in current value form or indeed the recasting of the profit and loss account through some smoothing method to produce a 'sustainable' earnings figure, will ever produce complete information about the future. The future is essentially uncertain and realistic expectations embrace a wide range of possible outcomes to which different users of accounts may choose to attach different probabilities. This difficulty would not matter if markets were perfect and complete, i.e. all uncertainties could be traded away; but this is not a realistic scenario. The idea that accounts could ever yield some single-valued measure of net present value was dismissed by accounting theorists nearly two decades ago (Bromwich, 1977; Peasnell, 1977; Beaver and Demski, 1979).

The incomplete nature of what accounts can tell us, particularly in relation to the future, draws attention to the potential problem of 'short-termism', i.e. undue focus on short-term performance, as measured by the accounts, at the expense of long-term performance. The effect of many creative accounting devices, such as window-dressing (including, more recently, off-balance sheet financing) and various income-smoothing devices, may be to improve the apparent short-term position as recorded by certain key ratios (possibly to the benefit of senior managers who may be rewarded on the basis of current performance), but this may mask potential problems of long-term performance. This does not have to be the case (e.g. income-smoothing devices could be applied in a prudent manner which led to an income figure which fairly reflected management's reasonable long-term expectations) but the temptation to exercise accounting discretion in favour of a good short-term performance must always be there if the use made of accounts (including managerial compensation packages) focuses too narrowly on a few key 'bottom line' figures.

The role for financial statements which emerges from this critique is that they provide useful, but incomplete, sets of information. The role of the user is to match this information with other relevant information and arrive at a subjective evaluation relevant to the purpose in hand. Neither a pure historical cost stewardship model nor a pure current value economic decision model can describe this process adequately.

The implication of this 'information set' approach to financial statements is that we should beware of simplistic use of aggregative measures such as 'bottom line' earnings. Careful use of dis-aggregated data, such as the principal components of earnings, in conjunction with non-accounting data (such as the state of the economy or special factors relating to the industry in which the firm is engaged) is the appropriate method of measuring performance from financial statements. Nevertheless, if financial statements are to convey information, rather than a confusing heap of data, they must contain elements of classification and summarisation on a meaningful basis. Moreover, the costs of processing information may be such that further summarisation may be appropriate, to reduce users' processing costs and to facilitate timely inter-pretation. In this spirit, we shall consider the use of summary measures of performance.

SUMMARY MEASURES OF PERFORMANCE

The basic measures of performance considered here are those which are the broad summary measures derived from the traditional accounting statements, the profit and loss account and the balance sheet. In our information set approach, this would be by more detailed analysis of the financial statements and data from outside the financial statements. There are also recently developed financial statements which provide relevant information, notably the cash flow statement (as in the international standard, IAS 7, and the national standards FRS 1 in the UK and SFAS95 in the USA) and, in the UK, the operating and financial review.

Profit measures

A profit measure is perhaps the most obvious potential measure of overall performance, summarising the transactions of an accounting period and netting them out to produce a single measure of performance: a profit or loss. A few years ago accounting theorists hoped to refine such measures to define a pure measure of 'true' economic profit. However, it soon became apparent that, in a world of uncertainty, there were a number of rival candidates for the truth, and David Solomons wrote, with great prescience, in 1961, that 'So far as the history of accounting is concerned, the next twenty-five years may subsequently be seen to have been the twilight of income measurement (p. 383). Thus, the emphasis on a single 'bottom line' profit has been eroded, and the profit statement is better regarded as producing several useful summary bottom lines.

This approach is adopted by the ASB's recent FRS 3, Reporting Financial Performance. This disaggregates the profit and loss account in a number of ways which are intended to give greater insight into the profit figure. For example, the effects of new acquisitions and discontinued activities are shown separately, so that the user of accounts can make better inter-period comparisons of the performance of the ongoing business and can better appraise the contribution of divestment and acquisition. An important disaggregation contained in FRS 3 is the distinction between the profit and loss account and the new statement of gains and losses. Partly for legal reasons and partly because of the transitional state of accounting practice, this distinction is not yet as clear as it might be, but the essential intention is to regard the full statement (including the statement of gains and losses) as leading to an aggregate measure of what is sometimes called 'comprehensive income'. The dichotomy between the two component parts should ideally capture the distinction between operating gains (the effect of the transactions which the firm undertakes as part of its routine business activities with the object of making a profit) and holding gains (the change in value of the assets and liabilities which are held in order to operate the business), as was proposed many years ago in the Sandilands Report (1975). This dichotomy, like many distinctions in accounting, is difficult to define at the margin, and its precise definition and significance may be different in different types of business activity. Nevertheless, it is part of the important endeavour of disaggregating a firm's activities in a way which offers deeper insights into the firm's performance.

Balance sheet measures

The balance sheet states the assets and liabilities at a point in time. The balance sheet at the end of the most recent accounting period is therefore the most up-to-date statement of the firm's position that is available to external users of financial statements. Possible uses of the information contained in the balance sheet are as an indication of the firm's net asset backing for borrowing (e.g. in the calculation of balance sheet gearing ratios), or as an indication of the resources available to generate future income. Both of these uses suggest that up-to-date valuations might convey more relevant information than historical cost, although the added relevance may have to be traded off against the greater unreliability and cost of current valuations.

However, even a balance sheet which contains reliable current valuations of assets and liabilities is unlikely to provide complete information. Self-generated goodwill, for example, is not typically recorded in balance sheets, and this draws attention to the fact that, in general, there may be an aggregation problem in valuation: the sum of the separately valued individual assets, less liabilities, may well not equal the market value of the net assets of the firm valued as a whole. Equally, the value of a group of assets may be different from the sum of the value of the individual items. Moreover, in the world of imperfect and incomplete markets described earlier, there may be considerable divergences between different methods of assessing current value, such as replacement cost, selling price or amount recoverable from use.

Thus, current valuation is not a panacea for all the limitations of the balance sheet. Current trends towards introducing more current valuations in the balance sheet may be welcomed as providing more relevant information, but that information will never be complete. As with the profit statement, the balance sheet needs to be interpreted using its components rather than merely concentrating on simple aggregates, such as net assets. Furthermore, even analysis of components, such as a gearing ratio or a liquidity ratio, must be sensitive to problems of measurement and must be interpreted in relation to other information in the financial statements; e.g., other things being equal, an adverse liquidity ratio is much less of a problem in a firm with a strong current and prospective cash inflow.

Rates of return

The rate of return is perhaps the most attractive single measure of the performance of a business, relating the 'bottom line' of the profit statement to that of the balance sheet, and it has been used for many years, despite persistent warnings that the accountant's measure of return is a very imperfect reflection of the rate of return on investment as conceived by economists. Accounting rates of return have been used not only by financial analysts but also by public sector regulators, e.g. in the regulation of public utilities (particularly in the USA), in monopoly investigations and in controlling public sector investment (as in the UK Treasury's various guidelines on the subject).

The debate on the precise significance of rate of return measures continues to evolve and to give mixed messages. Much of the earlier debate is reprinted in Brief (1986). The critique by Harcourt (1965), who showed that the accounting rate of return is not, in general, equal to the economist's internal rate of return on investment, was answered by Kay (1976), who showed that over long periods it was possible to relate the two when accounts are fully articulated (all gains passing through the profit and loss account). Harcourt's message was repeated by Fisher and McGowan (1983), whose work was a by-product of the IBM monopoly case in the USA, where rate of return was critical. They were answered by Edwards, Kay and Mayer (1987), who showed that current value based accounts, using the value to the business principle (sometimes called deprival value), could produce annual rate of return signals which were compatible with the economist's capital budgeting model. They were concerned with single period signals rather than the internal rate of return which dominated the earlier literature and was concerned with lifetime returns. However, the Edwards, Kay and Mayer approach assumes that accounts are fully articulated (all gains being recorded as returns) and that the value to the business method can and will be applied with a degree of precision which may not be possible, especially when the preparers of accounts have an incentive to produce a particular type of result (e.g. in the context of regulation, a low rate of return and a high capital value on which future returns will be based).

Some of these difficulties are discussed, in the context of UK utility regulation, in Whittington (1994). They turn mainly on the problems of applying value to the business. This constitutes replacement cost or recoverable amount, whichever is the lower. Replacement cost involves estimating the effects of technical progress, which, in the case of long-lived assets such as are owned by utilities, can be very substantial. It also raises particular aggregation difficulties in the network utilities, which have a high degree of interdependence between assets which constrains the form of replacement, and where there may be significant economies to replacing large sections. However, the more difficult problem is in assessing recoverable amount. In theory, this is the higher of sale value or value in use, but in practice it is likely to be the latter: sections of second-hand pipeline or individual pumping stations do not usually have a high second-hand value. Calculating recoverable amount involves taking a view on the present value of the future cash flows derived from using an asset. This raises another serious aggregation problem (as in Edey's (1974) classic example of valuing a tunnel on a railway), and all the problems of subjective estimation. More fundamentally, in the context of regulation, recoverable amount can become circular: if the regulator awards a fair rate of return on the recoverable amount, then *any* recoverable amount will be justified by subsequent returns. In the UK, utilities such as electricity, gas and water were privatised at large discounts on replacement cost, so that recoverable amount can be regarded as the relevant component of value to the business, and the problems of applying the Edwards, Kay and Mayer (1987) framework for performance evaluation are acute.

This critique of the use of accounting measures of profitability for regulation recalls the earlier debate on the use of the rate of return for regulatory purposes and for internal management controls such as those used to motivate divisional managers. It is widely recognised that the use of accounting rates of return in such contexts can create perverse incentives, such as the excessive expansion of the regulated asset base (the so-called Averch–Johnson effect: Averch and Johnson, 1962).

Thus, the rate of return provides a particularly good example of our general theme: that we should not rely on particular numbers or ratios to provide a total picture of performance. Rather, we should assess the particular number or ratio in the context of other information, and we should pay due attention to the problems of measurement.

Gearing

Much creative accounting effort appears to have been directed, in recent years, towards the gearing ratio in the balance sheet. This ratio can be regarded as a performance measure from the point of view of the lender, particularly the long-term lender, who may use it as a measure of the cover for repaying his stake in the business (interest payments plus repayment of the principal). As such repayments are made out of future cash flows, it might be expected that cash flow forecasts would be the ideal information to be used for this purpose, but such forecasts might be unreliable. If *ex post* data were to be used, then recent cash flows (as reported under the ASB's FRS 1) would seem relevant, and, among the traditional financial statements, income gearing (i.e. a measure of the extent to which interest payments are covered by current earnings) might be a key measure.

Thus, on the face of it, a balance sheet measure of gearing seems to be one of the less attractive methods of assessing the security of long-term debt repayments. If a static measure were to be chosen, we might choose the market value of debt in relation to the market value of equity (assuming that the debt and equity are traded in a reasonably deep market), on the ground that the market value of securities represents the discounted present value of the market's expectations of future cash flows. However, the market itself may rely on the information contained in financial statements, so that this does not avoid the need for better accounting measures. The introduction of current values into the balance sheet may make the balance sheet measure of gearing more useful than would be the case under historical cost, because current values give a better indication of the value of the assets available to generate cash flows to meet debt contracts. Nevertheless, balance sheet measures must necessarily give an incomplete picture, because they reflect the position at a single point in time.

In these circumstances, it may seem remarkable that debt covenants often make use of the balance sheet gearing ratio measured on a historical cost basis. This is less remarkable when we consider the importance of using reasonably reliable and objective information in contracts where one of the parties (the borrowing company) has both the incentive and the means to manipulate the information in its favour. Moreover, the breach of a covenant may well be only one signal which will influence the lender's actions: it is to be expected that this will trigger further investigation, which will include consideration of some of the other relevant data suggested above. Thus, consideration of the use of gearing measures confirms our earlier conclusions about the importance of not putting too much interpretative weight on single items in the financial statements, considered in isolation.

CONCLUSION

The conclusion of this discussion is that the assessment of performance involves taking what might be called a holistic view of the information available. This involves not only looking at the financial statements as a whole, but also taking account of all of the other information which is available and bears on the periodic performance and current financial state of the firm.

With regard to the financial statements themselves, this approach recognises not only that particular items in a given statement can be as important as aggregate summary figures (e.g. the importance of the dis-aggregated components of profit revealed by FRS 3), but also that the relationship between financial statements can be revealing. For example, in order to appreciate the effects of asset revaluations during a period, we may need to look at the fixed asset figures in the balance sheet, the depreciation charge in the profit and loss account, and the amount of revaluation in the statement of gains. Equally, we have already noted that the comparison of the cash flow statement with the traditional accrual-based accounts can reveal interesting contrasts (such as a high profit figure combined with negative cash flow) which provide signals for deeper investigation.

An application of the holistic approach to financial statements is that we should reject the commonly held view that accounting should concentrate on a single primary statement, typically the profit and loss account but sometimes the balance sheet, regarding the rest of the financial statements as merely residual data. Such a view is, for example, apparent in Ernst and Young's otherwise admirable treatise *UK GAAP* (Davies, Paterson and Wilson, 1994, p. 99), which takes the view that the profit and loss account is the primary statement, producing a key 'bottom line' earnings figure which, by a smoothing process, is reflective of the firm's long-term ability to sustain earnings. Within this framework, the balance sheet is reduced to the role of a mere accrual sheet, which provides a temporary home for the accruals generated by the earnings-measurement process. In contrast to this, the view advanced in this chapter is that the financial statements should attempt to reveal, as well as possible, both the gains during the period (in the profit and loss account) and the state of the business at the end of the period (in the balance sheet). The full articulation of the two statements (enabling shareholders' interests in the closing balance sheet to be related to their amount in the opening balance sheet and the gains during the year) will be revealed by the statement of gains and statement of movement on reserves, required by FRS 3.

With regard to information not contained in the financial statements, this will be extremely important in determining the background against which the financial statement information is evaluated. Some of this may be of unique relevance to the immediate financial state and prospects of the specific firm under consideration, e.g. if it relates to the prospective sales of the market in which the firm is involved, or the specific costs which it incurs. Other information will be of a more general kind, to do with the state of the economy (e.g. inflation rates, interest rates and exchange rates), and likely to impact on all businesses, albeit to different degrees. In fact these factors contribute a high proportion of the inter-temporal variability of share prices: this can be demonstrated by examining the day-to-day volatility of individual share prices, which occurs typically in the absence of any release of financial statement information.

With regard to the non-accounting information which has a specific impact on the assessment of the performance of the firm in question, clearly an 'insider', with detailed knowledge of the firm's business, has better opportunities for an accurate assessment than an 'outsider', who has access only to the published financial statements. The same comment applies, of course, to the insider's advantage due to the possession of more detailed accounting information than is published. Thus, a mechanism for externalising this internal 'know-how' would seem to be desirable. Financial analysts seem to have solved this problem partly by periodic meetings with senior management. Such meetings are, of course, constrained by the rules of the Stock Exchange, which forbid insider trading or the giving of privileged information. A way of extending the benefit of more informed judgement to a wider audience, while avoiding the suspicion that analysts may sometimes be given privileged information, is for the company to produce a published statement providing a wider interpretation of its performance and strategy. This is the objective of the operating and financial review recommended by the ASB.

In summary, this chapter has advocated the role of financial statements in performance measurement as a process of providing relevant, but incomplete, information upon which users will form judgements. An excellent description of this role was provided long ago by J. R. Hicks (1946, p. 171) in his celebrated discussion of income measurement, when he described the concepts of income, saving, depreciation and investment as 'rough approximations used by the business man to steer himself through the bewildering changes of situation which confront him. For this purpose, strict logical categories are not what is needed; something rougher is actually better.'

References

Accounting Standards Board (ASB) (1991) FRS 1: Cash flow statements, ASB, London.
Accounting Standards Board (ASB) (1992) FRS 3: Reporting financial performance, ASB, London.
Accounting Standards Board (ASB) (1993) *Operating and Financial Review*, ASB, London.
Accounting Standards Board (ASB) (1994) FRS 7: Fair values in acquisition accounting, ASB, London.
Accounting Standards Steering Committee (1975) *The Corporate Report*, ASSC, London.
Averch, H. A. and Johnson, L. L. (1962) Behaviour of the firm under regulatory constraint, *The American Economic Review* (December), pp. 1052–69.
Ball, R. and Brown, P. (1968) An empirical evaluation of accounting income numbers, *Journal of Accounting Research* (Autumn), pp. 159–78.
Beaver, W. H. and Demski, J. S. (1979) The nature of income measurement, *The Accounting Review* (January), pp. 38–46.

Brief, R. P. (ed.) (1986) *Estimating the Economic Rate of Return from Accounting Data*, Garland, New York.

Bromwich, M. (1977) The use of present value valuation models in published accounting reports, *The Accounting Review* (July), pp. 587–96.

Citron, D. B. (1992) The use of financial ratio covenants in UK bank loan contracts and the implications for accounting method choice, *Accounting and Business Research* (Autumn), pp. 322–35.

Davies, M., Paterson, R. and Wilson, A. (1994) *UK GAAP*, 4th edn, Ernst and Young/Macmillan, London.

Edey, H. C. (1974) Deprival value and financial accounting, in H. C. Edey and B. S. Yamey (eds.), *Debits, Credits, Finance and Profits*, Sweet and Maxwell, London, pp. 75–83.

Edwards, J. S. S., Kay, J. A. and Mayer, C. P. (1987) *The Economic Analysis of Accounting Profitability*, Clarendon Press, Oxford.

Egginton, D. A., Forker, J. J. and Tippett, M. J. (1989) Share option rewards and managerial performance: an abnormal performance index model, *Accounting and Business Research* (Summer), pp. 255–66.

Financial Accounting Standards Board (1987) SFAS95 – Statement of cash flows, FASB, Stanford, Conn.

Fisher, F. M. and McGowan, J. J. (1983) On the misuse of accounting rates of return to infer monopoly profits, *American Economic Review* (March), pp. 82–97.

Green Paper (1978) *The Future of Financial Reporting*, HMSO, London.

Harcourt, G. C. (1965) The accountant in a golden age, *Oxford Economic Papers* (March), pp. 66–80.

Hicks, J. R. (1946) *Value and Capital*, 2nd edn, Clarendon Press, Oxford.

International Accounting Standards Committee (1992) IAS 7, Cash flow statements, IASC, London.

Kay, J. A. (1976) Accountants, too, could be happy in a golden age: the accountant's rate of profit and the internal rate of return, *Oxford Economic Papers* (November), pp. 447–60.

Peasnell, K. V. (1977) A note on the discounted present value concept, *The Accounting Review* (January), pp. 186–9.

Sandilands, F. E. P. (Chairman) (1975) *Inflation Accounting: Report of the Inflation Accounting Committee*, Cmnd 6225, HMSO, London.

Solomons, D. (1961) Economic and accounting concepts of income, *The Accounting Review* (July), pp. 374–83.

Trueblood, R. (Chairman) (1973) *Objectives of Financial Statements* (the Trueblood Report), American Institute of Certified Public Accountants, New York.

Whittington, G. (1994) Current cost accounting: its role in regulated utilities, *Fiscal Studies* (November), pp. 88–101.

3

Regulating Change – The Role of the Conceptual Statement in Standard-Setting

SIR DAVID TWEEDIE

A standard-setter's lot is not a happy one! Standard-setters are beset by conflicting forces. On the one hand there are those who complain that advantages are being taken from them – on the other those who complain that change is far too slow. Broadly speaking, a standard-setter is concerned with change or restraint of change. Stand-fasters would have the standard-setter making only minor changes to the status quo. Crusaders would sweep away present practice and replace it with something radically different. Evolutionists would like gradual change but then argue over the pace and the direction of that change. The standard-setter is caught up in the swirl of these conflicting forces.

Standard-setters are constantly reminded about the economic consequences of their actions, which, some argue, will:

(1) jeopardise the credit market because of a loss of public confidence in banking companies or the financial institutions;
(2) have an adverse effect on the UK's balance of payments;
(3) lead to investment being reduced;
(4) lessen the availability of capital by removing leasing companies from the capital market;
(5) deny weak companies the opportunity to be acquired.

Others will attack the standard-setter on the grounds that the solution to the perceived ills of financial reporting is not more technical standards but that 'the root problem in financial reporting is moral and ethical' (Tietjen, quoted by Kirk, 1988, p. 10). Good ethical standards for the profession and greater independence for the auditor apparently would be the answer. Over the last 50 years or so, however, the emphasis has been on the reduction of technical accounting choice.

SETTING ACCOUNTING PRINCIPLES – THE EARLY STAGES

The American Institute of Accountants' (the American Institute of Certified Public Accountants from 1957) Committee on Accounting Procedures (1938–59) did attempt to reduce the number of then, almost limitless, extant accounting practices. Unfortunately, the end result was an overabundance of 'good practices' that survived the process of elimination. There were several alternatives for treatment of similar transactions as 'the Committee rarely met an accounting principle it didn't find to be acceptable' (Storey, 1990, p. 18). Early efforts to develop accounting principles were dominated by a belief that the principles were essentially 'a distillation of experience' (the subtitle of May, 1943).

A key feature in the Institute's study of accounting principles was the seminal book *An Introduction to Corporate Accounting Standards* by W. A. Paton and A. C. Littleton (1940). This monograph generally rationalised existing practice, giving it what many saw as the theoretical underpinning that had previously been lacking. Paton and Littleton accepted two major premises:

(1) that periodic income determination was the central function of financial accounting; and

(2) accounting was not essentially a process of valuation but the allocation of historical cost and revenues to the current and succeeding fiscal periods.

Paton and Littleton then gave a catchy name to these ideas – 'the matching principle'.

Under the matching principle most assets were deemed to be deferred charges to revenue, costs waiting to be matched with future revenues; that is, the factors applied to production which had not yet reached the point in the business process where they might be appropriately treated as 'cost of sales' or 'expense' were deemed to be 'assets' and were presented as such in the balance sheet. It was not to be overlooked, however, that these 'assets' were in fact 'revenue charges in suspense' awaiting some future matching with revenue as costs or expenses. This notion still holds sway in certain quarters:

> A non-monetary asset in a historical cost system is purely a deferred cost, a cost which has been incurred before the balance sheet date and, on an accruals basis, is expected (with sufficient certainty to jump the prudence hurdle) to benefit periods beyond the balance sheet date, so as to justify its being carried forward. This general description fits every non-monetary asset in the historical cost balance sheet, whether it be stock, repayments, tangible fixed assets, deferred development expenditure or whatever.
>
> (Paterson, 1988, p. 26)

The AICPA's Accounting Principles Board (1959–73) was the second major attempt by the Americans to reorganise their efforts in the area of accounting principles. Initially, Accounting Research Studies 1 and 3 (1961 and 1962) proposed dramatic changes to accounting but these scared the Board, which stated (April 1962): 'While these studies are a valuable contribution to accounting thinking, they are too radically different from present generally accepted accounting principles for acceptance at this time.' It was not the Accounting Principles Board's (APB) finest hour (Storey, 1990, p. 22). The Board did little more on accounting principles except to authorise a project that became Accounting Research Study 7, Inventory of Generally Accepted Accounting Principles – a list of acceptable practices (1965).

APB Statement No. 4 (1970), however, did attempt to give definitions of basic elements of financial accounting. Unfortunately, the definition of an asset or liability was defective since the only essential distinguishing characteristic of an asset (or liability) was that it was recognised and measured (as an asset or liability) 'in conformity with generally accepted accounting principles', i.e. assets and liabilities were what practice said they were.

The Financial Accounting Standards Board (FASB) (1973 to date) in commencing its work on the definitions of elements of financial statements found the APB's definitions circular and therefore of no guidance to a standard-setter in attempting to decide issues such as whether: research and development costs should be capitalised (i.e. was R&D an asset or an expense?); or should 'provisions' for self-insurance be created by charging through the profit and loss account (i.e. was self-insurance a liability or an appropriation of profit?).

Financial reporting in the early 1970s was increasingly governed by a comprehensive set of detailed rules and procedures. Such a situation is quite unsuitable for dealing with new situations where a standard frame of reference is required when existing procedures do not deal with the problem.

The FASB soon found that the conceptual superiority of definitions of assets and liabilities that describe resources and obligations in the real world rather than deferred charges and credits resulting from bookkeeping entries was strongly reinforced by Board members' experiences in trying to set financial accounting standards using a notion of assets characterised as the fall-out from periodic recognition of revenues and expenses – an approach they found too vague and subjective to be workable. A major challenge was made to the emphasis on financial accounting being primarily a process of matching costs and revenues. The FASB's intention was that no longer could deferred charges and credits that were carried forward for matching in future periods be included in assets and liabilities merely by meeting definitions no more restrictive than 'assets are costs and liabilities are proceeds' (Storey, 1990, p. 46).

This was the beginning of the differing perspectives of financial reporting: the 'asset–liability' view versus the 'revenue–expense' view, i.e. whether reported income resulted from measuring changes in assets and liabilities or whether assets and liabilities resulted from measuring income. Upon which concept reporting requirements should be based became a hotly debated question. Which would lead to more consistency in application and be better understood?

THE ACCOUNTING STANDARDS BOARD'S
DRAFT STATEMENT OF PRINCIPLES

If a conceptual framework does not exist a standard-setter is forced to fall back on his or her own experience of accounting. The problem with starting by using experience as a frame of reference is that no one can be sure of a common starting point as everyone's experience is different. Different experiences lead to different solutions and, consequently, financial accounting in the past became inundated with varied solutions to the same problems. In the past the predecessor of the UK's Accounting Standards Board (ASB), the Accounting Standards Committee, was faced with draft standards prepared by working parties, each of which approached its task from the collective background of its individual members' different experiences. The intention of the ASB's conceptual framework was that it would articulate definitions and concepts and, if possible, would remove the inconsistencies between standards for which standard-setters in the past have been criticised.

The ASB was required by the Dearing Committee (Dearing, 1988), which set out the basis of the UK's standard-setting process for the 1990s, to develop a conceptual framework for the UK. This impetus probably came from the pioneering work of Professor Solomons in his *Guidelines for Financial Reporting Standards* (1989) – produced for the Institute of Chartered Accountants in England and Wales at a critical time in the development of standard-setting in the UK. In its report the Dearing Committee (1988, p. 17) argued that

the lack of a conceptual framework is a handicap to those involved in setting accounting standards as well as to those applying them . . . We believe that work in this area will assist standard setters in formulating their thinking on particular accounting issues, facilitate judgements on the sufficiency of disclosures required to give a true and fair view, and assist preparers and auditors in interpreting accounting standards and resolving accounting issues not dealt with by specific standards.

The ASB's draft Statement of Principles is very similar to that proposed by Professor Solomons and, indeed, to those of the International Accounting Standards Committee and standard-setters in Canada and Australia, all of which ultimately derive from the pioneering work of the FASB in the USA.

The draft Statement of Principles is not intended to become an accounting standard but, rather, a statement of guidance for the Board, enabling it to ensure that it tackles new issues in a consistent manner. Ensuing standards will seek to implement the Statement. Each new standard is, in effect, a test of the principles. On occasion, a standard may not be in accordance with the Statement. In such cases the Board will have to consider how far the conflict is capable of being resolved by amending the standard and how far it points to a need to revisit the principles. Sometimes the Board will deliberately refrain from amending a standard, or amending it sufficiently to bring it into line with the principles, out of respect for its declared aim of pursuing evolutionary rather than revolutionary change. To the extent that further changes can be foreseen on the issue of a standard the Board would indicate that possibility. By such means the Board would allow practice to develop in a way that gradually accommodates more radical ideas instead of imposing an abrupt and contentious change in the name of conformity with its published principles.

The ASB's draft Statement of Principles consists of seven chapters.

(1) Objectives

The Board has deemed that the accounts should be aimed at the informed investor on the grounds that other major users of financial reports, such as creditors, would be interested in information similar to that supplied to a skilled investor. Research in the 1970s revealed that the private shareholder did not understand general-purpose financial statements (Lee and Tweedie, 1977) – a separate form of reporting is required for the layman.

The informed investor, however, is not simply interested in the objective of stewardship but is concerned to make decisions based on financial information. The draft Statement therefore deems that there should be a more forward-looking focus to financial information to enable decisions to be made. (The division of income in FRS 3 into continuing and discontinued components and the introduction of the operating and financial review are derived from this focus.)

(2) Qualitative characteristics

The major desirable features of financial information are that it should be reliable, relevant, understandable and comparable. Unfortunately, it is not possible to have all of these characteristics to the same degree. For example, while it is possible to produce a very reliable 1950 Edinburgh property cost this would probably be less useful for decision-making than a more relevant but more subjective 1994 property valuation. The ASB, therefore, has to choose between relevance and reliability as a prime characteristic and, broadly speaking, it has chosen relevance, although not at the price of unreliability.

(3) Elements of financial statements

The Board has adopted the international definitions of assets and liabilities, broadly that 'assets' are the rights to benefits resulting from a past transaction while 'liabilities' are obligations that will lead to resources leaving the organisation. These concepts have already assisted the Board in developing FRS 4, Capital Instruments, FRS 5, Reporting the Substance of Transactions and FRS 7, Fair Values in Acquisition Accounting. As mentioned below, however, these definitions have caused a certain amount of anguish for those who prefer the former 'matching' approach to the determination of assets and liabilities.

(4) Recognition

Recognition poses the question of when the assets and liabilities should be recognised in the financial statements. The answer is straightforward – when they can be measured reliably. In other words, given the same facts, three or four accountants would broadly agree on the measurement. Is this presently true in the case of certain assets currently shown in UK balance sheets – especially when there is little evidence of market activity to verify the valuations?

(5) Measurement

If the ASB is concerned with more relevant information it will tend to move more towards current values than historical costs. Board members are all, however, aware of the current cost accounting debate of the 1970s and early 1980s. The Board believes in general that, while financial reporting should move towards the use of current valuations, the Board should not introduce such a change at a speed that would obliterate familiar landmarks but only at a pace the financial community desires. In that sense I suspect that any move towards current values would be very piecemeal, similar to the movement to date whereby certain disposable assets (such as investment properties or commodities) may be revalued, leaving those assets which are the engine of a business, its core operating assets, at historical cost.

(6) Presentation

Changes in the accounts have already resulted from this chapter, which seeks to marry the identified demands of users of financial reports to the supply of information. As a result, the source and application of funds statement has been replaced by a cash flow statement, the profit and loss account has been restructured and the statement of recognised gains and losses has been introduced to highlight those items which previously bypassed the profit and loss account and went straight to reserves. This last statement adds no new information, it simply extracts important information previously buried in the notes and presents it prominently.

(7) The reporting entity

The final section of the draft Statement of Principles is concerned with the philosophy behind group accounts and the effect on a reporting group of strategic alliances (partnerships) between the group and other parties in the form of joint ventures and associated companies.

The core chapters of the draft Statement of Principles have been those concerned with elements, recognition and measurement. The chapters on elements and recognition have also been the most controversial,[1] mainly because they have challenged the predominant revenue – expense ('matching') view of financial reporting, traditionally the key concept underpinning financial reporting.

THE 'ASSET AND LIABILITY' APPROACH VERSUS 'MATCHING'

Criticism of the asset and liability viewpoint

Throughout this century there have been great changes in accounting thought. Until 1929, in the UK, only a balance sheet had to be laid before members in a general meeting and even after the Companies Act 1929 only the balance sheet along with the directors' and auditor's reports had to be sent to members. The Act contained nothing about the contents of the now required profit and loss account as statutory prescription for disclosure in accounts was disliked, although the Act did require in the balance sheet a summary of the share capital and an indication of the general nature of the liabilities and assets.

The Royal Mail Steam Packet case of 1931, however, had a major impact. The company had made substantial profits during the First World War and up to 1921, although thereafter the company's earnings had fallen considerably. During the years 1921 to 1927 the profit and loss accounts were credited with special items amounting to approximately £5 million which represented excess profit duty recoveries, obsolescence and deferred repairs allowances, excess taxation provisions and bonuses from subsidiaries paid out of past profits. As a result of crediting these items, which were effectively hidden from anyone reading the profit and loss account, large trading losses were disguised and healthy profits reported enabling the company to pay its debenture interest and dividends on its ordinary and preference shares.[2]

The case had a profound effect as the public conscience was greatly shocked and the lessons from it did much to shape the 1948 Companies Act. This, at last, set out the essential contents and the manner of presentation of the profit and loss account. There was therefore much concern in protecting the profit and loss account and the information required in that statement has gradually grown over the years.

The growing interest in reported earnings probably led to the income statement being deemed the most important accounting statement, a position it had held for many decades, when the FASB first challenged the revenue–expense (matching) viewpoint in the 1970s.

The issue became highly emotional. Many defenders of the revenue–expense view could not believe that the FASB's concern was to obtain a set of definitions that assisted the standard-setter to produce consistent accounting standards (an issue to which we shall return later in the chapter). Definitions of assets and liabilities had not been important in the revenue–expense review, which focused on the need to avoid distortion of periodic net income and to emphasise 'profit' and 'matching'; assets and liabilities were simply those residual costs and revenues not included in the profit and loss account. Unfortunately, the absence of a previous need for asset and liability definitions under the matching principle led to other explanations for the FASB's decision. In particular two arguments came forward – arguments also used against the ASB's draft Statement of Principles.

The first charge was that the FASB was deemed to be downgrading the importance of net income by making the balance sheet more important than the income statement.

The ASB's draft Statement of Principles, which reflects much of what the FASB has produced in its Statements of Concepts, reveals that it is simply untrue that the ASB believes income to be unimportant:

> Information about the performance of an enterprise, in particular its profitability, is required to assess potential changes in the economic resources that it is likely to control in the future. Information about variability of performance is important in this respect. Information about performance is useful in predicting the capacity of the enterprise to generate cash flows from its existing resource base. It is also useful in forming judgements about the effectiveness with which the enterprise might employ additional resources.
>
> (ASB, 1991, chap. 1, para. 17)

The ASB does believe, however, that to obtain the full picture of what is happening to an enterprise changes in assets and liabilities have to be considered:

> In assessing the overall financial performance of an enterprise during a period, all changes in equity of the enterprise from activities or events need to be considered. The total of such changes, excluding those deriving from capital contributed by or payments to shareholders, is referred to as total recognised gains and losses.
>
> Profit or loss of a period is a component of total recognised gains and losses and focuses on revenues for its output (income) that the enterprise has earned and recognised and what it has sacrificed to obtain that output (expenses). It should be noted that gains that are realised in a period but recognised in previous periods are not components of total recognised gains and losses of the period under review.
>
> (ibid., chap. 6, paras. 16–17)

The second charge against the FASB's conceptual stance was that the Board was deemed to be supplanting accounting based on completed transactions and matching of costs with a new accounting based on the valuation of assets and liabilities at current values.

While the ASB has added a new statement, the statement of total recognised gains and losses, which adds to profits those items which previously would have been reserve accounted, the Board has made no move to change the basic measurement process inherent in accounting. Despite the accusation that the

Board is concerned solely with the balance sheet and that income would be derived by comparing the current balance sheet with that for the previous year, the facts are that changes in balance sheets (ignoring, as we do, for the purposes of the statement of total recognised gains and losses, capital injections and distributions) are caused either by transactions or by other events involving increases or decreases in the value of assets (revaluations or impairments) and liabilities (increases and decreases in obligations). Transactions will continue to form the bedrock of accounting.

Chapter 5 of the ASB's draft Statement of Principles – Measurement in financial statements – states (1993, para. 5):

> total recognised gains and losses can be derived either by considering each event or transaction affecting the entity individually (a 'transactions-based approach') or by considering the transactions in aggregate by comparing the opening and closing capital of a period. Whichever approach is used, the same overall measure of the total recognised gains and losses of a period will result. In practice, accounting is transactions-based and does not simply compare opening and closing capital of a period to measure gains and losses. In addition, the transactions-based approach, unlike the aggregate approach, reveals the components of the changes in an entity's net assets during a period and gives users of financial statements important information in the form of a detailed breakdown of profit and other gains and losses. Such components of the gains and losses give users information about the quality of particular gains and losses and can indicate whether they are realised, relate to readily realisable assets or liabilities or relate to assets essential to the entity's operations which are unlikely to be sold.
>
> (ASB, ch. 5, 1993, para. 5)

In answer to the charge that current values are to replace historical costs the chapter on measurement indicates that, while the Board prefers current values, it is not willing to move faster than the financial community believes to be appropriate (ibid., para. 61):

> no single valuation method can cater for every need or would be sufficiently reliable for financial reporting in all circumstances. Hence, it is desirable to apply a system that chooses the valuation method appropriate to the circumstances. The 'cost or net realisable value whichever is the lower' rule is an example of such a method which has a well established tradition in accounting practice. The current value concept which is equivalent to this is the value to the business concept. This can be interpreted loosely as current cost or market value whichever is the lower . . . value to the business is the soundest method of valuing assets at the second (remeasurement) stage of recognition; similar arguments apply to the valuation of liabilities. This conclusion at the level of general principles is consistent with an evolutionary development of eclectic valuation methods in response to developing user needs.

The comprehensive measurement question that is commonly characterised as current value versus historical cost has yet to be resolved. This is not an issue on the Board's present agenda and will return to haunt accountants the next time inflation or deflation strikes. It is a question that merits serious consideration on its own account but is not something that is hidden in the asset–liability approach.

British accounts have continually moved in the direction of adopting current values on a piecemeal basis. The Board believes that that is the right direction in which to travel as such information is, in its opinion, more useful to a user than some outdated historical cost. The changes have been made voluntarily so far. The Board has to decide how such gradual change should be managed.

The ASB has faced a charge, additional to the above, made against its draft Statement of Principles, namely that the Board intends that the balance sheet should give the value of a business. Yet the draft Statement states (ibid., chap. 6, para. 27):

> a balance sheet does not purport to show the value of a business enterprise. As a result of limitations from reliability of measurement and cost–benefit considerations, not all assets and not all liabilities are included in a balance sheet (e.g. some contingent liabilities are not included), and some assets and liabilities that are included may be affected by events, such as price changes or other increases or decreases in value through time, that are not recognised or are only partly recognised. Even if all recognised assets and liabilities were to be included at up-to-date values, the total of assets less the total of liabilities would not, except by coincidence, equal the value of the business. However, together with other financial statements and other information, balance sheets should provide information that is useful to those who wish to make their own assessments of the enterprise's value.

The Board is not guilty of the charges made against it. It is keen to disclose more relevant information. The major changes made to the profit and loss account in FRS 3 are indicative of this fact; namely, the division of income into continuing and discontinued items, new income from acquisitions, the statement of recognised gains and losses revealing reserve movements previously hidden – a movement away from the previous obsession with the 'bottom line' by breaking income into its components. Similarly, the balance sheet, too, is part of the new campaign for relevance. The 'bottom line' of a balance sheet, for the reasons set out in chapter 6 of the draft Statement of Principles, can no more give the value of a company than the 'bottom line' in a profit and loss account can encapsulate in a single figure all that is important about a company's performance.

'Whatsits' – criticism of the revenue–expense viewpoint

The key aspect of the debate over the principle of matching concerns the definition of an asset and a liability. A debit can only be an asset or an expense;

a credit can only be a liability or income. It would not seem to matter which element of the debit or credit is defined as the other will be the residual. The Board's view is that it is easier to assess assets and liabilities than it is to assess income and expenditure. Even one of the supporters of the income and expense viewpoint outlined on page 19 states that an asset 'is expected to benefit periods beyond the balance sheet date' (Paterson, 1988, p. 26). The definitions of both sides therefore have common aspects. The major difference lies in supporters of the revenue–expense approach deeming certain deferred costs and revenues to be forms of assets and liabilities respectively, simply to smooth income.

The Board's intention is that what appears in accounts must be rooted in the real world. Some deferred costs and revenues are recorded in the balance sheet not because they represent anything in the real world, but because they are said to 'match' costs and revenues properly and avoid 'distorting' periodic net income. Assets, therefore, are revenue charges in suspense yet most of us know an asset or liability when we see one. The problem is in accounting, not in our basic perceptions. Concepts have to be rooted in the real world. Accounts should not devise imaginary assets or liabilities. We need veracity in the balance sheet. The balance sheet should not be 'a mausoleum for the unwanted costs that the double entry system throws up as regrettable by-products' (Baxter, 1962, p. viii).

If the balance sheet is not based on the real world, if stocks do not actually represent assets in warehouses, then we are going to be in trouble. The existence of phantom assets must be questioned. (Can you explain it to Mum? Would you buy it?) Robert Sprouse (1988, p. 126) used the term 'what-you-may-call-its' (here 'whatsits') to describe certain 'deferred charges' and 'deferred credits'. These items are included in balance sheets without much consideration of whether they are actually assets or liabilities. These are a result of 'proper matching', 'non-distortion of periodic net income' and the 'assets are costs' view.

It is, however, extremely difficult for a standard-setter to pin down what respondents mean by 'proper matching' and 'periodic income distortion'.

What follows is paraphrased from the FASB's hearings on research and development and similar costs and accounting for contingencies (see FASB, 1974, Vol. 1, Part 2, pp. 171–2, 189–90; Vol. 3, Part 2, pp. 18–19, 65).

(1) *Q.* In other words, you would focus on the measurement of income? You would not be concerned about the balance sheet?
    A. Yes, I think that is the major focus.
(2) Much of the controversy over accrual of future losses has focused on whether a company had a liability for future losses or not. However, the impact on income should be overriding. The credit that arises from a provision for self-insurance is not a liability in the true sense, but that in and of itself should not keep it out of the balance sheet. APB Opinion 11 recognised deferred tax credits in balance sheets even though all agreed that the credit balances were not liabilities. Income statement consid-

erations were considered paramount in that case, and similar thinking should prevail in accounting for self-insurance.

(3) Defining assets does not really solve the problem of accounting for research and development expenditures and similar expenses. If some items that do not meet the definition of an asset are included in expenses of the current period, they may well distort the net income of that period because they do not relate to the revenues of that period. That accounting also may distort the net income of other periods in which the items more properly belong. The Board should focus on deferability that gets away from the notion of whether or not those costs are assets and concentrates on the impact of deferral on the determination of net income.

(4) Q. One of your criteria for capitalisation is that net income not be materially distorted. Do you have any operational guidelines to suggest regarding material distortion?
A. The profession has been trying to solve that one for a great many years and has been unsuccessful. I really do not have an answer.
Q. Then, is material distortion a useful criterion that we can work with?
A. Yes, I believe it is. Despite the difficulty. I think it is necessary to work with that criterion. It is a matter of applying professional judgement.

The implication was that 'proper matching' and 'non-distortion of income' were like beauty and lay in the eye of the beholder. The non-distortion of income, of course, does assume that we know what net income ought to be and achieve it by 'proper' matching of costs and revenues and the removal of whatever would distort. Periodic income would presumably be determined by 'gut-feel', experience, management intent or similar 'sound' concepts. The 'whatsits' are at the heart of some of our interesting accounting questions. Practices that have avoided 'distorting' net income include deferring losses, providing for future losses, providing for reorganisation expenses, providing for the cost of relining blast furnaces, major overhauls, dry-docking ships, and self-insurance provisions.

Deferral of losses
Some companies capitalise start-up losses, i.e. the losses incurred in the initial period of operation. Are these losses really assets? Presumably the argument would be that such losses are unavoidable in such a business situation and are essential if future profits are to be obtained. On this basis, of course, in the sure and certain expectation of future profits to come, all trading losses could be capitalised as assets as a signal that the company is a going concern! Trading losses occur in a period and should be recorded there. Management can explain that such initial losses are normal for the type of business and let the investor decide whether to accept the explanation. It has to be remembered that some companies with initial start-up losses never become profitable and die soon after birth.

Provisions for future losses
In the past companies may have made provisions when future trading losses

were anticipated. If such losses reflect the impairment of an asset then clearly the asset value should be diminished. If, however, they merely reflect an expected dip in trading performance, this is a feature of the years to come and has nothing to do with the present year's results. Investors would clearly like to be warned about expected poor performance in the future but this could be done through the operating and financial review. As no liability exists, however, no charge should be made in the profit and loss account.

Provisions for reorganisation expenses

Management may intend to reorganise the business, to incur redundancies, to close certain factories, but accounting, if it is to reflect reality, cannot be based on intention. Such accounting has been famously deemed by a past chairman of the Securities and Exchange Commission, as 'psycho-analytic accounting'. Should accounts be based on management's current thoughts? Management may change its mind! Does this year's charge become next year's income? Intentions do not result in liabilities but commitments do. Once a company is committed and cannot withdraw from a course of action then a liability clearly exists and a charge should be made.

Blast furnace provisions and dry-docking

Proper practice for some accountants would be to spread such costs over a reasonable period of time but companies do not incur the liabilities for relining blast furnaces or dry-docking ships while they are using the assets. They incur such costs when the repair work is begun. Until then no liability exists. The assets may suffer impairments in value but there is no obligation to reline a blast furnace or dry-dock a ship. Consequently, no liability exists but a diminution of the asset's value should be reflected in the accounts.[3] To some this might be mere geography in the financial statements but then lack of concern about whether assets are impaired or liabilities are created is irrelevant if the primary concern is with the matching of income and expenditure and a focus on the bottom line.

Self-insurance provisions

Not even those who advocated accruing self-insurance provisions would normally argue that these were liabilities. Such accruals are appropriations not charges. There is no liability existing at the time the charge for self-insurance is shown in the profit and loss account. No incident has occurred resulting in a commitment to ensure resources will leave the organisation. The fact is the company is uninsured and in the future an incident may happen which will cause a fall in income. Management making self-insurance provisions clearly believes that it would be cheaper not to insure and to bear the risk of future costs. Yet it is concerned about the volatility of income: a concern perhaps that shareholders would prefer a smooth level of income. In that case why does the company not insure?

The fact is that management is taking a risk and hiding that risk from users who may not want to be involved in companies that have a potential downside associated with a lack of insurance. It is probably cheaper for airlines not to insure their passengers on a flight and take a chance that none of their aircraft will crash. Every flight that lands is a bonus – the company got away with it! Would shareholders, being ignorant of the lack of insurance, be happy to continue to invest in a company which, in these litigious times, could be suddenly faced with a massive legal claim even though so-called insurance premiums had passed through its accounts? An airline that is uninsured is, *ceteris paribus*, presumably better off in cash flow terms than one that does insure – until the aircraft crashes!

It is understandable that management is concerned about volatility of profit. Finance directors responsible for financial planning, for regular reporting, find an unpredictable event that upsets those plans difficult to accept. For those who believe that such volatility affects the company's share price then clearly it is to be avoided at all costs; indeed if, as has been the case in the past, executive remuneration is tied to income, the desire to avoid it may become quite overwhelming.

Minimising the effects of erratic events is a job for management. To the extent volatile events occur and affect market prices we should reflect them in financial statements. Transparency is all-important – otherwise accounts will never reflect the actual risk to which investors and creditors are exposed. It is no argument in opposing a proposed standard to say that implementation might cause managers or investors to act differently. If the standard is deemed to reflect the situation appropriately, to oppose it would mean that it is better to hide reality. An appropriate presentation may, of course, mean the cost of borrowing is higher and the price of the company shares is lower. A major purpose of financial statements, however, is to help lenders and investors in their comparisons of alternative investments. If stability or volatility is important to users of financial statements, all the more reason that the degree of stability or volatility should be faithfully recorded.[4]

The fact is that companies do not have the same stability of earnings. We would expect certain companies to have different patterns of income – some industries (e.g. commodities) are inherently more risky than others – the need is to tell the story as it is. Financial information has to be neutral.

> To be reliable, the information contained in financial statements must be neutral, that is, free from bias. Financial statements are not neutral if, by the selection or presentation of information, they influence the making of a decision or judgement in order to achieve a pre-determined result or outcome.
>
> (ASB, 1991, chap. 2, para. 31)

Financial reporting is not financial analysis. Assessments of income may help investors to value management's performance. Future income potential assists investors in deciding whether to risk investing in a company. Consequently, measures of income should be useful for these and similar purposes. However, 'smoothed' income providing measures of income other than evaluations of actual performance probably does not assist in the prediction of income. It is up to investors, creditors and other users – and not the role of the accountant – to undertake evaluation and to average out distortions. The concept of earning power and the techniques of estimating it are part of financial analysis and not within the scope of financial reporting. The profit and loss account should reflect the volatility of performance, the balance sheet should show the genuine assets and liabilities of the business (the platform for future performance) and the ASB Statement, Operating and Financial Review (1993) should be used by management to explain the volatility and the 'revenue investment' for the future.

CONCLUSION – THE ROLE OF THE CONCEPTUAL FRAMEWORK

The Board's conceptual framework essentially involves asking the following questions:

(1) What is the asset?
(2) What is the liability?
(3) Does an asset or a liability or its value change?
(4) Does it increase or decrease?
(5) By how much?
(6) Did the change result from: investment by owners, distribution to owners, income, expense, unrealised gain or loss?

It is difficult to start at the bottom and work up but it is quite easy to start from the top and work down.

It should be said, however, that answers to all problems will not be derived from the conceptual framework. The intention is that the Board should approach problems in a consistent manner to move in a similar direction. A conceptual framework will disappoint those who expect it to lead unequivocally to a single answer to a problem. It is not a search for the ultimate truth but a search for consistency and useful concepts based on real-world experience.

It is high time to stop thinking about assets as costs in accounts and to start thinking of the resources that benefit an enterprise. It is time to ask whether descriptions and numbers we put in financial statements actually represent something that exists and are not simply something we insert in accounts. It will not be easy to change. We should challenge every non-separable asset that presently exists in accounting – does it make sense to the non-accountant?

We traditionally have had to be dragged kicking and screaming to accept every significant change in financial reporting – this is a natural human characteristic, but I suspect just as students in my time became familiar with Paton and Littleton and the matching principle, gradually students in this age will become familiar with the concepts of assets and liabilities and a different form of accounting will eventually evolve.

It is interesting to note that at a celebration of his 80th birthday, Paton stated that he wished that he had never been involved in the Paton and Littleton (1940) monograph or that it had gone out of print 25 years earlier. He had altered his view and now believed that the central element in business was the resources in hand or in prospect and the main objective of operations was the efficient utilisation of available assets. (The celebration of Paton's 80th birthday was clearly to enable the gentleman in question to give his views on the contemporary scene in case he would not be around much longer. Such fears proved to be entirely false. He died in 1990 at the age of 101!)

The draft Statement of Principles has profoundly affected the ASB's decisions. The Board's debates nowadays centre not so much on its members' experience but on whether something is, or gives rise to, an asset or a liability. That is the way I see accounting developing – is there a right to a stream of benefits? (an asset); or is there an obligation which will lead to resources leaving the organisation? (a liability). If the answer to either question is in the negative the item should not be included in the balance sheet.

The ASB's draft Statement of Principles is not a revolution nor is it unique to the UK – it broadly follows international views. Evolution is the key to the Board's approach. Standard-setters do sometimes accept that the world is not actually ready for some changes to existing practice. Hence no standard-setter has yet demanded all leases be capitalised (although we are thinking about it!). Similarly, so far only the Australian standard-setters have suggested that the pension cost for each year should measure the full amount of the apparent change in the net liability at the end of that year. The draft Statement of Principles will result in a development of practice. The ASB wants to move at the pace with which the financial community feels comfortable. The standards which put the principles into practice may not go as far as the ultimate goal indicated by the principles. The ASB may press the pace a bit by putting a shoulder to the wheel when the wagon seems to have stopped or is moving too slowly. Ultimately the future of our profession depends on describing financial performance and position as they really are. I am not sure at present we are actually doing that. The ASB still needs to push a little at this time!

Notes

1. Measurement may well become an issue but perhaps has not done so yet as a result of the ASB publishing contemporaneously with the draft chapter on measurement principles a discussion paper, *The Role of Valuation in Financial Reporting* (March 1993), which proposed a pragmatic approach to the incorporation of current values in financial statements.

2. For a detailed account see Jones , E. (1995) *True and Fair: A History of Price Waterhouse*, pp. 145–57, Hamish Hamilton, London.

3. The costs of repairs which add to the value of an asset can be capitalised when they are incurred.

4. This argument echoes that of Sprouse (1987).

References

Accounting Standards Board (ASB), ASB, London (July 1991) Exposure Draft, chs. 1 and 2, *The objectives of financial statements and the qualitative characteristics of financial information.*

Accounting Standards Board (ASB), ASB, London (December1991) Exposure Draft, ch. 6, *Presentation of financial information.*

Accounting Standards Board (ASB), ASB, London (July 1992) Discussion Draft, ch. 3, *The elements of financial statements.*

Accounting Standards Board (ASB), ASB, London (July 1992) Discussion Draft, ch. 4, *The recognition of items in financial statements.*

Accounting Standards Board (ASB), ASB, London (March 1993) Discussion Draft, ch. 5, *Measurement in financial statements.*

Accounting Standards Board (ASB), ASB, London (July 1994) Discussion Draft, ch. 7, *The reporting entity.*

Accounting Standards Board (ASB) (1993) Statement: Operating and Financial Review, ASB, London.

Baxter, W. T. (1962) Introduction, to W. T. Baxter and S. Davidson (eds.), *Studies in Accounting Theory*, Sweet & Maxwell, London, pp. viii–xii.

Dearing, R. (1988) *The Making of Accounting Standards: Report of the Review Committee under the Chairmanship of Sir Ron Dearing, CB*, ICAEW, London.

FASB (1974) *Public Record*, 2 vols., FASB, London.

Kirk, D. J. (1988) Looking back on fourteen years at the FASB: the education of a standard setter, *Accounting Horizons* (March), pp. 8–17.

Lee, T. A. and Tweedie, D. P. (1977) *The Private Shareholder and the Corporate Report*, ICAEW, London.

May, G. O. (1943) *Financial Accounting: A Distillation of Experience*, Macmillan, London.

Paterson, R. (1988) Building the right framework, *Accountancy* (October), pp. 26–7.

Paton, W. A. and Littleton, A. C. (1940) *An Introduction to Corporate Accounting Standards*, American Accounting Association, Ann Arbor, Michigan.

Solomons, D. (1989) *Guidelines for Financial Reporting Standards*, ICAEW, London.

Sprouse, R. T. (1987) Commentary on financial reporting – economic consequences: the volatility bugaboo, *Accounting Horizons* (March), pp. 87–90.

Sprouse, R. T. (1988) Commentary on financial reporting, *Accounting Horizons* (December), pp. 121–27.

Storey, R. K. (1990) The framework of accounting concepts and standards: in *Accountant's Handbook*, D. R. Carmichael, S. B. Lillien and M. Mellman (eds.), 7th edn, Wiley, New York.

4

Assets' Versus Firm's Value: What if the Parts Exceed the Whole?

WILLIAM T. BAXTER

INTRODUCTION

We tend to assume that a healthy firm's profits are big enough to lift its value as a whole (e.g. its takeover price) to more than the sum of its separate net asset values. Thanks to this excess, an enlightened firm that wants to raise assets to current values can usually do so with few qualms.

But an interesting question arises where a firm is in the opposite situation – where it is doing badly, so that the whole's value drops to less than the balance sheet total of its net assets. Some accountants hold that here the assets – even if otherwise sound enough – ought to be written down. Should they? And, if so, on what basis, and which of them should be the sacrificial lambs?

When we hear of such a firm, we naturally think that it probably should sell off its assets and close down, or put the assets to other uses. We think too that nobody would now start an enterprise that earns so little.

But sometimes the managers will not share such gloomy thoughts, and will doggedly struggle on. They may believe the firm's troubles to be temporary; they may be anxious to avoid staff unemployment, or to preserve their own pickings. So they continue to trade and to replace old assets, and see little need for write-downs.

To reach the kernel of our problem, however, we must suppose that the setback is indeed permanent, and the owners recognise this.

CURRENT VALUE

It is not unreasonable to think that, if the firm revalues, it will somehow make the new figures reflect the low profits now expected. Normally, however, accounting does not link each asset's current value to the firm's profits but to the asset's market price. We must consider whether we should abandon this practical rule where profits are bad.

Let us assume that the revaluation will be guided by the widely accepted rules of 'value to the business', i.e. deprival value (DV). This does indeed stress the need to write down unfruitful assets. As we all know, it regards value as the likely ill-effects on cash flow of an asset's hypothetical loss (e.g. of stores used up in production). Thus valuers behave like a thoughtful manager who is costing materials on hand for a job. Traditionally, he is said to select, in the light of the facts, from three possible figures: DV is the lower of:

(1) cost (i.e. potential outlays on replacement): if the firm were deprived of an asset, it would usually have to buy another; the cardinal advantage of ownership is that it obviates this payment; and
(2) (where the asset is not worth replacing) the higher of:
    (a) net realisable value (NRV), and
    (b) value in continued use (future benefits).

If a firm intends to stay in business, it will probably replace any lost asset. So DV is normally the obviated cost of replacement (RC), and not one of the other two possible figures. This is fortunate. While RC is not free from difficulties, it is simple and objective in comparison with the other values. By relying on the market's replacement price, the appraiser is spared the need for research (or guesswork) about prices in scrap markets or the asset's benefits (future cash flows).

In an unsuccessful firm, however, there is an obvious likelihood that assets will not be replaced. If they will not, then they can no longer be valued at RC, but will have to be shown at NRV or use value. Accountants find this a distasteful prospect. In particular, measurement of use value is repugnant because it demands speculation about the asset's future cash flows and then their discounting (DCF). Accountants dislike such speculation and, till recently, most of them were completely innocent of DCF calculation; the idea of using DCF versions of wealth was dismissed as 'sheer insanity', and use value was warily given labels such as 'economic value' (EV) – though all the other values are surely 'economic' too.

TYPES OF AILING FIRMS

Ailing firms can for our purposes be conveniently classified in three groups.

Firms with very short life expectancy

Where a firm faces a sombre future, its plans will depend in part on how much money it could raise by selling off its assets piecemeal.

Investment has been likened to a rat-trap: cash slips in more easily than it wriggles out again. Escape becomes less difficult if the assets can be sold off quickly and at high prices. Where they can, a depressed firm is more likely to turn them into cash, and to stop trading.

When such a sell-off is planned, assets should indeed be revalued. The DV of each is now its NRV. Conveniently, total NRVs here equal the whole firm's value.

Survivors with low profits

Suppose instead that the assets would fetch negligible prices. Here, escape from the rat-trap is less easy. The owners' strategy will depend largely on the firm's yearly pattern of cash receipts and payments.

Consider first a trading firm with cash, debtors, stocks, etc. (but no machines or buildings). With these assets, receipts and replacement payments go almost hand in hand during the trading cycle – which make the possible strategies very clear. Where profits are low, owners should estimate the likely proceeds of a closing-down sale, and the cost of paying off staff, etc., and then they must decide whether such net receipts outweigh the low net receipts from staying in business.

If they decide to stay, later profit figures will look incongruously small compared with the assets. But these will still be replaced in the course of ordinary trade. Accounting rules and common sense both tell us that the cash, stocks, etc. can hardly be valued at any figure save face value or RC; there is small scope for write-offs. So here the accountant must shrug his or her shoulders and accept that the odd-looking figures faithfully match the facts.

The same reasoning may apply to a firm with many fixed assets if their replacement dates and costs are spread out smoothly, leaving positive net cash flows. Here, however (if the owners decide to carry on), the idea of writing down fixed assets becomes alluring; low figures seem cautious and wise. But such bookkeeping would in fact flout logic. There is no reason for picking on the fixed assets except that their current values will not be obvious to the accounts' readers. There is likewise no rational way for determining the write-off from each asset; and mere rule-of-thumb deductions would be allocation at its worst. Deprival would here still lead to replacement; so DV is still RC. Again, the odd figures match the facts.

Survivors that will later face irregular outlays

Where a weakly firm faces big payments at irregular intervals, each payment prospect brings a powerful inducement to get out of the rat-trap. Payments for replacement of depreciating assets are an obvious example.

Suppose that revenue has fallen to a point at which profits (after depreciation) can still be earned, but at such a low level that entry to this kind of business would not be justified (i.e. profits would not cover opportunity cost). Here the low gains will prompt thoughts of closure. The grounds for closure get still stronger where the small profits sink into losses.

However, DCF budgets may show that the firm should carry on until some costly asset must be renewed (perhaps many years later). The firm should enjoy its net receipts as long as ageing assets can be coaxed to work. Depreciation is a bygone; cash budgets here give wiser advice than income statements.

ASSETS THAT WILL NOT BE REPLACED

Where an asset will not be replaced, the valuer (as we have seen) must abandon RC and study benefits. This rule applies alike to an ailing firm and a prosperous one (e.g. where the latter owns a semi-obsolete type of computer).

If the asset will be sold quickly, the benefits are now NRV. If it will instead be kept in service, the valuer would at first sight seem forced to estimate and discount its cash flows, i.e. to use the unloved EV.

But (something ignored by those who hold forth on this topic) such reasoning must often founder over an awkward new factor – jointness. A firm's assets very often work as a close-knit team; assets that earn in isolation are somewhat rare, and firms with only one asset are still rarer. A team's revenue cannot be unscrambled; its total can be valued, but not each asset's contribution (how much revenue is earned by the office filing cabinet?).

Suppose the ailing firm's assets include X and Y. How do we find X's value? We must distinguish between the two possibilities:

(1) X and Y are a team (as is usual), and earn jointly;
(2) X and Y are not a team but earn on their own.

In (1), separate benefits from X cannot be found. So the valuer is forced back to our fundamental question: what harm would deprival inflict on cash flows? We face trouble at once. If lack of X would make the firm close down, we may be tempted to say that X's value is the present value of all the firm's flows. But we could with equal justice say the same of Y; so, by this reasoning, the sum of the two asset values would be twice the firm's value. Which is absurd.Clearly neither X nor K can be valued at EV. Likewise any other written-down figure that purports to reflect separate benefits must be meaningless.

But fortunately there may often be an escape route from this difficulty. The firm deprived of X or Y would probably find means of continuing to trade for a while, e.g. by buying a second-hand asset or using extra labour. Then deprival's consequence would be the need to pay for such 'replacements'; benefits are once more irrelevant, and EV gives way to the accountant's old friend RC, now defined somewhat loosely.

In (2), an asset's benefits can be identified. The valuer must ask how a deprived owner could best 'make himself or herself whole' by getting a like set of flows. Sometimes a cheaper physical asset (e.g. a second-hand machine) would yield them; DV is then its price (again a much-stretched form of RC).

With other types of asset, the benefits may have to be measured directly as cash flows, i.e. DV seems to be pure EV. Now, EV is commonly thought to mean the owner's estimate of future benefits, discounted at his or her discount rate. But the market can estimate the value of cash flows; if we respect the usual accounting rule (stressing market value rather than benefits), surely we ought to reject the owner's estimate and instead use the market's – e.g. the price of shares, in companies of comparable risk, that would yield the market's estimate of the flows. This price may well be less than the owner's estimate.

By this reasoning, then, EV again gives way to (or is redefined as) market price of a different asset. It is still a form of RC.

Thus the grounds for ever using EV seem weak. Where an asset will not be sold or literally replaced, normally it can (and should) be given a value that is not EV but a redefined version of RC. The accountant's value formula is wrong.

CONCLUSION

These arguments suggest that accountants should not embark lightly on a downward revision of an ailing firm's balance sheet. Such a write-down would in some cases be irrational, even if the assets' total exceeds the firm's going-concern value; only if assets will not be replaced is a write-down justified.

So can anything be done where the figures look incongruous? Probably the least unsatisfactory plan would be to leave alone the separate DVs, and to deduct a blanket provision from the sum of a group of asset values. In this way, the balance sheet total could be cut down to the firm's low going-concern value (but, if valuation of each asset may be difficult and contentious, valuation of the firm is many times more so).

Maybe we here face a problem that defies tidy solution.

5

On the Microeconomic Foundations of Financial Ratio Analysis

HUW RHYS and MARK TIPPETT

INTRODUCTION

In a series of earlier papers, Tippett (1990), Rhys and Tippett (1993) and Tippett and Whittington (1995) have investigated the properties of financial ratios on the assumption that the underlying financial aggregates from which ratios are constructed are generated by some form of diffusion process.[1] That this assumption is useful stems from the fact that it provides a certain amount of analytical convenience and tractability. It remains unclear, however, what microeconomic structures, if any, might be consistent with such processes, and so our objective here is to investigate this issue in further detail. To this end, the chapter considers a firm which invests in a risk-free asset and a portfolio of risky assets. The ratio of the monetary investment in two of these assets is taken as an exemplar of the more general financial ratios modelled in the earlier papers.

The remainder of the chapter is organised into four sections. The first of these introduces the continuous time theory, which describes how firms allocate capital among a portfolio of risky assets. The next section examines the implications of this theory for the evolution of a firm's financial ratios. The third section explores how the theory may be applied in an empirical context. The final section contains our summary conclusions.

THEORY OF THE FIRM AND FINANCIAL RATIOS

Suppose a firm's opportunity set consists of two kinds of asset. The first is a risk-free asset (the borrowing and lending rate) with a sure return of r (per annum). The second is composed of risky investments. We follow Merton (1969, 1971, 1973) and others in assuming the risky asset return dynamics to be described by a geometric Brownian motion with instantaneous expected returns vector, $\mu = \begin{pmatrix} \mu_1 \\ \mu_2 \\ \mu_3 \\ | \\ \mu_n \end{pmatrix}$, for μ_j, the expected return on the jth risky asset. The

instantaneous variance–covariance matrix of asset returns is defined by

$$\Omega = \begin{pmatrix} \sigma_{11} & \sigma_{12} & ---- & \sigma_{1n} \\ \sigma_{21} & \sigma_{22} & ---- & \sigma_{2n} \\ | & | & | & | \\ \sigma_{n1} & \sigma_{n2} & ---- & \sigma_{nn} \end{pmatrix}$$

where σ_{jk} is the covariance between the returns on the jth and kth risky assets. These assumptions imply that the instantaneous return to the firm's equity capital, $W(t)$, is described by the following stochastic differential equation:

$$\frac{dW(t)}{W(t)} = [r + \alpha^{\mathrm{T}}.(\mu - \hat{r})]dt + \alpha^{\mathrm{T}}.dQ(t) \tag{5.1}$$

where $dW(t)$ is the instantaneous change in the firm's capital, $\alpha = \begin{pmatrix} \alpha_1 \\ \alpha_2 \\ \alpha_3 \\ | \\ \alpha_n \end{pmatrix}$ is the

vector containing the proportionate investments in the risky assets and α^{T} is its

transpose, $\hat{r} = \begin{pmatrix} r \\ r \\ r \\ | \\ r \end{pmatrix}$ is a vector, all of whose elements are the return to the

risk-free asset and $dQ(t) = \begin{pmatrix} dQ_1(t) \\ dQ_2(t) \\ dQ_3(t) \\ | \\ dQ_n(t) \end{pmatrix}$ is the vector of the risky asset 'white noise'

terms (Hoel, Port and Stone, 1972, p. 141; Tippett, 1990, p. 78). It follows that the instantaneous return to equity will be normally distributed with instantaneous mean $[r + \alpha^{\mathrm{T}}.(\mu - \hat{r})]$ and variance $\alpha^{\mathrm{T}}\Omega\alpha$.

Now suppose the managers of the firm determine the 'optimal' investment strategy by recourse to the 'bequest' function, $B(W,t) = e^{-\rho t}J(W)$. The bequest function measures the 'satisfaction', $J(W)$, obtained from bequeathing a given amount of capital to 'future generations', discounted at the 'own' rate of ρ (per annum). Using the principle of optimality from dynamic programming in conjunction with a limiting argument on a Taylor series for $B(W,t)$, shows that the proportionate investments, α, will be computed so as to maximise the following version of the Bellman–Dreyfus equation (Merton, 1969; Dreyfus and Law, 1977, p.198):

$$[r + \alpha^T.(\mu - \hat{r})]WJ'(W) - \rho J(W) + \frac{1}{2}\alpha^T\Omega\alpha W^2 J''(W) = \phi(\alpha) = 0$$

Differentiating this equation with respect to α shows the optimum vector of proportionate investment to be

$$\alpha = \frac{-J'(W)}{WJ''(W)}\Omega^{-1}(\mu - \hat{r})$$

where Ω^{-1} is the inverse of the variance–covariance matrix, Ω. Substituting this expression back into $\phi(\alpha)$ gives the *optimised* value of the Bellman–Dreyfus equation, namely:

$$0 = rWJ'(W) - \rho J(W) - \frac{1}{2}(\mu - \hat{r})^T\Omega^{-1}(\mu - \hat{r})\frac{[J'(W)]^2}{J''(W)} \tag{5.2}$$

This is a second-order non-linear ordinary differential equation and the initial condition $J(0) = 0$ taken in conjunction with the non-satiation requirement $J''(W) < 0$, implies *a unique class of solutions* of the form $J(W) = \beta W^\gamma$, where $\beta > 0$ and $0 < \gamma < 1$ are parameters; a detailed proof is contained in the appendix to this chapter. The Pratt–Arrow measure of relative risk aversion for preference functions of this type is $-\dfrac{WJ''(W)}{J'(W)} = (1 - \gamma)$. This in turn implies that the optimal vector of proportionate investments is independent of wealth, or:

$$\alpha = \frac{-J'(W)}{WJ''(W)}\Omega^{-1}(\mu - \hat{r}) = \frac{\Omega^{-1}(\mu - \hat{r})}{1 - \gamma} \tag{5.3}$$

It would, perhaps, help to clarify matters if the above theory were cast in terms of a numerical example.

Suppose, therefore, a firm is to make a portfolio decision involving two risky assets. The relevant variance–covariance matrix is assumed to take the following form:

$$\Sigma = \begin{pmatrix} 0.07 & 0.05 \\ 0.05 & 0.25 \end{pmatrix}$$

Hence, the variance of the returns on the first asset is contained in the first row and first column of the matrix and amounts to 0.07. Similarly, the covariance of the return between the first and second asset is contained in the first row, second column (or second row, first column) and amounts to 0.05. Similar considerations dictate that the variance of the return on the second asset is 0.25. We also assume the vector of asset expected returns to be given by:

$$\mu = \begin{pmatrix} 0.10 \\ 0.20 \end{pmatrix}$$

Hence, the expected return on the first asset is 10%, whilst for the second asset it amounts to 20%. Suppose also the return to the risk-free asset is $3^1/_3$%. From this it follows that the vector of asset risk premia is given by:

$$(\mu - \hat{r}) = \begin{pmatrix} \dfrac{1}{10} \\ \dfrac{1}{5} \end{pmatrix} - \begin{pmatrix} \dfrac{1}{30} \\ \dfrac{1}{30} \end{pmatrix} = \begin{pmatrix} \dfrac{1}{15} \\ \dfrac{1}{6} \end{pmatrix}$$

Finally, consistent with previous analysis, the bequest function is taken to be of the form $J(W) = \beta W^\gamma$ where $\gamma = \dfrac{1}{9}$.

The above data imply that the optimal vector of proportionate investments is:

$$\alpha = \frac{\Omega^{-1}(\mu - \hat{r})}{1 - \gamma} = \frac{9}{8} \begin{pmatrix} 0.07 & 0.05 \\ 0.05 & 0.25 \end{pmatrix}^{-1} \begin{pmatrix} \dfrac{1}{15} \\ \dfrac{1}{6} \end{pmatrix}$$

or:

$$\alpha = \frac{9}{8} \begin{pmatrix} \dfrac{50}{3} & -\dfrac{10}{3} \\ -\dfrac{10}{3} & \dfrac{14}{3} \end{pmatrix} \begin{pmatrix} \dfrac{1}{15} \\ \dfrac{1}{6} \end{pmatrix} = \begin{pmatrix} \dfrac{5}{8} \\ \dfrac{5}{8} \end{pmatrix}$$

Hence, the firm will invest a proportion of $\alpha_1 = \alpha_2 = \dfrac{5}{8}$, or 62.5% of its capital in both risky assets and finance this investment by borrowing the equivalent of $(1 - 2*0.625) = \dfrac{1}{4}$ of its capital through the capital market. In other words, the firm's debt to equity ratio will be 0.25. Finally, the ratio of the firm's investment in the two risky assets will be $\dfrac{0.625}{0.625} = 1$, whilst the ratio of the firm's investment in each risky asset to its investment in the risk-free asset will be $\dfrac{-0.625}{0.25} = -2.5$.

FINANCIAL RATIOS AS DETERMINED OR STOCHASTIC FUNCTIONS OF TIME

These results enable us to determine the distributional properties of the firm's asset holdings. Equation (5.3), for example, implies that $x = \alpha W = \dfrac{\Omega^{-1}(\mu - \hat{r})}{1 - \gamma} W$ will be the vector of *monetary* investments in the risky assets. In other words, the amount invested in the jth risky asset will be $x_j = \alpha_j W$, where, as previously, α_j is the jth element of the vector α, the proportion of the firm's equity capital invested in the *j*th risky asset. From this we have $dx_j(t) = \alpha_j dW(t)$, and we can use this in conjunction with equations (5.1) and (5.3) to show that:

$$\frac{dx_j(t)}{x_j(t)} = [r + \frac{(\mu - \hat{r})^T \Omega^{-1}(\mu - \hat{r})}{1 - \gamma}]dt + \frac{(\mu - \hat{r})^T \Omega^{-1}}{1 - \gamma}dQ_j(t) \tag{5.4}$$

In other words, the optimised proportionate change in the monetary investment in the *j*th risky asset will evolve as a geometric Brownian motion with instantaneous mean $[r + \dfrac{(\mu - \hat{r})^T \Omega^{-1}(\mu - \hat{r})}{1 - \gamma}]$ and variance $\dfrac{(\mu - \hat{r})^T \Omega^{-1}(\mu - \hat{r})}{(1 - \gamma)^2}$.

Tippett (1990, pp. 77–9) develops a theory of financial ratios based on the assumption that a firm's asset portfolio stochastically evolves in accordance with an equation like (5.4). However, the continuous time-rebalancing mechanism which underpins equation (5.4) implies that proportionate changes in a given asset will be perfectly correlated, both with changes in capital, $W(t)$, and, more importantly, with proportionate changes in the other assets composing the firm's portfolio of risky assets. This in turn implies that the firm's investment policy will be conducted in such a way that the ratio of its investments in any two assets will be constant through time. Hence, contrary to Tippett's (1990) analysis, the continuous time model presented her implies that financial ratios will *not* be stochastic functions of time.[2]

The key assumption which underpins the above analysis, of course, is that the investment policy is continuously revised. Rebalancing, however, is a costly exercise and, in any event, is not always completely within a firm's control. Hence, it is more likely that the continuous time-rebalancing model presented here represents an 'ideal' towards which the firm will periodically 'target' its investment policy (Lev, 1969; Boyle and Emmanuel, 1980; Leland, 1985). The revision mechanism implied by such periodic targeting means it is unlikely that proportionate changes in the value of a firm's assets will be perfectly correlated. Indeed, it opens up the possibility that the investment dynamics might well be described by a number of processes but two, in particular, stand out as potential candidates. The first is the geometric Brownian motion which underpins most of our analysis to date, and the second is the elastic random walk.

EMPIRICAL IMPLICATIONS

Consistent with previous analysis, assume that risky asset returns are generated by geometric Brownian motions but that the firm rebalances its asset portfolio on a periodic basis only. It then follows that in intervening periods, the firm's investment in the *j*th risky asset, will evolve in accordance with the stochastic differential equation (Tippett, 1990, pp. 77–9):

$$\frac{dx_j}{x_j} = \mu_j dt + dQ_j(t) \tag{5.5}$$

where, as previously, μ_j is the expected return to an investment in the *j*th risky asset and $dQ_j(t)$ is a white-noise process with variance and covariance parameters σ_j^2 and σ_{jk}, respectively. It also follows that in intervening periods the ratio, $r_{jk} = \dfrac{x_j}{x_k}$, of the monetary investment in the jth and kth assets will be described by the stochastic differential equation (Tippett, 1990, p. 78):

$$\frac{dr_{jk}}{r_{jk}} (\mu_j - \mu_k - \sigma_{jk} + \sigma_k^2)dt + dQ_j(t) - dQ_k(t) \tag{5.6}$$

In other words, instantaneous proportionate variations in the ratio will be normally distributed with mean $(\mu_j - \mu_k - \sigma_{jk} + \sigma_k^2)$ and variance of $\sigma_j^2 + \sigma_k^2 - 2\sigma_{jk}$. The solution to this equation, and hence the stochastic specification for the ratio, is (Tippett, 1990, p. 78):

$$r_{jk}(t) = r_{jk}(0)\exp[(\mu_j - \tfrac{1}{2}\sigma_j^2)t - (\mu_k - \tfrac{1}{2}\sigma_k^2)t + Q_j(t) - Q_k(t)] \tag{5.7}$$

where $Q_j(t)$ is normally distributed with mean zero and variance σ_j^2. Taking logarithms across equation (5.7) shows:

$$\log[r_{jk}(t)] = \alpha_{jk} + \beta_{jk}t + \varepsilon_{jkt} \tag{5.8}$$

where $\alpha_{jk} = \log[r_{jk}(0)]$ is the logarithm of the ratio at the start of the period under investigation, $\beta_{jk} = (\mu_j - \tfrac{1}{2}\sigma_j^2) - (\mu_k - \tfrac{1}{2}\sigma_k^2)$ and $\varepsilon_{jkt} = Q_j(t) - Q_k(t)$ is a stochastic error term. Tippett (1990, p. 81) notes, however, that ε_{jkt} is heteroscedastic (i.e. the variance increases through time) and it may also be shown that it is serially correlated in time. Hence, the standard OLS estimation procedures will be inefficient.

Alternative procedures, involving the estimation of less parameters, are also available. To illustrate, from equation (5.8), we have:

$$\log\frac{r_{jk}(t + \Delta t)}{r_{jk}(t)} = \beta_{jk} + \zeta_{jkt} \tag{5.9}$$

where $\beta_{jk} = [(\mu_j - \tfrac{1}{2}\sigma_j^2) - (\mu_k - \tfrac{1}{2}\sigma_k^2)]\Delta t$ and $\zeta_{jkt} = [Q_j(t + \Delta t) - Q_j(t)] - [Q_k(t + \Delta t) - Q_k(t)]$. Taking expectations across the above expression, it follows that the logarithm of the first difference in the ratio is a serially uncorrelated normal variate with mean $[(\mu_j - \tfrac{1}{2}\sigma_j^2) - (\mu_k - \tfrac{1}{2}\sigma_k^2)]\Delta t$ and variance $(\sigma_j^2 + \sigma_k^2 - 2\sigma_{jk})\Delta t$. Hence, if the geometric Brownian motion-based model is a satisfactory representation of the process from which a financial ratio is generated, we would expect the first differences in the logarithm of the ratio to be independent and identically distributed normal variates.

The targeting procedures implied by the discrete time-rebalancing interpretation of the model outlined in the second section of the chapter suggests, however, that a second class of processes could well provide a better description of the way firms implement their investment policies (Davis and Peles,

1922; Bliss, 1923; Boulding, 1950; Lev, 1969; Peles and Schneller, 1989). To illustrate, suppose $\frac{x_j}{\alpha_j W(t)} < 1$, so that the firm has less invested in the jth risky asset than is optimal. It will then attempt to increase its investment in this asset by partly liquidating its holdings in 'over-represented' assets (Friedman, 1956). Similarly, should $\frac{x_j}{\alpha_j W(t)} > 1$, the firm will attempt to decrease its investment in the asset. The following adjustment mechanism is consistent with such a rebalancing process:

$$\frac{dx_j}{x_j} = -\lambda \log[\frac{x_j}{\alpha_j W(t)}]dt + dZ_j(t) \tag{5.10}$$

where $dZ_j(t)$ is a white-noise process with variance and covariance parameters δ_j^2 and δ_{jk}, respectively. Note that this is an elastic random walk in the sense that x_j has a greater tendency to revert to its target value, $\alpha_j W(t)$, the further it is removed from it. The intensity with which it is drawn back to target is measured by the parameter $\lambda > 0$, which Lev (1969), Tippett (1990) and others define as the 'speed of adjustment' coefficient.

Using Ito's lemma in conjunction with equation (5.10) shows that the ratio of the firm's investment in any two assets will evolve in accordance with the stochastic differential equation (Tippett, 1990, p. 79):

$$\frac{dr_{jk}}{r_{jk}} = (\delta_k^2 - \delta_{jk} - \lambda \log \frac{r_{jk}}{\eta_{jk}})dt + dZ_j(t) - dZ_k(t) \tag{5.11}$$

where $\eta_{jk} = \frac{\alpha_j}{\alpha_k}$, for α_j the optimal proportionate investment in the jth asset, is the target ratio. In other words, instantaneous proportionate variations in the ratio will be normally distributed with mean $(\delta_k^2 - \delta_{jk} - \lambda \log \frac{r_{jk}}{\eta_{jk}})$ and variance $\delta_j^2 + \delta_k^2 - 2\delta_{jk}$. The solution to this equation, and hence the stochastic specification for the ratio, is (Tippett, 1990, pp. 79–80):

$$r_{jk}(t) = \eta_{jk} \exp[\gamma_{jk} - \frac{\delta_j^2 - \delta_k^2}{2\lambda}] \tag{5.12}$$

where $\gamma_{jk}(t) = \int_0^t e^{-\lambda(t-s)}[dZ_j(s) - dZ_k(s)]$. Now it can be shown that $\gamma_{jk}(t)$ is normally distributed with mean zero and variance $\frac{\delta_j^2 + \delta_k^2 - 2\delta_{jk}}{2\lambda}(1 - e^{-2\lambda t})$ (Hoel, Port and Stone, 1972, pp. 133, 147). From this it follows that the ratio is log-normally distributed and will fluctuate around its optimal value, η_{jk}, with $\gamma_{jk}(t)$ being in the nature of a 'noise' term.

Tippett (1990, p. 81) shows that if we take the logarithmic first difference across equation (5.12), then we have:

$$\log \frac{r_{jk}(t + \Delta t)}{r_{jk}(t)} = \alpha_{jk} + \beta \log[r(t)] + \varepsilon_{jkt} \tag{5.13}$$

where $\beta = -(1 - e^{-\lambda\Delta t})$, $\alpha_{jk} = \beta(\dfrac{\delta_j^2 - \delta_k^2}{2\lambda} - \log\eta_{jk})$ and

$\varepsilon_{jkt} = e^{-\lambda(t + \Delta t)} \int_{t}^{t +\Delta t} e^{\lambda s}[dZ_j(s) - dZ_k(s)]$. Furthermore, since it may be shown that the ε_{jkt} are serially uncorrelated with constant variance, it follows that the standard regression assumptions are satisfied.

A significant problem with the above approach, however, is that it assumes that the underlying expected returns and the variance–covariance matrix are time stationary and, as such, fails to allow for technological innovation. Nelson and Kang (1984, p. 78) suggest that one way of overcoming this is to incorporate time as an independent variable. This implies that we need to amend Tippett's (1990) analysis so that the basic regression equation takes the form:[3]

$$\log\frac{r_{jk}(t + \Delta t)}{r_{jk}(t)} = \alpha_{jk} + \beta\log[r(t)] + \theta_{jk}t + \varepsilon_{jkt} \qquad (5.14)$$

Since it may be shown that the ε_{jkt} are serially uncorrelated with constant variance, it follows that the standard regression assumptions are satisfied (Tippett, 1990, p. 81). Hence, if standard OLS methods were to be applied using the above model, we would expect the residuals to be consistent with an independent and identically distributed normal distribution. Furthermore, we would expect the parameters α_{jk}, β and θ_{jk} to be constant through time, with $\beta = (e^{-\lambda\Delta t} - 1)$ being negative.

SUMMARY CONCLUSIONS

This chapter has sought to place recent work on the stochastic evolution of financial ratios in a microeconomic context. The assumption that returns on risky investments evolve as geometric Brownian motions leads to the conclusion that the firm's optimal investment strategy will result in determined, and constant, investment ratios. To explain the apparently random behaviour of such ratios in reality it is necessary to relax an implausible assumption of the model that firms continuously rebalance their investments to maintain the optimal strategy. It is assumed, instead, that firms rebalance perfectly only at intervals, and that their investments evolve stochastically during the intervening periods, an assumption that is more consistent with the observed behaviour of such ratios.

The assumption that investments evolved as geometric Brownian motions, as did their returns, implied that the firm's investment policy in the intervening periods was not influenced by changes in the underlying optimal investment strategy. The assumption that investments evolved as an elastic random walk, however, enabled the model to encompass the possibility that firms, while not perfectly rebalancing continuously, do attempt 'on average' to make the investment decisions which draw the overall investment portfolio towards the optimal one.

MATHEMATICAL APPENDIX:
SOLUTION OF BELLMAN–DREYFUS EQUATION

For the equation:

$$rWJ'(W) - \rho J(W) - c\frac{[J'(W)]^2}{J''(W)} = 0$$

where $c = \frac{1}{2}(\mu - \hat{r})^T \Omega^{-1}(\mu - \hat{r})$, make the change of variable $z = \dfrac{J}{W\dfrac{dJ}{dW}}$ from which it follows:

$$\frac{dW}{W} = \frac{1 - \dfrac{\rho}{r}z}{1 - \dfrac{(r + \rho + c)}{r}z + \dfrac{\rho}{r}z^2}dz$$

Now the two roots of the denominator of the above equation have the property that $\gamma_1 + \gamma_2 = \dfrac{(r + \rho + c)}{r}$ and $\gamma_1\gamma_2 = \dfrac{\rho}{r}$, where γ_1 and γ_2 are the reciprocals of the roots. Hence, we can represent the above equation as:

$$\frac{dW}{W} = \frac{1 - \gamma_1\gamma_2 z}{(1 - \gamma_1 z)(1 - \gamma_2 z)}dz$$

integrating through the above expression implies:

$$\lambda W = (1 - \gamma_1 z)^{\frac{-A}{\gamma_1}}(1 - \gamma_2 z)^{\frac{-B}{\gamma_2}}$$

where λ is a constant of integration and $A + B = 1$, $A\gamma_2 + B\gamma_1 = \gamma_1\gamma_2$. Using the fact that $z = \dfrac{J}{W\dfrac{dJ}{dW}}$ implies the above result can be restated as:

$$\lambda = \frac{dJ}{dW}[W\frac{dJ}{dW} - \gamma_1 J(W)]^{\frac{-A}{\gamma_1}}[W\frac{dJ}{dW} - \gamma_2 J(W)]^{\frac{-B}{\gamma_2}}$$

Further, since $\dfrac{1}{J(W)} \cdot \dfrac{dJ}{dW} = \dfrac{1}{Wz}$, it follows that:

$$\frac{dJ}{J} = \frac{dW/dz}{Wz}dz = \frac{dz}{zW\dfrac{dz}{dW}} = \frac{1 - \gamma_1\gamma_2 z}{z(1 - \gamma_1 z)(1 - \gamma_2 z)}dz$$

Integrating through the above expression implies:

$$\theta J(W) = z(1 - \gamma_1 z)^{-A}(1 - \gamma_2 z)^{-B}$$

where θ is a constant of integration. Again, since $\dfrac{1}{J(W)} \cdot \dfrac{dJ}{dW} = \dfrac{1}{Wz}$, it follows that:

$$\theta = [W\frac{dJ}{dW} - \gamma_1 J(W)]^{-A}[W\frac{dJ}{dW} - \gamma_2 J(W)]^{-B}$$

Substituting $W = 0$ in the expression for λ implies:

$$\lambda = \frac{-J'(0)}{J(0)\,(\gamma_1)^{A/\gamma_1}(\gamma_2)^{B/\gamma_2}}$$

Similarly,

$$\theta = \frac{-1}{J(0)\,(\gamma_1)^A(\gamma_2)^B}$$

From these results it follows:

$$[J(W) - \frac{W}{\gamma_1}\cdot\frac{dJ}{dW}]^{\frac{A}{\gamma_1}}\,[J(W) - \frac{W}{\gamma_2}\cdot\frac{dJ}{dW}]^{\frac{B}{\gamma_2}} = \frac{\frac{dJ}{dW}\cdot J(0)}{J'(0)}$$

and:

$$[J(W) - \frac{W}{\gamma_1}\cdot\frac{dJ}{dW}]^A[J(W) - \frac{W}{\gamma_2}\cdot\frac{dJ}{dW}]^B = J(0)$$

These two equations give the general solution to the Bellman–Dreyfus equation under given initial conditions for $J(W)$ and $J'(W)$. Now suppose we set $J(0) = 0$, in which case we have $J(W) = \frac{W}{\gamma_1}\cdot\frac{dJ(W)}{dW}$ or $J(W) = \frac{W}{\gamma_2}\cdot\frac{dJ(W)}{dW}$ or both. Solving these equations implies that the general solution of the Bellman–Dreyfus equation is:

$$J(W) = \beta_1 W^{\gamma_1} + \beta_2 W^{\gamma_2}$$

where β_1 and β_2 are constants.

To obtain more information about the nature of this solution, note that letting $J(W) = \beta W^\gamma$ in the Bellman–Dreyfus equation implies $\psi(\gamma) = r\gamma^2 - (r + \rho + c)\gamma + \rho = 0$ with $r, \rho, c > 0$. The two roots of this equation, γ_1 and γ_2 have the property that $\gamma_1 + \gamma_2 = \frac{(r + \rho + c)}{r}$ and $\gamma_1\gamma_2 = \frac{\rho}{r}$. Further, note that $\psi'(\gamma) = 2r\gamma - (r + \rho + c)$ whilst $\psi''(\gamma) = 2r > 0$ and so the polynomial has a single stationary point which is a minimum. Further, $\psi(0) = \rho > 0$ and $\psi(1) = -c < 0$ and so one root, say γ_1, lies between zero and one. Note that for this root, $J'(W) = \beta\gamma_1 W^{\gamma_1 - 1} > 0$ and $J''(W) = \beta\gamma_1(\gamma_1 - 1)W^{\gamma_1 - 2} < 0$, provided $\beta > 0$ and so it satisfies standard 'marginal utility' assumptions. The other root, γ_2, exceeds unity and implies $J'(W) < 0$ and $J''(W) > 0$ (wealth satiation) and so need not be considered further.

Hence $J(W) = \beta W^\gamma$ with $\beta > 0$ and $0 < \gamma < 1$ is the 'unique' solution to the Bellman–Dreyfus equation under the initial condition $J(0) = 0$.

Notes

1. A diffusion process is a Markov process which involves continuous changes of state. In the present context this implies that changes in financial aggregates are 'small' and serially independent. Cox and Miller (1965, p. 203) and Crank (1975, p.1) provide particularly readable introductions to this area, including several examples.

2. Following Tippett (1990, p. 85) we can apply Ito's lemma to the ratio $r = \frac{x_j}{x_k}$ to give $\frac{dr}{r} = \frac{dx_j}{x_j} - \frac{dx_k}{x_k} + (\frac{dx_k}{x_k})^2 - (\frac{dx_j}{x_j} \cdot \frac{dx_k}{x_k})$. However, since both x_j and x_k are generated by equation (5.4), it follows that $\frac{dx_j}{x_j} = \frac{dx_k}{x_k}$ and $(\frac{dx_k}{x_k})^2 = (\frac{dx_j}{x_j} \cdot \frac{dx_k}{x_k}) = \frac{(\mu - \hat{r})^T \Omega^{-1} (\mu - \hat{r})}{(1 - \gamma)^2}$.

Hence $\frac{dr}{r} = 0$ which implies that the ratio is constant through time.

3. Assuming the investment dynamics take the form $\frac{dx_j}{x_j} = \lambda[\log\frac{x_j}{k} - \mu_j t]dt + dZ_j(t)$, implies that the ratio will take the form given by equation (5.14). It may also be shown that $\theta_{jk} = -\beta(\mu_j - \mu_k)$, can be interpreted as a kind of drift term.

References

Bliss, J. (1923) *Financial and Operating Ratios in Management*, Ronald Press, New York.

Boulding, K. (1950) *A Reconstruction of Economics*, John Wiley, New York.

Boyle, P. and Emmanuel, D. (1980) Discretely adjusted option hedges, *Journal of Financial Economics*, Vol. 8, no. 3, pp. 259–82.

Cox, D. and Miller, H. (1965) *The Theory of Stochastic Processes*, Chapman & Hall, London.

Crank, J. (1975) *The Mathemathics of Diffusion*, Clarendon Press, Oxford.

Davis, H. and Peles, Y. (1992) Further remarks on 'The duration of the adjustment process of financial ratios', *Review of Economics and Statistics*, Vol. 74, no. 3, pp. 557–8.

Dreyfus, S. and Law, A. (1977) *The Art and Theory of Dynamic Programming*, Academic Press, New York.

Friedman, M. (1956) The quantity theory of money – a restatement, in M. Friedman (ed.), *Studies in the Quantity Theory of Money*, Chicago University Press, Chicago.

Hoel, P., Port, S. and Stone, C. (1972) *Introduction to Stochastic Processes*, Houghton Mifflin, Boston, Mass.

Leland, H. (1985) Option pricing and replication with transactions costs, *Journal of Finance*, Vol. XL, no. 5, pp. 1283–1301.

Lev. B. (1969) Industry averages as targets for financial ratios, *Journal of Accounting Research*, Vol. 7, no. 2, pp. 290–9.

Merton, R. (1969) Lifetime portfolio selection under uncertainty: the continuous time case, *Review of Economics and Statistics*, Vol. LI, no. 3, pp. 247–57.

Merton, R. (1971) Optimum consumption and portfolio rules in a continuous-time model, *Journal of Economic Theory*, Vol. 3, no. 4, pp. 373–413.

Merton, R. (1973) An intertemporal capital asset pricing model, *Econometrica*, Vol. 41, no. 5, pp. 867–87.

Nelson, C. and Kang, H. (1984) Pitfalls in the use of time as an explanatory variable in regression, *Journal of Business and Economics Statistics*, Vol. 2, no. 1, pp. 73–82.

Peles, Y. and Schneller, M. (1989) The duration of the adjustment period of financial ratios, *Review of Economics and Statistics*, Vol. LXXI, no. 3, pp. 527–32.

Rhys, H. and Tippett, M. (1993) On the steady state properties of financial ratios, *Accounting and Business Research*, Vol. 23, no. 92, pp. 500–10.

Tippett, M. (1990) An induced theory of financial ratios, *Accounting and Business Research*, Vol. 21, no. 81, pp. 77–85.
Tippett, M. and Whittington, G. (1995) An empirical evaluation of an induced theory of financial ratios, *Accounting and Business Research*, Vol. 25, no. 99, pp. 208–18.

6

Directors' Perceptions of the Effects and Values of Share Option Rewards

DON EGGINTON, GEOFFREY ELLIOTT,
JOHN FORKER and PAUL GROUT

INTRODUCTION

Grants of share options to directors and company executives have become an established feature of corporate reward packages. This relatively recent development has been accompanied by anxieties over the disclosure and corporate governance implications of option rewards (e.g. FASB, 1981; ABI, 1987; Cadbury, 1992; ABI/NAPF, 1993; SEC, 1993) as well as a variety of research into issues relating to executive share options (ESOs).

Among the advantages that can be advanced for executive share options are the alignment of management rewards directly with those of shareholders' share values over the option period, and the longer time horizon of ESOs compared with the conventional annual earnings measures on which bonuses are commonly based. Conventional short-term earnings performance measures can be open to manipulation of the sort which features in the accounting policy choice literature (e.g. Watts and Zimmerman, 1986, chap. 11), and such measures can also encourage management to focus on activities which bring quick results at the expense of long-term benefits, in ways documented in the behavioural literature (e.g. adopting cost-reduction rather than productivity-raising strategies which take longer to mature: Likert, 1967, chap. 5).[1] Thus option rewards, which depend on the 'neutral' measurement of the market and require managers to take a view of several years, can have positive potential in countering both the manipulative potential and the 'short-termism' of conventional performance measures. However, ESOs also pose problems which will be considered in this chapter, and the potentially unbounded rewards that could arise from share price increases, together with some well-publicised cases of substantial option packages, cause unease over the relationship between option rewards and management effort.

In essence the central concern over ESOs is whether they give value for shareholders' money. One approach to this issue is to examine the performance of companies with share option plans, but the relationships are complex and the results of research are mixed. For example, support for the existence of a positive link between share options and 'long-termism' arises from findings that, on the announcement of mergers, US bidding firms with long-term compensation plans experience high abnormal returns (Tehranian, Travlos and Waegelein, 1987; Travlos and Waegelein, 1993). UK research into the association between employee share ownership schemes and corporate performance (Richardson and Nejad, 1986) indicate that UK companies setting up such schemes had a faster than average subsequent increase in share price. However, causality is not clear, because such schemes may be more likely to be initiated when a company's prospects are good. On the other hand, research into changes in option plans of US companies showed that subsequent cumulative abnormal stock market returns declined for about two-thirds of the companies (DeFusco, Zorn and Johnson, 1991), which suggests that changes in option plans tend to occur when a company's prospects are poor.

This chapter addresses 'value for money' differently. One issue to be examined involves the perceptions of directors on the motivational effects of ESOs compared with conventional performance rewards. The other issue, which is the main concern of the chapter, relates to the values which directors themselves place on ESOs in their companies, compared with estimates of the option value sacrificed by shareholders. Although the focus is on directors' rewards, the results also have implications for executive rewards in general.

Certain forms of share options are traded, and have explicit market prices. But ESOs, which are specific to an individual, are not tradeable. Price estimation based on the Black–Scholes (1973) option pricing model works well in replicating market values, so an option pricing model approach can be used to estimate the value shareholders forgo when non-traded options are granted to directors. Given directors' own valuation on the grant of an ESO, comparisons can be made between 'shareholder cost' and 'director benefit'. However, there are different views on the applicability of the conventional option pricing model to ESOs and the implications of these arguments for the present study are considered.

Both the motivation and valuation issues are then explored in a survey of directors of UK listed companies. The results provide support for some motivational benefits of options, but with significant differences between the views of executive and non-executive directors. On the fundamental issue of value, in the majority of cases values assigned by the directors to options were below estimates of shareholder costs derived from the option pricing model. However, there was very considerable dispersion and a substantial proportion of directors gave values in excess of those derived from the option pricing model. Consequently, the results point to the need for option rewards to be correctly focused in terms of both motivation and recipient valuation if they are to be cost-effective.

IMPLICATIONS OF SHARE OPTIONS REWARDS

The use of ESOs brings advantages and disadvantages for both shareholders and directors. The fact that they feature so widely in reward packages[2] suggests that the balance of advantage is considered to be favourable, although it need not be the case that both the director and shareholder groups are net beneficiaries.

Considering the shareholder viewpoint first, there are four main categories of potential advantage over conventional bonus payments:

(1) ESOs potentially motivate directors to act in the shareholders' interest by offering a reward for performance which is directly aligned with a major shareholder objective: increase in share price (the other major objective being dividend payments).

(2) ESOs have a longer time horizon (typically three to five years to exercise) than the annual earnings measures on which more conventional bonus payments are based, and can therefore act as an antidote to 'short-termism' in decision-making as well as an incentive for executives to remain with the company.

(3) There are tax advantages for option schemes which are approved for tax purposes in the UK, in that any tax is not payable on the grant of an option but is deferred until shares are sold and any gains then arising are taxed as capital gains. For some years the benefit was substantial, because gains were taxed at a rate below the marginal rate of highly paid individuals.[3] Gains are now taxed at taxpayer's marginal income tax rate, but there remains a benefit where the capital gains annual exemption limit[4] has not otherwise been exhausted.

(4) Share price is less vulnerable to director manipulation than measures based on conventional accounting profits, such as changes in earnings per share.

Against these advantages there are problems with share option rewards from the shareholder viewpoint:

(1) Macroeconomic factors affect stock market prices and may have little or nothing to do with the performance of directors. Thus directors who perform very well within their company in difficult circumstances in a 'bear' market may not get any reward from ESOs, but in a 'bull' market directors get rewards from share options with minimal effort. A fairly common solution in a bear market is the practice of voluntary lapsing, whereby ESOs are reissued at a new lower exercise price reflecting market changes, but there is a notable absence of a corresponding practice in a bull market. There are better devices to overcome this problem,[5] but they do not feature in conventional option schemes which are under consideration here.

(2) Options could motivate directors to take greater risks (e.g. accept projects with a much greater dispersion of returns) which could increase the company's beta without the knowledge of existing shareholders.

(3) Directors may adjust their own asset portfolios when options are granted. Specifically they may well reduce their holdings of company shares and exercise existing options in the company when they are granted fresh options. A one-for-one sale for every option granted will have no positive effect on incentives.

(4) Options could encourage directors to exploit information asymmetries to the detriment of shareholders (e.g. delaying adverse actions until after the exercise of options and sale of shares) although the same problem arises with conventional director shareholdings.[6]

(5) The grant and exercise of an option need not involve a cash flow from the company, where the common practice is adopted of satisfying exercise by the issue of new shares. In the absence of UK rules for disclosing estimated cost of options,[7] the value sacrificed by shareholders is never made explicit. Thus excessive rewards are less liable to scrutiny.

There are, of course, other problems concerning options (e.g. uncertainty over the impact of one individual's efforts on a company's performance) but they can apply equally to conventional bonuses and therefore are not relevant to a comparison between the two.

The first three items in the shareholder list of option advantages have potentially positive implications for directors. On the other hand, only the first of the shareholder problem list has potentially adverse effects for directors. But even those effects apply only in a bear market, where the practice of voluntary lapsing is available for the benefit of directors. Thus the simple listing suggests a balance of benefits which is far greater for directors than for shareholders.

Whether options achieve overall 'value for money' for shareholders depends on how directors' behaviour is affected by options, and on the value which directors themselves place on option rewards relative to the sacrifice of value by shareholders. These issues require some preliminary consideration before turning to the survey.

Effects of options on performance and tenure

Of the potential advantage to shareholders of option rewards discussed above, the first two are particularly dependent on the behaviour of directors in response to such rewards. The effects of options on both the performance and time horizons of directors will depend on the personal perceptions of individual directors and their consequent behaviour.

Appropriate perceptions by directors on these issues are a prerequisite for favourable shareholder results, although of course perceptions do not ensure that results will be favourable. In other words director perceptions consistent with the hypothetical advantages of options are a necessary, although not sufficient, condition for directors to achieve benefits which will accrue to shareholders.

There is little evidence on these issues and it was decided to ask directors for their attitudes to the performance and tenure effects of options as part of our survey. For comparison purposes attitudes to the performance and tenure effects of conventional rewards were also included in the survey.

In considering directors' options there is an important distinction between executive directors who receive such awards and non-executive directors who are not active in management (of the company concerned) and do not normally[8] have options as part of their remuneration. Non-executive directors are, however, active in the remuneration committees which decide on the rewards structure for executives. Thus executive and non-executive directors have somewhat different interests in option issues. It was therefore decided to question executive and non-executive directors separately.

Option values to shareholders and directors

An ESO granted to a director or any other employee is effectively a call option on the company's shares (Noreen and Wolfson, 1981). For traded call options the option pricing model (OPM) developed by Black and Scholes (1973) has been shown to give good estimates of traded values. Copeland and Weston (1988, p. 285), referring to empirical investigations with market price of options, comment that 'the Black and Scholes OPM predicts option prices very well indeed'.[9] Thus the OPM can provide a means of estimating untraded ESO values (e.g. Foster, Koogler and Vickrey, 1991).

However, ESOs are not identical to call options tradeable on the stock market, for reasons which are analysed by Jennergren and Naslund (1992, 1993), Foster, Koogler and Vickrey (1993) and Hemmer, Matsunaga and Shevlin (1994). There are two major sources of difference:

(1) Unlike conventional call options, ESOs have stochastic lives because they are subject to cancellation if the grantee ceases to be employed by the company. That may happen as a result of resignation, death or takeover. This will be referred to as the premature cancellation effect on value.

(2) An ESO is specific to an individual, so the holder does not have a readily marketable asset. The holder cannot liquidate, so that the ESO has limitations similar to that of a non-transferable term bond. A related consequence is that the holder's portfolio cannot be fully diversified,[10] so that for the holder ESOs will have undiversifiable risk. This will be referred to as the illiquidity effect on value.

Both of these elements can reduce value to the holder. But only the first affects value from the shareholders' viewpoint. The premature cancellation effect cuts shareholder cost identically with the reduction in value to the grantee, since the probability of cancellation reduces the prospect that shares will be delivered on the exercise of the option. However, there are a number of grounds for believing that the financial effect on option value will rarely be material. The departure of executive directors from companies is exceptional rather than normal; for example Main, O'Reilly and Crystal (1994) disclose that the average time current chief executives had already served with their companies was 19 years in the UK and 23 years in the USA, suggesting substantial stability of tenure. If directors leave voluntarily they will usually have flexibility in timing, which can allow the exercise of options before departure. When executive directors leave involuntarily the managerial labour market operates to give protection from corporate opportunism regarding the director's long-term contribution (Fama, 1980; Williamson, 1985, chap. 12). In particular, service contracts provide compensation for loss of office compensating prematurely departing directors for options held prior to the date of exercise. Finally, even in the case of the employing company being taken over, it is usual for executives in the 'victim' company to be given benefits which preserve or compensate for their existing options.[11] For all these reasons we consider that the prospect of premature cancellation will rarely have a material impact on option value. The same conclusion is reached by Foster, Koogler and Vickrey (1993) by different means.

The illiquidity effect on option value, arising because ESOs are not tradeable, applies only to the holder's financial flexibility during the life of the ESO. For shareholders the prospective sacrifice from having to supply shares on the eventual exercise of the option is in no way diminished by the holder's lack of flexibility. Therefore when an ESO is granted there is an asymmetry between value to the holder and shareholder cost in terms of prospective sacrifice of value.

Thus so far as the *shareholder* is concerned, the difference in characteristics between ESOs and call options tradeable on a stock market are not material for valuation purposes. Option pricing approaches developed for tradeable options can be used to estimate the costs of ESOs to shareholders. But where directors are concerned, it is to be expected that values of ESOs to directors will be lower than equivalent tradeable options as a result of the illiquidity effect.

Our survey took the approach of asking directors for the value they would attach to an option in their company, which could then be compared with estimates of the sacrifice of value by shareholders. The illiquidity effect was expected to reduce directors' values below shareholder value, but the extent of the differences might allow an assessment of the hidden costs of this form of reward. A more fundamental consideration was the extent to which directors fully understood the value implications of share options, and for this purpose the survey included a question on values of three-year and five-year options. The latter would have higher values under the OPM and director awareness of relative values could provide an indicator of their understanding of option value implications in general.

THE SURVEY AND RESULTS

The survey was conducted by a postal questionnaire which was sent with a personally addressed letter to all directors of a sample of 100 large listed UK companies.[12] The questionnaire, reproduced in the appendix to this chapter, had marginal differences in wording between executive directors and non-executive directors.[13] Nine hundred and ten questionnaires were dispatched and 373 replies were received (253 from executives and 120 from non-executives), a response rate of 41%. However, a substantial number of respondents did not give usable replies on all questions, particularly on option values. Only 300 replies were usable for all questions (209 from executives and 91 from non-executives), a usable response rate of 33%. The questionnaire did not identify individual respondents but a company identifier was used which allowed option value calculations from the responses.

Effects of options on performance and tenure

Directors were asked to respond on the performance and tenure effects of three different types of reward. The summary of responses, together with chi-square statistics for association between pairs of responses (responses E1a against E2a, etc.), appear in Table 6.1.

Executive directors were first asked if they held options under a scheme in their company. Those who did were asked if they thought the effect of holding options on their performance was very favourable, favourable, negligible or unfavourable. The same choice of responses was then offered for the effect of options on how long the directors were likely to stay with the company. The results appear as 'Effects on performance' and 'Effects on tenure' in Table 6.1, in the column headed 'Option rewards E1'.

The next questions asked if executive directors received any financial rewards based on accounting measures of group performance, such as profit or earnings per share. For those who received these rewards the same choice of responses was offered for performance and tenure as before. The results appear in the column headed 'Group rewards E2' in Table 6.1.

The directors were then asked if they received any financial rewards on individual or unit performance below group level, such as divisional return on capital employed. Those who received such rewards were again offered the choice of responses for performance and tenure. These results appear in the column headed 'Individual unit rewards E3' in Table 6.1.

The questions posed to non-executive directors differed only in that they asked the respondents to give their opinions on the performance and tenure effects for executive directors in their companies.[14] Thus, whereas the responses of executive directors related to their own behaviour, the responses of non-executives were generalised responses on their perceptions of the effects on their colleagues. The results for non-executive directors are shown in the middle section of Table 6.1 under the headings N1, N2 and N3.

It was anticipated that self-interest would lead directors generally, and executive directors in particular, to respond favourably on the effects of different rewards. The main implications of the results were expected to lie in the differences in perceptions between categories. Although differences between categories yield some strong results in Table 6.1, there are surprises in the degree of director scepticism over the effects of rewards, bearing in mind that all responses related to reward structures in their own companies.

Turning first to the responses of executive directors, column E1 shows that almost a quarter of executive directors in companies with option schemes saw

Table 6.1 Responses of directors on the motivation effects of alternative rewards

Executive directors	Option rewards E1	χ^2 statistics	Group rewards E2	χ^2 statistics	Individual or unit rewards E3	χ^2 statistics
Number participating in each form of reward	240		204		51	
(a) Effects on performance (%):						
Very favourable	24.6		32.8		39.2	
Favourable	52.1	[E1a]:[E2a] 5.40	50.0	[E2a]:[E3a] 0.74	45.1	[E3a]:[E1a] 4.95
Negligible	22.9		17.2		15.7	
Unfavourable	0.4		0.0		0.0	
χ^2 statistics	[E1a]:[E1b] 0.32		[E2a]:[E2b] 31.85*		[E3a]:[E3b] 6.15	
(b) Effects on tenure (%):						
Very favourable	22.5		21.1		27.5	
Favourable	52.9	[E1b]:[E2b] 19.23*	36.3	[E2b]:[E3b] 1.04	35.3	[E3b]:[E1b] 6.00
Negligible	24.2		42.6		37.3	
Unfavourable	0.4		0.0		0.0	

Non-executive directors' opinions on effects for executive directors	Option rewards N1	χ^2 statistics	Group rewards N2	χ^2 statistics	Individual or unit rewards N3	χ^2 statistics
Number of non-executive directors responding that executive directors in their companies received a particular form of reward	116		111		53	
(a) Effects on performance (%):						
Very favourable	24.1		24.3		24.5	
Favourable	59.5	[N1a]:[N2a] 3.73	67.6	[N2a]:[N3a] 1.09	71.7	[N3a]:[N1a] 5.51
Negligible	16.4		8.1		3.8	
Unfavourable	0.0		0.0		0.0	
χ^2 statistics	[N1a]:[N1b] 5.75		[N2a]:[N2b] 20.23*		[N3a]:[N3b] 12.07*	
(b) Effects on tenure (%):						
Very favourable	12.9		13.5		15.1	
Favourable	66.4	[N1b]:[N2b] 5.23	55.0	[N2b]:[N3b] 0.20	56.6	[N3b]:[N1b] 2.29
Negligible	19.8		31.5		28.3	
Unfavourable	0.9		0.0		0.0	

Association of responses of executive and non-executive directors	Option rewards χ^2 statistics	Group rewards χ^2 statistics	Unit rewards χ^2 statistics
Effects on performance	[E1a]:[N1a] 2.88	[E2a]:[N2a] 9.81†	[E3a]:[N3a] 8.74†
Effects on tenure	[E1b]:[N1b] 7.09‡	[E2b]:[N2b] 10.38†	[E3b]:[N3b] 5.07

* Significant at 1%.   † Significant at 5%.   ‡ Significant at 10%.

options as having negligible effects on their performance (22.9%) and tenure (24.2%). The performance effects of conventional group and unit rewards (E2a and E3a) produced consistently more favourable responses, although the differences were not statistically significant. These more favourable responses for group and unit rewards are consistent with behavioural theory that motivation is influenced by (among other things) an individual's expectations that effort can achieve a particular goal and that achievement of the goal will eventually be rewarded.[15] The link between effort and achievement is more transparent for an operating unit than for a group of such units (the former offers less scope for free-riders) and the receipt of conventional awards is less uncertain than the outcome of option rewards, which are subject to market-wide factors outside the control of management.

But executive directors thought options had much more favourable effects on their tenure than group rewards (E1B:E2b = 19.23, significant at 1%). As a counterpart to that executives saw group rewards as having more favourable effects on performance than on tenure (E2a:E2b = 31.85, significant at 1%). On the other hand, no strong differences emerged from the tenure comparison between options and unit rewards or between the performance and tenure effects of unit rewards. Thus the strongest executive perception of options was that they are more effective than conventional group rewards in inducing the recipients to stay with a company.

The responses of non-executive directors was less dispersed and strongly bunched at 'favourable' for all questions. This may suggest that non-executive directors were less discriminating in their perceptions, which would raise doubts about the effectiveness of non-executives in remuneration committees.[16] In fairness to non-executives it must be said that they were asked for their opinions of the effects on executive directors as a whole in their company, whereas the executives responded for their own individual circumstances. It is therefore to be expected that the executive responses would be more dispersed. But the non-executive responses did not reflect an unbiased centralising of executive views. Whereas 24% of both classes of directors thought the performance effects of options was very favourable and there was no significant difference between the two classes on this question (E1a:N1a = 2.88), the non-executives were less sanguine for 'very favourable' effects on tenure. Responses overall were significantly different at the 10% level (E1b:N1b = 7.09). On group rewards the non-executives gave responses which roughly centralised those of the executives, but the answers on both performance and tenure were significantly different at the 5% level. On unit rewards the non-executive responses were again significantly different for performance at the 5% level (E3a:N3a = 8.74) but paradoxically there was no significant difference between executives and non-executives on the impact of unit rewards on tenure.

In summary there were three noteworthy results for this section of the study. Substantial proportions of both classes of director considered that options (as well as other forms of incentive rewards) had negligible effects on performance or tenure. Neither group of directors believed options had performance effects significantly different from the other forms of incentive reward, but executives said that options had significantly more favourable impact on their tenure than other rewards at group level. Finally, there were significant differences between the responses of executive and non-executive directors, which raises doubts about the expertise on the incentive effects of executive rewards which non-executive directors bring to corporate remuneration committees.

Directors' valuations of options

The valuation section of the survey asked respondents to give estimates for values of options in their companies. The section had two main purposes. One was to obtain directors' personal values which could be compared with estimates of cost to shareholders based on the Black and Scholes (1973) OPM; these results will be considered in the light of the earlier discussion of Jennergren and Naslund (1993), Foster, Koogler and Vickrey (1993) and Hemmer, Matsunaga and Shevlin (1994). The other purpose was to test the directors' perceptions of option pricing relativities, by asking for values for two identical options of different duration.

The question (number 5 in the Appendix) asked respondents to state the percentage of today's share price which they would be prepared to pay for options in their company which would be exercisable in three and five years' time. The use of a percentage value was adopted as a result of pilot studies in two companies, which showed that executives could more readily give a percentage than an absolute value for an option. The percentage approach also had computational advantages, to be explained later.

The Black and Scholes (1973) OPM gave a basis for calculating a second set of values. These OPM values represented estimated costs to shareholders of granting the options, which could then be compared with the director's values.

Using the OPM notation of Copeland and Weston (1988, p. 268), the value of a call option c is given by:

$$c = SN(d_1) - Xe^{-r_f t}N(d_2) \tag{6.1}$$

where:

c is the value of a European call option (i.e. can be exercised only on maturity),
S is the share price at valuation of the option,
t is time to maturity of the option,
X is the exercise price,
r_f is the risk-free rate of interest,
$N(d)$ is the cumulative normal density function, and

$$d_1 = \frac{\ln(S/X) + r_f t}{\sigma\sqrt{t}} + \frac{1}{2}\sigma\sqrt{t}$$

$$d_2 = d_1 - \sigma\sqrt{t} \tag{6.2}$$

where σ is the standard deviation of the continuously compounded annual rate of return on the share.

However, the Black and Scholes OPM must be adjusted for anticipated dividends payable before the options can be exercised. This can be done following Hull (1989, p. 135), where the OPM expression for a call on a share paying known dividend yield is:

$$c = Se^{-qt}N(d_1) - Xe^{-r_f t}N(d_2)$$

(6.3)

and

$$d_1 = \frac{\ln(S/X) + (r_f t - q)t}{\sigma\sqrt{t}} + \frac{1}{2}\sigma\sqrt{t}$$

(6.4)

where q is the continuously compounded dividend yield.

As respondents were asked to give a percentage value c/S; and were asked to assume an exercise price (X) equal to the share price, dividing the OPM formula by S gives:

$$\frac{c}{S} = \frac{S}{S}N(d_1) - \frac{X}{S}e^{-r_f t}N(d_2)$$

(6.5)

$$= N(d_1) - e^{-r_f t}N(d_2)$$

and

$$d_1 = \frac{(r_f t - q)t}{\sigma\sqrt{t}} + \frac{1}{2}\sigma\sqrt{t}$$

(6.6)

There were computational advantages in using this version of the OPM formula. The second expression in equation (6.5) does not contain the share price, so that values could be calculated without having to identify each company's share price at the time corresponding to the respondent's valuation. The expression was used to calculate the OPM values[17] as percentages of the share price, which could then be compared with the respondents' values.

The results for directors' valuations of three-year and five-year options in their companies appear in Figure 6.1. It can be seen that responses were bunched towards the lower end of the valuation scale. For both three-year and five-year options the respondents' median values were 10%. Thus the majority of directors gave low values to options in their companies.

Whether the majority view was low relative to estimated values to shareholders will be considered later, but there were some values which were irrationally low. There were 23 directors who gave zero values to both three-year and five-year options. Yet a call option on the shares of a solvent company must have *some* value (since there must be some non-zero probability that the future share price will be higher than the current share price). At the other extreme 11 directors gave a value of 100% or more of the current share price for three-year options and 17 directors who gave corresponding values for five-year options. It would be irrational to pay as much as, or more than, the current share price for a call option, since the share itself could be bought

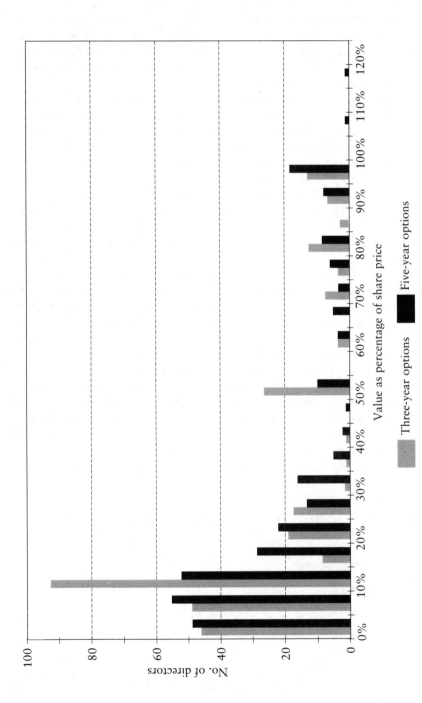

Figure 6.1 *Directors' valuations of options*

for the same money. Whereas an option will become valueless if the share price is below exercise price when the option is exercisable, a share will (excepting insolvency) retain some value. Thus there were some directors who disregarded option values whilst others had grossly inflated views of values. These were minority views but they provide extreme examples of the difficulties which would face a corporate compensation committee in assessing the impact of providing option rewards.

A comparison of each respondent's values for three-year and five-year options provides further insight into directors' option value perceptions. Option pricing theory would give a higher value to the longer-lived option, as that offers more opportunities for share price to exceed exercise price. However, Figure 6.1 does not show any marked tendency for five-year options to be more highly valued than three-year options.

Table 6.2 shows that 99 directors, 33% of the respondents, gave the anticipated response of valuing a five-year option more highly than a three-year option. The remainder gave values to five-year options which were equal to or less than those for three-year options. This suggests a lack of awareness of the relativities of option values on the part of the majority of the directors. However, in making these comparisons between three-year and five-year options the possibility of a belief in 'inside information' must be mentioned. It is possible that directors who gave a higher value to a three-year option believed they could predict that their companies would have declining fortunes from year 3 onwards, and those who gave equal values to both options believed in a static future from year 3. But that such an explanation applies to two-thirds of the directors seems highly implausible, and the principle of Occam's razor leads us to prefer the simpler explanation that the majority of directors displayed some naivety in their approach to option values.

Non-executive directors gave a higher proportion of responses in accord with option pricing theory (40.7% against 29.7% for executives), which might suggest more sophistication in financial matters among non-executive directors. A chi-square test for association between the executive and non-

Table 6.2 *Directors' valuations of three-year relative to five-year options*

	Executive directors	Non-executive directors	All directors
Five-year values greater than three-year values	62 (29.7%)	37 (40.7%)	99 (33.0%)
Five-year values equal to three-year values	83 (39.7%)	36 (39.6%)	119 (39.7%)
Five-year values less than three-year values	64 (30.6%)	18 (19.8%)	82 (27.3%)
	209 (100%)	91 (100%)	300 (100%)

executive responses gave a value of 5.048, so that the null hypothesis of independence could not be rejected at the 5% level (critical value 5.99). Thus there is insufficient statistical support for the view that non-executive directors were more financially sophisticated.

The principal benchmark against which responses were compared was the OPM value expressed in equation (6.5). This value was adopted as the estimate of the cost to shareholders of the grant of an option. The approach assumes that the possibility of premature cancellation of the ESOs is not a material valuation factor, for reasons discussed earlier. However, from the viewpoint of a director who was asked in the survey to give a buying price for an option, any gains from the option would be taxable. Thus a rational buying price for the director would be given by $(1 - g)V$, where g is the tax rate applicable to the gains from the option and V is the expectation of the value of the option. The best available estimate of V is, of course, the OPM value. Gains from UK ESOs are taxable at the individual's marginal tax rate, with a current maximum of 40%; although there are reliefs and avoidance devices which can reduce that maximum. Thus directors who made *maximum* allowance for the tax liability would give a value of $0.6V$, so that 0.6 of the OPM value becomes a benchmark against which to compare the directors' responses.

OPM values were computed for each company, scaled by 0.6 for estimated tax on gains, and compared with the responses of directors. Summary statistics of the responses received are provided in Table 6.3, where values are expressed as a proportion of share price except those in the final row, which show directors' over- or undervaluations as a proportion of the after-tax OPM values. The results of these comparisons for three-year and five-year options are summarised in Figures 6.2 and 6.3 respectively, which shows directors' over- or undervaluations as percentages of the after-tax OPM values.

The top section of Table 6.3 shows that the average non-executive director was consistent with OPM theory in valuing a three-year option below a five-year option (medians 0.1 and 0.15 respectively). In contrast, the medians for executive directors was 0.1 in both cases. This again raises the issue, discussed in connection with Table 6.2, of whether non-executives were more sophisticated than executives in their understanding of the options. The Mann–Whitney U test z statistics for three-year or five-year option responses are supportive of this view in direction (0.8987 for executives against 0.3044 for non-executives) but the evidence is inadequate because non-executives failed to produce a significant difference between three-year and five-year option values.

The most revealing statistics in Table 6.3 are in the final line. This shows the median undervalues are very close in both cases: 28.5% for three-year options and 29.4% for five-year options. Thus the majority of directors undervalued substantially relative to the OPM, even after allowing for *maximum* tax effects. Some undervalue was to be expected in view of the illiquidity effects of ESOs discussed earlier, and the valuation model developed by Hemmer, Matsunaga and Shevlin (1994) produced an estimated valuation difference for US ESOs averaging (mean and median) 21.5%. However, whatever the reason,

Table 6.3 *Comparison of directors' and option pricing model values of share options*

	Three-year options				Mann–Whitney U test	Five-year options			
	N	Median	Mean	S.D.	z statistic	N	Median	Mean	S.D.
Directors' values as proportion of share price									
Executive directors	209	0.1	0.2319	0.2701	0.8987	209	0.1	0.2453	0.2976
Non-executive directors	91	0.1	0.2428	0.3069	0.3044	91	0.15	0.2632	0.3137
All responses	300	0.1	0.2352	0.2813	0.6679	300	0.1	0.2507	0.3021
	max 1.0 min 0.0					max 1.2 min 0.0			
After-tax OPM values as proportion of share price	300	0.14	0.1446	0.0347		300	0.17	0.1712	0.0506
	max 0.282 min 0.072					max 0.359 min 0.058			
Directors' over/(under)valuation as proportion of after-tax OPM values	300	(0.285)	0.763	2.264	0.2947	300	(0.294)	0.705	2.418
	max 9.337 min (1.0)					max 15.62 min (1.0)			

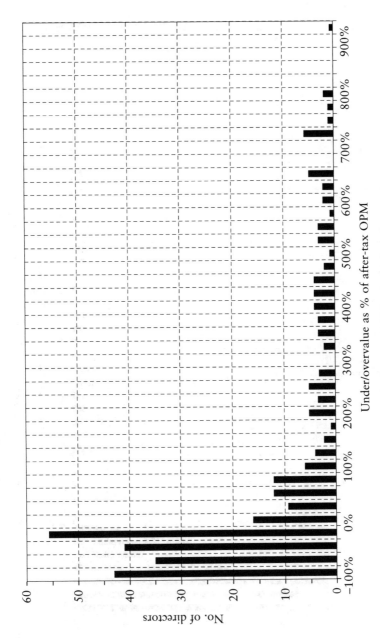

Figure 6.2 *Directors' values compared with after-tax OPM values: three-year options*

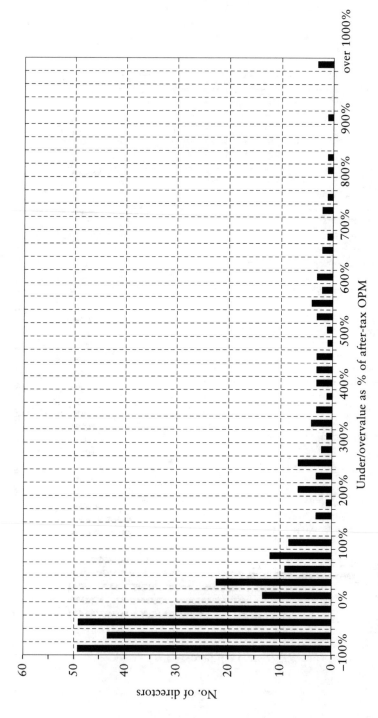

Figure 6.3 *Directors' values compared with after-tax OPM values: five-year options*

an undervalue of more than a quarter must raise serious doubts about shareholder 'value for money' compared with conventional rewards which do not suffer the discount effect.

Although the majority of directors placed a lower value on options than the implied cost to shareholders, the results were widely dispersed. The last line of Table 6.3 shows large standard deviations of 226.4% and 241.8% for three- and five-year options respectively and the minority of directors who valued above the after-tax OPM benchmark included some who valued options very highly indeed (see Figures 6.2 and 6.3). Consequently the *mean* valuation differences in the last line of Table 6.3 are positive, overvaluing by 76.3% for three-year options and 70.5% for five-year options. Thus in terms of *mean* valuation differences it can be said that directors' average valuations exceeded the average costs to shareholders, but the valuation of the average director (i.e. the *median*) substantially undershot the average costs to shareholders.

The illiquidity effect on the value of ESOs discussed earlier does, of course, lead to an expectation that directors' values should be somewhat lower than those from the OPM. But illiquidity alone as an explanation would suggest a discount from the after-tax OPM which did not fluctuate wildly between individuals, whereas the directors' values are greatly dispersed relative to the after-tax OPM. Moreover, if illiquidity is the cause of the general downward bias in director values, the median discount value of some 29% for both classes of option implies quite strong effects. The alternative explanation, which is lent support by the irrational valuers, is that most directors have difficulty placing realistic values on ESOs.

Whatever the cause, the valuation disparities raise serious difficulties for a recent financial reporting proposal by Sunder (1994). He proposes (p. 110) that firms (in effect the directors) 'should be free to assign whatever value they consider appropriate to such stock options [in financial reports] subject to one restriction: the firm must be willing to sell up to a specified number of *similar* options at the same date at a price equal to the stated compensation value to its own shareholders (and perhaps to the public)'. Our study suggests that, in the absence of strong incentives to the contrary, the average director would be prone to underprice substantially, bringing dangers of either an influx of unusable cash or (more likely) problems in rationing a restricted number of options between shareholders. Sunder's proposal is made in the US context of the FASB's intention (FASB, 1993) to base a P&L charge in the accounts on the 'fair value' of the option, which might also lead directors to prefer low valuations. However, the dispersion of responses in our study suggests there could also be problems in reaching a consensus between the directors with disparate views on values. The Sunder proposal does have an incentive to assign a high price to the options, to avoid dilution of the directors' interests, but it is far from clear that the balance of incentives would yield a valuation reflecting the cost of ESOs to shareholders.

The results of directors' valuations raise important issues for corporate governance, with regard to the process of awarding ESOs to individual directors. Whereas a minority of directors were ascribing values to options in excess of the costs to shareholders, with motivational benefits implicitly exceeding costs, that was not the case for the majority of directors. This suggests that the blanket provision of ESOs for all directors may not be the most cost-effective approach to remuneration packages. A selective approach which seeks to identify those individuals who are likely to place high values on option rewards could be more beneficial. The implication is that the motivational benefits of options could be focused on appropriate individuals, using other, more easily valued, forms of reward for the majority of directors who are prone to undervalue option rewards.

CONCLUSIONS

Three main facets of directors' ESOs have been addressed in this chapter, all having a bearing on the issue of cost-effectiveness. First was the listing of advantages and problems of ESOs, which produced four major categories of advantage but also five problem areas from the shareholder viewpoint. Although most of the advantages also benefited directors, it was evident that directors were largely immune from the problems. Thus ESOs are potentially far more problematic for shareholders than for directors.

The second area concerned the perception of directors of the effects of options on performance and tenure. Given the advantageous nature of director ESOs, it was expected that self-interest would yield generally favourable responses and that more would be revealed by differences between categories. Surprisingly, almost a quarter of executive directors replied that ESOs had negligible effects on their performance and tenure. The executives considered options had a more favourable effect on tenure than conventional group rewards, whereas group rewards had greater impact on performance than on tenure. Thus there was some support for the view that option rewards can act as a counter to the 'short-termism' of conventional rewards. However, it would seem likely that the motivational effects of ESOs will diminish as the date of exercise draws closer. Thus the divergences in executives' responses may have arisen from a 'roller-coaster' effect on motivation, with high impact for directors with newly minted options but negligible effects on directors with options close to exercise. This would suggest that there could be merit in replacing the usual practice of lumpy sporadic grants of options with a more modest annual programme on a rolling basis. In this way smoothing of the motivational effects could be achieved.

As far as non-executives were concerned, their answers were at variance from executives in certain respects, notably on the tenure effects of options and both the performance and tenure effects of conventional group rewards. Since non-executives were responding on their perceptions of the effects of rewards on executive directors, the disparities between executive and non-executive responses raises some doubts about the role of the latter in corporate remuneration committees.

The third area related to directors' valuations of options. The results gave differences between directors' values and option pricing principles in three respects. About one director out of eight gave irrational values to ESOs and almost two-thirds of directors valued three-year options equal to or higher than five-year options. The third, and most important, disparity from option pricing principles arose from a comparison of directors' and after-tax OPM values. Not only was there no association between the two sets of values, but there was a median undervaluation of some 29%. Although the illiquidity of ESOs gives an expectation that holders will value lower than the OPM, the size of the median discount raises doubts about 'value for money' compared with conventional rewards which do not suffer the discount effect. Moreover, wide dispersion of the value differences casts doubts on the realism of many of the directors' valuations.

The results of this study show that there are big differences between directors in both their perceptions of the motivational effects and their valuations of ESOs. A substantial proportion of directors thought ESOs had negligible performance and tenure effects, and the majority of directors gave surprisingly low values to ESOs. On the other hand the majority of directors thought ESOs had positive performance and tenure effects, and a substantial number of directors gave surprisingly high values to ESOs. Overall the results cast doubt on the cost-effectiveness of ESOs for the average director, although they also suggest that new benefits would accrue to shareholders if combination cases of high motivation and high ESO valuation by individual directors can be identified.

APPENDIX: EXECUTIVE DIRECTOR'S QUESTIONNAIRE

The non-executive director's questionnaire differed only in the wording shown in italics.

FINANCIAL REWARDS SURVEY   Company number ......

Confidential: The responses to this questionnaire are not identifiable to individuals, and will be used only for overall statistical analysis.

Please assume 'your company' refers to the Stock Exchange listed parent company to which this letter is addressed.

1. Please tick if you own:

   01 _____ Shares in your company
   02 _____ Shares in other companies

2. Do you hold share options under a scheme in your company
   Does your company have an executive share option scheme

   03 _____ Yes
   04 _____ No

If yes, do you think the effect of holding options:
(a) on your performance for your company is
     on the performance of executive directors in your company is

      05 _____ Very favourable
      06 _____ Favourable
      07 _____ Negligible
      08 _____ Unfavourable

(b) on how long you are likely to stay with your company is
     on how long executive directors are likely to stay with your company is

      09 _____ Very favourable
      10 _____ Favourable
      11 _____ Negligible
      12 _____ Unfavourable

3. Do you receive any financial rewards based on accounting measures of group performance (such as profit or earnings per share)
   Do executive directors in your company receive any financial rewards based on accounting measures of group performance (such as profit or earnings per share)

      13 _____ Yes
      14 _____ No

If yes, do you think the effect of the group reward system
(a) on your performance for your company is
     on the performance of executive directors in your company is

      15 _____ Very favourable
      16 _____ Favourable
      17 _____ Negligible
      18 _____ Unfavourable

(b) on how long you are likely to stay with your company is
     on how long executive directors are likely to stay with your company is

      19 _____ Very favourable
      20 _____ Favourable
      21 _____ Negligible
      22 _____ Unfavourable

4. Do you receive any financial rewards based on individual or unit performance below group level (such as divisional return on capital employed)
   Do executive directors in your company receive any financial rewards based on individual or unit performance below group level (such as divisional return on capital employed)

23 _____ Yes
24 _____ No

If yes, do you think the effect of that reward system
(a) on your performance for your company is
on the performance of executive directors in your company is

25 _____ Very favourable
26 _____ Favourable
27 _____ Negligible
28 _____ Unfavourable

(b) on how long you are likely to stay with your company is
on how long executive directors are likely to stay with your company is

29 _____ Very favourable
30 _____ Favourable
31 _____ Negligible
32 _____ Unfavourable

5. Assume that you could buy a share option in your company and that this involved two payments:
   (i) A payment *now* for the opportunity to buy a share in 3 years' time; and
   (ii) A payment in *3 years' time* equal to today's price if you decide to buy the share.
   Please write the percentage of today's share price that you would be prepared to pay under (i) above:

33 _____ %

If the option allowed you to buy the shares in 5 years' time, instead of 3 years, please write the percentage of today's share price you would be prepared to pay under (i) above:

34 _____ %

Date _____ (please complete)

Notes

1. See also Emmanuel, Otley and Merchant (1990), pp. 232–3 for a summary of potential defects of accounting measures. That summary is made from an internal control standpoint, but many aspects are equally relevant to performance of corporate management.

2 For example, a survey by the CBI (1988) of 862 companies reported that 34% had executive share option schemes and 29% had employee share ownership schemes, while Egginton, Forker and Grout (1993) reported that 97% of the top 100 UK companies had option schemes.

3. This benefit prevailed from the inception of executive share option schemes in the Finance Act 1984 until the taxation of capital gains at the taxpayer's marginal rate in the Finance Act 1990.

4. £6,000 in 1994/5. In line with indexation, the Chancellor has announced in the 1995 Budget Speech an increase in the annual exemption to £6,300.

5. For examples see Egginton, Forker and Tippett (1989), Bickford (1990) and Laier and Riley (1991).

6. Although, conversely, executive shareholdings can reduce agency problems; see Agrawal and Mandelker (1987).

7. There are disclosure rules in the USA, where SEC (1993) requires disclosure of the fair value of all forms on non-cash compensation to directors and executive officers.

8. The Cadbury Report (1992) reinforces normal practice by recommending that non-executive directors should not be granted options in a company in which they serve as a non-executive director. However, proposals to amend the 1995 Finance Bill to prevent non-executive directors from participating in option schemes aroused strong opposition from the Institute of Directors, which argued that it would 'strike a blow against the unitary board system which is the bedrock of the way UK companies are run' (*Financial Times*, 9 March 1995).

9. Copeland and Weston are referring here to the results of studies by Galai (1997) and Bhattacharya (1980). However, they also refer to studies by MacBeth and Merville (1979) and Beckers (1980), which show that the Black–Scholes OPM has a bias towards underpricing (overpricing) 'in-the-money' ('out-of-the-money') options which increases to the extent that options are 'in-the-money' (out-of-the-money). This bias decreases as the time to expiration decreases.

10. In theory this illiquidity problem can be avoided if capital markets are perfect and executives are able to sell call options with an equivalent time structure. In practice that is not feasible for directors or executives generally. The markets do not provide long-life options, and executives are restricted in their financial dealings in company shares by legal restrictions and company contracts.

11. For example, when the Hong Kong and Shanghai Bank took over the Midland Bank in1992, holders of ESOs were allowed to trade their Midland options into HKSB options or exercise existing option rights.

12. The sample was randomly selected from the Times Top 1,000 Companies 1987–8, and the questionnaires were dispatched in January 1991. Replies were received in the period January–March 1991. All responses were received as a result of the original mailing; no reminders were sent. The survey was preceded by pilot studies in two companies, which led to substantial changes in the design of the questionnaire.

13. Separate questionnaires were sent to those executive and non-executive directors whose roles were identified by company reports. However, in 60 cases the director's role was not identified; these directors were sent a copy of both questionnaires and were asked to respond to the questionnaire which was appropriate to their role.

14. For the precise wording of the non-executive questionnaire see the appendix to this chapter.

15. These behavioural assumptions are specified in the expectancy theory of motivation (see House, 1971, and Ronen and Livingstone, 1975) which hypothesises that an individual's motivation will depend, *inter alia*, on the expectations (subjective probabilities) that effort will achieve a task and that achievement will in fact be rewarded.

16. Support for this interpretation is provided by the findings (Main and Johnston, 1993) that UK remuneration committees have no effect on the incentive structure of directors' remuneration.

17. To adjust OPM values for the payment of dividends before the exercise date continuously compounded dividend yields were calculated from the dividend yield of each company on the date of the dispatch of the questionnaire.

References

Accounting Standards Board (ASB) (1994) Disclosure of directors' share options, Urgent Issues Task Force, Abstract 10, ASB, London.

Agrawal, A and Mandelker, G. N. (1987) Management incentives and corporate investment and financing decisions, *Journal of Finance* (September), pp. 823–37.

Association of British Insurers (ABI) (1987) *Share Options and Profit Sharing Schemes: Summary of Revision to Guidelines to Requirements of Insurance Offices as Investors*, ABI, London.

Association of British Insurers (ABI) and National Association of Pension Funds (NAPF) (1993) *Share Scheme Guidance: A Joint Statement from the Investment Committees of the ABI and the NAPF*, ABI/NAPF, London.

Beckers, S. (1980) The constant elasticity of variance model and its implications for option pricing, *Journal of Finance* (June), pp. 661–73.

Bhattacharya, M. (1980) Empirical properties of the Black–Scholes formula under ideal conditions, *Journal of Financial and Quantitative Analysis* (December), pp. 1081–106.

Bickford, L. C. (1990) Rewarding executives for value creation, *Journal of Compensation and Benefits* (September/October), pp. 53–5.

Black, F. and Scholes, M. (1973) The pricing of options and corporate liabilities, *Journal of Political Economy*, Vol. 81, pp. 637–54.

Cadbury Report (1992) *Report of the Committee on the Financial Aspects of Corporate Governance*, Gee & Co., London.

Confederation of British Industry (CBI) (1988) *Special Survey – Executive Share Option Schemes*, CBI, London.

Copeland, T. E. and Weston, J. F. (1988) *Financial Theory and Corporate Policy*, Addison-Wesley, Reading, Mass.

DeFusco, R. A., Zorn, T. S. and Johnson, R. R. (1991) The association between executive stock option plan changes and managerial decision making, *Financial Management* (Spring), pp. 36–43.

Egginton, D., Forker, J. and Grout, P. (1993) Executive and employee share options: taxation, dilution and disclosure, *Accounting and Business Research*, Corporate Governance Special Issue, pp. 363–72.

Egginton, D., Forker, J. and Tippett, M. (1989) Share option rewards and managerial performance: an abnormal performance index model, *Accounting and Business Research* (Summer), pp. 255–66.

Emmanuel, C., Otley, D. and Merchant, K. (1990) *Accounting for Management Control*, Chapman & Hall, London.

Fama, E. F. (1980) Agency problems and the theory of the firm, *Journal of Political Economy*, Vol. 88, pp. 288–307.

Financial Accounting Standards Board (FASB) (1981) *Interpretation No. 28: Accounting for Stock Appreciation Rights and Other Variable Stock Option or Award Plans*, FASB, Stanford, Conn.

Financial Accounting Standards Board (FASB) (1993) *Accounting for Stock-Based Compensation: Proposed Statement of Financial Accounting Standard – Exposure Draft*, FASB, Norwalk, Conn.

Foster, T. W., Koogler, P. R. and Vickrey, D. (1991) Valuation of executive stock options and the FASB proposal, *Accounting Review* (July), pp. 595–610.

Foster, T. W., Koogler, P. R. and Vickrey, D. (1993) Valuation of executive stock options and the FASB proposal: an extension, *Accounting Review* (January), pp. 184–9.

Galai, D. (1977) Tests of market efficiency of the Chicago Board of Options Exchange, *Journal of Business* (April), pp. 167–97.

Hemmer, T., Matsunaga, S. and Shevlin, T. (1994) Estimating the 'fair value' of employee stock options with expected early exercise, *Accounting Horizons* (December), pp. 23–42.

House, R. J. (1971) A path goal theory of leader effectiveness, *Administrative Science Quarterly* (September), pp. 321–38.

Hull, J. (1989) *Options, Futures, and Other Derivative Securities*, Prentice-Hall, Englewood Cliffs, NJ.

Jennergren, L. P. and Naslund, B. (1992) *Valuation of Executive Stock Options*, Ekonomiska Forskningsinstitutet, Stockholm.

Jennergren, L. P. and Naslund, B. (1993) A comment on valuation of executive stock options and the FASB proposal, *Accounting Review* (January), pp. 179–83.

Laier, D. W. and Riley, L. (1991) Real gains from phantom stocks, *Small Business Reports* (November), pp. 19–22.

Likert, R. (1967) *The Human Organization: its Management and Value*, McGraw-Hill, New York.

MacBeth, J. and Merville, L. (1979) An empirical examination of the Black–Scholes call option pricing model, *Journal of Finance* (December), pp. 1173–86.

Main, B. G. M. and Johnston, J. (1993) Remuneration committees and corporate governance, *Accounting and Business Research*, Corporate Governance Special Issue, pp. 351–62.

Main, B. G. M., O'Reilly, C. A. III and Crystal, G. S. (1994) Over here and over there: a comparison of top executives pay in the UK and the USA, *International Contributions to Labour Studies*, Vol. 4, pp. 115–27.

Noreen, E. and Wolfson, M. (1981) Equilibrium warrant pricing models and accounting for executive stock options, *Journal of Accounting Research* (Autumn), pp. 384–98.

Richardson, R. and Nejad, A. (1986) Employee share ownership schemes in the UK – an evaluation, *British Journal of Industrial Relations* (July), pp. 233–50.

Ronen, J. and Livingstone, J. L. (1975) An expectancy theory approach to the motivational impact of budgets, *Accounting Review* (October), pp. 671–85.

Securities and Exchange Commission (SEC) (1993) *New Executive Compensation Disclosure Rules* (Act Release Number 6932), SEC, New York.

Sunder, S. (1994) Economic incentives as a substitute for detailed accounting requirements: the case of compensation value of stock options, *Accounting Horizons* (June), p. 110.

Tehranian, H., Travlos, N. G. and Waegelein, J. (1987) Management compensation contracts and merger-induced abnormal returns, *Journal of Accounting Research*, Supplement, pp. 51–76.

Travlos, N. G. and Waegelein, J. (1993) Executive compensation, method of payment and abnormal returns to bidding firms at takeover announcements, *Managerial and Decision Economics*, Vol. 14, pp. 493–501.

Watts, R. L. and Zimmerman, J. (1986) *Positive Accounting Theory*, Prentice-Hall, Englewood Cliffs, NJ.

Williamson, O. E. (1985) *The Economic Institutions of Capitalism*, Free Press, New York.

The authors gratefully acknowledge financial support from the Research Board of the Institute of Chartered Accountants in England and Wales.

7

The Measurement of Audit Quality

DAVID HATHERLY and TOM BROWN

INTRODUCTION

Following a number of recent spectacular business failures (notably Polly Peck, Maxwell and BCCI) the role of the auditors and the quality of the audit have come increasingly into question. Proposals to strengthen the independence of the auditor have come from ICAS (1993) the APB (1992) and Cadbury (1992). The Scottish Institute and the APB put forward the idea that an audit panel independent of the directors should be influential in the appointment and remuneration of auditors. Cadbury suggests that all listed companies should have audit committees with a majority of non-executive directors. Whereas executive directors work closely with auditors and have an opportunity to gauge the quality of the audit first hand, audit panels and non-executive directors along with shareholders do not have such a first-hand knowledge and yet clearly need to be able to assess audit quality to fulfil their responsibility for the appointment of auditors.

The first part of this chapter discusses economic models of the auditor's choice of audit quality. These suggest that auditors will compete on image and on cost rather than directly on audit quality unless audit quality is made much more visible than is the case at present. The second part examines the potential of 'free form' audit reporting as a vehicle for increasing the visibility of audit quality.

ECONOMIC ARGUMENTS

The Moizer thesis

Peter Moizer (1993a) provides a comprehensive review of economic models of the auditor's choice of audit quality. His analysis suggested the following:

(1) there is no economic incentive for auditors to undertake audits of a quality level in excess of the minimum prescribed by the profession;

(2) that audit firms therefore compete for audits through image-building activities rather than through the quality of their audit work;
(3) that audit standard-setters under the control of the profession have little incentive to increase the minimum level of audit quality, since to do so might increase the litigation risk faced by the profession;
(4) that the monitoring activities of the profession in essence serve a compliance function reinforcing the minimum levels of audit quality.

A lack of economic incentive

To support proposition (1) there is a number of theoretical perspectives, from which Moizer draws heavily on Simunic and Stein (1984). In their model the inability of users to observe the audit process results in the external users' quality assessment being based on brand name and reputation. In these circumstances the actual effort level chosen by the auditor is that necessary to protect or enhance the audit firm's reputation. Moizer argues (1993a, p. 83) that since audit effort is unobservable, it is more cost-effective for an audit firm to protect and enhance its reputation through general image-building activities than directly through audit effort. Simunic and Stein recognise that the unobservability assumption, on which the above argument rests, breaks down in the event of litigation if as a result the auditor's work becomes visible and the auditor's reputation may be damaged. They therefore use avoidance of litigation as a key driver of the audit firm's reputation and the level of audit effort is influenced by the need to avoid litigation. Out of court settlements are a complicating factor in this argument since, as Moizer points out, they may be used to avoid the public visibility of audit work and hence to protect the auditor's reputation. Nevertheless, the weakness of the professional indemnity insurance market makes the out of court settlement very expensive for the partners. Litigation levels currently provide a potentially strong economic incentive for audit firms to maintain the quality of audit work above a level likely to lead to litigation, although an alternative response is to avoid high-risk audit clients. So far, the only visible response of the large auditing firms to the litigious environment has been to lobby for lessening of auditor exposure to claims. Whether or not they have raised audit quality as a response is not visible.

Image-building activity

Given that executives are, *de facto*, influential in the appointment and remuneration of auditors, it is logical for the auditors to direct their image-building activity at company executives. In a recent study Beattie and Fearnley (1995) found that the auditor characteristic most highly rated by executives was technical competence, with value for money as the second most important. This begs the question of what executives regard as auditor competence. However, an interesting finding of the Beattie and Fearnley study is that fee level is the most cited reason for consideration of a change in auditor and fee reduction by the incumbent auditor is the most cited reason for not changing auditors after considering a change. Thus in terms of competition between auditors it is the level of the fee which is the most important consideration, with competence being relegated to second place. A plausible explanation for this shift in positions is that executives, at least as far as the big audit firms are concerned, tend not to distinguish competence but take it as given, leaving competition to take place on cost. Using data that relate back to 1982–7, Chan (1993) demonstrates that the overall level of audit fees declined over that period and anecdotal evidence from practitioners suggests that cost competition has intensified since. Moizer (1993b), however, reports that audit fees were not particularly squeezed during 1990 although in 1991 audit fees for 50 of the largest UK companies rose by only 1 per cent (Bagnall, 1992).

Moizer (1993a) surveyed company financial executives to identify the dimensions of their image of an auditing firm. The dimensions in the order in which they emerged were labelled effectiveness, prominence, enterprise, self-importance, Americanisation, social status, flexibility and relevatory power. His study revealed that the financial executives did not distinguish the quality of service provided by the big, at the time of study (eight), auditing firms in terms of effectiveness but that there were significant differences in the perceptions of the other dimensions of image for the big firms.

To summarise, the Moizer, and Beattie and Fearnley studies, taken together, suggest that executives regard technical competence as the most important audit quality but do not distinguish between the big auditing firms on quality, that the auditing firms successfully differentiate themselves on other aspects of image, but that cost is the most important consideration in the current competitive market for audits. Given cost pressures it is questionable whether auditing firms will feel able, in response to the litigious environment, to improve audit quality beyond the minimum standards set by the profession.

Standard-setting

A detailed study of the standard-setting process employed by the Auditing Practices Committee in respect of three guidelines has been made by Pong and Whittington (1994). They used three criteria to investigate quality. First, they considered the extent to which the relevant guideline defined standard practice more precisely. Second, they considered the internal consistency and clarity of exposition of the guideline. Third, they considered the extent to which the guideline made an original contribution as opposed to simply describing or copying other guidelines. They assessed the guideline on analytical review as not being innovative or prescriptive, the guideline on fraud as essentially a conservative document preserving the status quo as perceived by the profession and the guideline on insurance companies as a necessary technical document but minimising the circumstances in which the auditor should report direct to a third party. Thus the findings of Pong and Whittington provide strong evidence of a minimalist approach to standard-setting by the Auditing Practices Committee. In 1991 the Auditing Practices Committee, which was dominated by practitioners and could only develop standards for issue by the CCAB bodies, was replaced by the Auditing Practices Board. The Board is committed to consultations with the professional institutes but can issue standards in its own name. Approximately half of its members are not practising auditors and one of the authors, having served for three years on the Auditing Practice Committee and for four years on the Board, can report that there is a much better and balanced debate within the APB than there was (at least latterly) within the APC. The APB gave itself a positive mission to enhance the quality of auditing and set about establishing its independence from the professional bodies. This led to strains between the APB and the English Institute in particular. There are many difficulties but the concept of a partnership between auditors and other interests remains the basis on which, hopefully, the APB can deliver on its mission of enhancing audit quality – though much is still to be done.

Monitoring
The work of the Joint Monitoring Unit (JMU) of the English, Scottish and Irish Institutes is conducted around the following eight issues (ICAEW, ICAS, ICAI, 1994, p. 12):

(i)	Properly registered	–	is control by qualified individuals and does the firm have adequate insurance arrangements?
(ii)	Integrity	–	is audit work under the control of responsible individuals?
(iii)	Independence	–	is the firm independent from audit clients?
(iv)	Firm's procedures	–	does the firm have procedures to ensure that audit work is properly carried out and subject to quality control?
(v)	Assessment of individual competence	–	are staff and principals competent and do they maintain their technical knowledge?
(vi)	Quality assurance	–	does the firm have procedures to monitor the quality of its own work?
(vii)	Proper performance	–	are individual audit assignments being properly carried out?
(viii)	Other ethical matters	–	does the firm comply with ethical and other guidance?

On the key question of proper performance, the JMU examines the conduct of individual audit assignments in terms of compliance with the auditor's operational and reporting standards and the disclosure requirements for the financial statements. The effect is to reinforce the message that proper performance equals compliance with (arguably minimalist) auditing standards.

Policy implications

In essence the analysis to date suggests that audit firms do not compete on audit quality but attempt to satisfy through compliance with auditing standards. The auditing profession attempts to control and minimise the quality of auditing standards in order to keep the litigation risk to firms as low as possible. Although compliance with standards is visible to the JMU, audit quality is not visible to the financial statement users. In any event financial statement users are less influential than company executives when it comes to the appointment and remuneration of auditors. The Moizer (1993a) and Beattie and Fearnley (1995) studies suggest that executives do not discriminate between large auditing firms on grounds of quality but encourage competition on cost. Competition on cost constrains the ability of audit firms to raise quality beyond the minimum consistent with auditing standards, although firms might otherwise wish to do so in order to reduce negligence claims.

The policy implications are that audit quality should be made visible to financial statement users and that financial statement users should, *de facto* as well as *de jure*, control the appointment and remuneration of auditors. These two measures would encourage a market for audit services based on quality as well as cost competition, giving value for money to those for whom the service is intended. There are a number of proposals affecting control of the audit appointment. One possibility is that the appointment should be recommended to the annual general meeting by an audit committee of non-executives. For this purpose the audit committee should function as independent representatives of the shareholders rather than as members of a unitary board. This duality of role may be hard to sustain – hence the alternative idea of a shareholder panel consisting of shareholder representatives who are not members of the board. Evidence on the performance of audit committees in promoting audit quality is hard to find. However, evidence that executives in companies with audit committees had different perceptions from other executives is found by Beattie and Fearnley (1995). In companies which had audit committees, the executive directors surveyed rated the ability to provide consultancy services as significantly less important than did executives in companies without an audit committee. Executives in companies with an audit committee rated the following characteristics as significantly more important: integrity of audit firm, technical competence, quality of working relationships, value for money of audit service, ethical standards, ability of auditor to detect problems, quality of advice to management, a big six audit firm, and specialist knowledge of the industry. This may provide evidence demonstrating the audit committee's ability positively to influence executives in favour of quality. Alternatively, it may be that companies whose executives had more virtuous perceptions of audit quality were also the companies more likely to have an audit committee. In any event Beattie and Fearnley found no evidence to demonstrate that audit committees influenced the executives' stated reason for considering a change of auditor, i.e. cost.

MAKING AUDIT QUALITY VISIBLE

The second part of the chapter explores the argument that audit quality visibility would be improved if the auditor adopted a 'free form' report explaining the audit approach taken and why, the problems found and how they were dealt with. Estes (1982) argued strongly in favour of a free form report in order to avoid investor conditioning in which the auditor loses interest in audit reports because of their excessive standardisation. Thus a free form report has the potential to provide interest and visibility. At present large audit firms offer 'free form' reports after the audit as a private service to the board. A specimen provided by Touche Ross reported a financial analysis of the company's results, audit issues arising, adjustments booked and not booked on grounds of materiality, and constructive recommendations (management letter points). Audit issues arising covered, *inter alia*, areas of judgement identified during planning, areas of judgement identified during the audit, and financial reporting issues. A research project is currently under way at the Universities of Edinburgh and Dundee, sponsored by the English Institute, to examine the impact which a free form report based on the Touche Ross specimen has on the perceptions of its readers. These perceptions are being surveyed using the 18 scales employed in Hatherly, Innes and Brown (1991). They cover perceptions of audit effectiveness in terms of input, process and outputs.

The free form audit report should allow the reader to judge quality in terms of the reasonableness of the audit approach, the problems found and their disposal. It can provide a basis for the reader to judge audit quality in terms of the likelihood that the auditor would discover a material error and correctly deal with the error. These are the joint probabilities used by De Angelo (1981) and Knapp (1991) in their well-known definitions of audit quality. The position taken in this chapter is that it is preferable to make audit quality visible rather than have financial statement users or their representatives rely on surrogates for audit quality such as a firm's name (Dopuch and Simunic, 1980) or length of tenure (Knapp, 1991).

A framework for audit quality assessment

This section goes beyond the definitions of De Angelo (1981) and Knapp (1991) to develop a framework for audit quality assessment around which the 'free form' report might be structured. The suggested framework is given in Figure 7.1 in respect of company X. Level 1 represents the hypothetical state of company X's financial statements if there were no external audit requirement, whilst level 2 represents the actual but unobservable state of company X's financial statements prior to the audit. The notional distance between these levels is the preventive effect of the audit, an important dimension of the audit's preventive purpose. Since it lies between the hypothetical and the unobservable, the preventive quality of company X's audit is difficult to establish with confidence.

Level

1   State of financial statements if no audit requirement

PREVENTIVE EFFECT

2   State of financial statements prior to audit

CORRECTIVE VALUE

3   State of financial statements after audit

AUDIT EXPOSURE

4   State of financial statements as conveyed by the audit opinion

Figure 7.1   *The audit performance framework*

Level 3 represents the actual state of X's financial statements after all adjustments including additional disclosures have been made on the basis of the findings of the audit. The distance between levels 2 and 3 equals the audit adjustments (inclusive of new disclosures) and is both a known and reportable dimension of the audit. This distance is the corrective value of the audit. Level 4 represents the state of X's financial statements as reported in what is presently the opinion section of the audit report. This opinion is arrived at by the auditor after evaluating all the findings of the audit, whether or not they lead to financial statement adjustments or disclosures. The distance between levels 3 and 4 represents the audit exposure.

The preventive effect
Evidence in support of the preventive effect might come from a declining profile over time of audit adjustments. Second, it might be supported whenever improvements by the auditee in respect of corporate governance, internal control or accounting policies can be traced to recommendations by the auditor. It is not suggested that all management letter points be included in the free form audit report – only those which are taken up by the auditee. To include all management letter points would put pressure on management to adopt all such points even when they considered them to be cost-ineffective. In any event suggestions not taken up do not belong in the preventive section. In essence the preventive effect requires the auditor to report a profile of improvements over time and this is in itself an innovative development for audit reporting since it regards each audit as updating a series. The difficulty is knowing for how long a current audit can claim performance through sustaining improvements made by the auditee in the past. This may have to be left to the judgement of the audit report reader. A further difficulty is knowing to what extent a fall in audit adjustments may be attributable to improvements in corporate governance which would have taken place irrespective of the existence of an external audit.

The corrective value

The adjustments made as a result of the audit findings form a key element of the specimen Touche Ross board report referred to earlier. In a market where shareholders or their representatives control the audit appointment there is a significant incentive for the auditor to demonstrate competence and independence by visibly finding problems and arguing for adjustments, suitable disclosures or suitable accounting policies. This is quite different from a market where the audit appointment is controlled by executives. In this case incentives, arguably, operate to discourage auditors from finding problems and pursuing adjustments if the result is to upset the executives with possible loss of the audit and consultancy assignments. However, the corrective value has to be seen alongside both the preventive effect and the assessment of audit exposure. A high level of adjustments indicates corrective value but the adjustments might indicate a preventive failure for previous audits. In terms of the audit exposure it has to be remembered that the significance of discovered problems is not necessarily found in the adjustments but in what the problems might indicate in respect of the state of the financial statements as a whole including transactions and balances not directly examined by the auditor.

The audit exposure

To judge the audit exposure the audit report reader needs to know the audit approach and its rationale in order to judge whether the audit work provides the auditor with representative evidence from which to assess the state of the financial statement as a whole, after agreed adjustments. The reader needs to see all potentially significant problems encountered by the auditor, whether or not they resulted in adjustments, and how the problems found influenced the final state of the accounts and the auditor's opinion thereof. Problems encountered should cover control weaknesses, errors in balances and trans-actions and any auditor doubts concerning the auditee's choice of accounting policies. The latter may be especially pertinent in circumstances where a second opinion has been obtained by the auditee. Since it is the audit exposure which generates the litigation risk there is a strong incentive for the auditor to frame this section of the audit report with great care. It is doubtful whether this incentive should be removed by a removal of liability, although some limitation of liability may be desirable in order to avoid over-cautious reporting.

CONCLUSION

The first part of this chapter reviewed economic analyses which suggest that audit quality will not advance beyond minimum standards unless (1) that quality is visible and (2) those in whose interest audit quality should be pursued are influential in the appointment and remuneration of auditors. These two factors are necessary to establish an audit market where there is competition on quality as well as on cost. It is argued that standard-setting will have only a marginal effect on audit quality unless non-practitioners are a major influence. Monitoring regimes merely enforce compliance with the standards.

The chapter puts forward the proposition that the visibility of audit quality might be enhanced through 'free form' reporting and the second part of it discusses an audit performance measurement framework around which the free form report might be constructed. This framework suggests that the audit report be in three parts corresponding to (1) the preventive effect of the audit, (2) the corrective value of the audit and (3) the audit exposure, plus of course the opinion on the financial statements required by statute. The free form report need not necessarily be issued to shareholders and therefore become effectively a public document. In particular during an initial, experimental, learning period it might be appropriate to test the concept by reporting 'free form' only to shareholders' representatives such as an audit committee or shareholder panel, provided those representatives were sufficiently independent of the executives. Ultimately there should be competition between firms not only on the preventive, corrective and exposure qualities of their audits but also on their audit reporting skills – a fourth and vital audit quality upon which the visibility of the first three depends. The role of the Auditing Practices Board in these circumstances is to articulate the framework within which appropriate competition can take place. The role of the JMU is to monitor whether the audit reports are a bona fide reflection of the audit work actually conducted.

References

APB (Auditing Practices Board) (1992) *The Future Developing of Auditing: A Paper to Promote Public Debate*, APB, London.

Bagnall, S. (1992) Competitive fees reveal price war, *Accountancy Age* (30 April), p. 10.

Beattie, V. and Fearnley, S. (1995) The importance of audit firm characteristics and drivers of auditor change in UK listed companies, *Accounting and Business Research* (Autumn), pp. 227–39.

Cadbury (1992) *Report of the Committee on the Financial Aspects of Corporate Governance*, Gee and Co., London.

Chan, P. W. K. (1993) The determinants of UK audit fee, unpublished M. Phil. thesis, University of Wales.

De Angelo, L. E. (1981) Audit size and audit quality, *Journal of Accounting and Economics* (December), pp. 183–99.

Dopuch, N. and Simunic, D. (1980) The nature of competition in the auditing profession: a descriptive and normative view, in J. Buckley and F. Weston (eds.), *Regulation and the Accounting Profession*, Lifetime Learning Publications, Belmont, California.

Estes, R. (1982) *The Auditors' Report and Investor Behavior*, Lexington Books, Lexington, Mass.

Hatherly, D., Innes, J. and Brown, T. (1991) The expanded audit report – an empirical investigation, *Accounting and Business Research* (Autumn), pp. 311–20.

ICAEW, ICAS, ICAI (1994) *Audit Regulation: Report to the DTI for the year ended 30 September, 1994*, ICAEW, London.

ICAS (1993) *Auditing into the Twenty-First Century*, ICAS, Edinburgh.

Knapp, M. C. (1991) Factors that audit committee members use as surrogates for audit quality, *Auditing: A Journal of Practice and Theory* (Spring), pp. 35–52.

Moizer, P. (1993a) Audit quality and auditor reputation: a theoretical and empirical investigation. Unpublished, Ph.D. thesis, University of Manchester.

Moizer, P. (1993b) The response of UK auditing firms to a changing environment. Paper presented to the Workshop on the Organisation and Management of Professional Service Firms, University of Alberta, May 21–23.

Pong, C. and Whittington, G. (1994) The working of the Auditing Practices Committee – three case studies, *Accounting and Business Research* (Spring), pp. 157–75.

Simunic, D. A. and Stein, M. (1984) *Product Differentiation in Auditing: A Study of Auditor Effects in the Market for New Issues*, University of British Columbia Working Paper, No. 1067.

Simunic, D. A. and Stein, M. (1987) *Product Differentiation in Auditing: Auditor Choice in the Market for Unseasoned New Issues*, Research Monograph No. 13, The Canadian Certified General Accountants' Research Foundation.

8

Activity Performance Measures and Tableaux de Bord

JOHN INNES

This chapter stems from two of my current research projects, namely surveys and case studies of activity-based costing (ABC) and cost management (ABCM) in the UK (with Falconer Mitchell of the University of Edinburgh) and a Franco-British case study of ABC and ABCM together with a case study of *tableaux de bord* with Pierre Mévellec of the University of Nantes. The discussion will be mainly in the context of a manufacturing organisation but both the activity-based approach and the *tableaux de bord* are also applicable to service organisations. After giving an overview of the activity-based approach and the resulting performance measures, the meaning and development of *tableaux de bord* will be discussed and a case will be made for combining the activity-based approach and the *tableaux de bord* system.

ACTIVITY-BASED APPROACH

The activity-based approach applies to an organisation's overheads – which have been an increasing percentage of total costs for many organisations. For example, a 1990 survey by the Confederation of British Industry of 13 manufacturing and 34 service companies revealed that overheads exceeded 30 per cent of total costs for 70 per cent of the companies surveyed. Furthermore, this survey showed that since 1970 overheads had increased by 70 per cent in real terms. However, despite such an increase, 90 per cent of the manufacturing companies surveyed still used traditional volume-related overhead recovery methods such as direct labour hours.

There is some debate about how new the activity-based approach really is (see, for example, Horngren, 1990; Staubus, 1990), but it was in the mid-1980s that Cooper and Kaplan started to attract attention to the current activity-based approach with their Harvard case studies and other writings (see, for example, Cooper, 1985; Kaplan, 1987; Cooper and Kaplan, 1987; Cooper and Kaplan, 1988). The first published UK activity-based case studies were in Innes and Mitchell (1990). Cooper and Kaplan do not claim to have invented the activity-based approach to overheads but to have found it in operation in American companies. The essence of the activity-based approach stems from two main features. First, instead of collecting overhead costs by departments, various activities (such as material handling, inspection and purchasing) are identified and costs are collected in terms of these activity cost pools. Second, a cost driver is identified for each cost pool. Some of these cost drivers may in practice be volume-related but generally most of them are not directly related to the volume of production output. Typical cost drivers may be the number of material movements, the number of inspections or the number of purchase orders rather than the volume of production output. This enables cost-driver-based rates to be calculated, such as £x per material movement. These rates can then be used to cost the overhead element of individual product lines.

The early activity-based cases concentrated on the objective of unit product costing and one significant later development has been the suggestion by Cooper (1992) of cost layering, which was a refinement of the activity-based costing approach. Cost layering suggests that certain overhead costs (such as machine power) are driven at the unit level, some (such as set-up) at the batch level, some (such as product specification) at the product line level and some (such as factory heat and light) at the facility level. This cost layering emphasises that although ABC may give a more 'accurate' unit cost than traditional product costing, it is very much an estimate and does still involve some overhead allocations. Management accountants cannot give managers a completely 'accurate' unit product cost. However, the evidence from ABC cases suggests that managers generally believe that an activity-based unit product cost is closer to 'reality' than a traditional unit product cost.

As ABC developed it soon became clear that the activity-based approach gave managers a new understanding of overhead costs and some organisations began to use the activity-based approach for cost management (see, for example, Innes and Mitchell, 1991). A recent survey of the UK largest companies by Innes and Mitchell (1995) has shown that for the activity-based approach the cost-management objective is at least as important as the unit product costing objective. Of 251 usable replies (a 25% response rate) just under 49 (i.e. 20% of respondents) had adopted the activity-based approach. Table 8.1 summarises the different activity-based applications in these 49 companies.

The table shows that 43 of these 49 companies used the activity-based approach for cost reduction or cost management. Indeed some organisations adopted the activity-based approach only for cost reduction or cost management and did not attempt to use it for unit product costing.

Two common classifications of activities have emerged in practice for cost-management purposes. The first is to split activities into core, support or diversionary activities (see, for example, Bellis-Jones, 1992). For a travelling salesperson a core activity would be finalising the sale with a customer; a support activity would be driving to meet the customer; and a diversionary activity would be listening to a customer's complaints about the previous order. Bellis-Jones (1992, p. 115) has suggested that such an analysis of activities commonly shows 30% core, 35% support and 35% diversionary activities. One objective

Table 8.1   *Activity-based applications*

	Proportion of activity-based users adopting this application*		Importance rating†		Success rating†	
	No.	%	Average rating	S.D.	Average rating	S.D.
Stock valuation	14	28.6	4.0	0.9	4.1	0.3
Product/service pricing	32	65.3	4.8	0.5	4.0	0.8
Output decisions	23	46.9	4.2	0.8	3.8	0.7
Cost reduction	43	87.8	4.5	0.5	3.9	0.6
Budgeting	29	59.2	4.4	0.6	4.0	0.7
New product/service design	15	30.6	4.5	0.8	4.1	0.6
Customer profitability analysis	25	51.0	4.2	0.7	4.0	0.6
Performance measurement/improvement	33	67.3	4.4	0.6	3.9	0.7
Cost modelling	30	61.2	3.9	0.6	3.8	0.6
Other applications	8	16.3	4.9	0.8	n/a	–

* This represents the number of users applying the activity-based approach for this particular purpose as a percentage of all activity-based users, i.e. 49 respondents.
† These ratings are computed from 5-point scales ranging from very important/successful (5 points) to very unimportant/unsuccessful (1 point).

is, therefore, to eliminate or at least to minimise diversionary activities and to concentrate on the core activities. The second common classification of activities is into value added or non-value added. This is value added from the customer's viewpoint. Again the objective is to eliminate or minimise these non-value added activities, such as dealing with problems which should not have arisen in the first place. Brimson (1992, p. 64) has suggested that 'most companies have between twenty and forty per cent of total cost consumed in performing non-value added wasteful activities'.

A natural extension of activity-based cost management is activity-based budgeting, where the overhead budget is set on the basis of the activities rather than the departments in an organisation. From this activity-based budgeting some organisations developed activity performance measures usually based on their activity cost drivers. Indeed Table 8.1 shows that, in this particular survey, performance measurement was the second most popular application of the activity-based approach after cost reduction. Some of these activity performance measures may be expressed in non-financial terms such as percentage of suppliers who are quality approved or volume of purchase orders but usually these activity performance measures are financial, such as cost per purchase order. Such activity performance measures include both the inputs (resource costs of each activity) and the outputs (service volumes of each activity). For example, cost per purchase order reflects the resource costs of purchasing and the service volumes in terms of the number of purchase orders processed. Obviously such an activity performance measure is incomplete on its own and would be combined with other performance measures.

As with all performance measures, the behavioural aspects must be considered. For example, it is possible to reduce the cost per purchase order by halving the quantity on each purchase order and doubling the number of purchase orders while at the same time increasing the cost of purchasing by say 25%. This certainly reduces the cost per purchase order but it is dysfunctional behaviour because the total costs of purchasing have risen by 25% without any benefits. As with all performance measures, activity performance measures must be used with care.

In practice managers find that activity performance measures can be used not only to control existing activities but also to encourage problem-solving and improvement. One of the most important advantages of the activity-based approach is the fact that activities cross departmental boundaries. For example, the activity of purchasing involves not only the purchasing department but also the various requisitioning departments, finance department (assessing financial viability of suppliers), stores (receiving orders), inspection (material receipts), accounts department (creditors) and cashier's department (payment of suppliers). The activity-based approach therefore helps to overcome the problem of departmental boundaries which exists in many organisations. Indeed some organisations have been so convinced of the benefits of the activity-based approach that they have actually reorganised so that individuals are responsible for activities or processes across the organisation instead of the more traditional departmental basis. Other organisations have compromised and become matrix organisations combining the activity or process approach with their existing departmental structure. In summary, therefore, the important feature of activity performance measures is that they cross departmental boundaries and give a view horizontally across the organisation.

The activity-based approach in the UK has been affected by developments in the USA. Indeed British accounting developments have generally been influenced more by North American than by European developments. One such European accounting development which has been in existence since the beginning of this century is the French *tableaux de bord*. The following section discusses the meaning and development of these.

TABLEAUX DE BORD

The French *tableaux de bord* are based on an organisation's departmental structure but within departments there may be *sections homogènes*, which are homogeneous cost pools. An example of a homogeneous sub-department within an overhead department would be the vehicle maintenance section. Originally these homogeneous sub-departments came from the Taylor approach to scientific management in the early part of this century when these sub-departments basically performed one operation and all the costs were collected for that one operation. The significance of these sub-departments today is that each develops its own *tableau de bord*. Lebas (1993, pp. 6–7) has defined the *tableau de bord* as 'the managerial information system that supports the achievement of performance just like the dashboard on a car allows the driver to reach his destination . . . These indicators are not all expressed in the same unit, their coherence comes from a model of the car operating system.'

Saulou (1982) gives further details of how to install a *tableau de bord* and Greif (1993) shows how the *tableaux de bord* are actually used in French factories. A *tableau de bord* for a sub-department includes key performance measures for that particular part of the organisation. Usually these are non-financial performance measures which the managers within that sub-department have identified as being critical to its successful operation. An important feature of the *tableau de bord* system is that it is not part of the formal accounting reporting system. It operates very much on the basis of self-control and also self-reporting. The managers themselves select the non-financial performance measures within their *tableaux de bord* and then monitor the results from these performance measures. It is very much a participative management style based on decentralised management.

The development of a *tableau de bord* for a sub-department requires much time and thought. Managers need to consider the sub-department's role in the organisation and its links with the organisational strategy. For example, in a recent case study of *tableaux de bord* implementation, managers spent their time approximately as follows:

(1) 50% on defining the objectives of the sub-department in relation to the strategy of the company;
(2) 20% on deciding the critical success factors for their sub-department;
(3) 30% on selecting detailed performance measures for their own *tableau de bord* and also on its presentation.

As circumstances change the *tableaux de bord* are revised and the self-control and self-reporting aspects of the *tableaux de bord* system give managers a great deal of flexibility in allowing them to make changes to their own *tableau de bord*.

The managers in a sub-department decide their own critical success factors – for example, for the export distribution sub-department it might be delivery on time. One performance measure for this particular sub-department might therefore be the number of late deliveries to export customers – probably expressed as a percentage of all export deliveries. Performance measures such as the number of late deliveries to customers indicate that it is not just internal but also external 'value to the customer' performance measures which are critical for the long-term survival of the organisation. For the vehicle maintenance sub-department, performance measures might include the number of vehicle breakdowns and the total time vehicles are off the road. For the warehouse receiving sub-department the performance measures might include the number of material receipts, the weight of materials received and the number of containers received. Very often such non-financial performance measures in the *tableaux de bord* are indicators of costs. However, the relationship between non-financial performance measures and financial measures is an area requiring much more research.

A *tableau de bord* usually has:

(1) several performance measures;
(2) mainly non-financial performance measures;
(3) the results presented in the form of charts.

All employees within the sub-department have access to the results of these performance measures and generally physical measures are better understood than financial measures. Similarly, by presenting the results in the form of wall charts it is relatively easy for everyone to see what is happening and to take corrective action as soon as a performance measure suggests that a problem is beginning to appear.

Gray and Pesqueux (1993) compared *tableaux de bord* in French organisations and responsibility accounting in American organisations. This comparison revealed a lot of similarities although the French organisations did make more use of presenting the results of their non-financial performance measures in the form of charts. However, a major difference was that the American management information system was much more centralised than the more localised French reporting system based on its *tableaux de bord*.

Another important feature is the systematic approach to the *tableaux de bord* system. Although each sub-department selects its own performance measures, the process of considering the objectives of the sub-department in relation to the organisation's strategy forces managers themselves to develop links with other sub-departments. This means that the *tableaux de bord* in effect become linked together vertically up through each department by means of some selected performance measures. Recently, a few French organisations have begun to experiment with the activity-based approach and are finding that this approach and the *tableaux de bord* system are in fact complementary. The *tableaux de bord* give the basis for non-financial performance measures with which French employees have been familiar for many years on a sub-departmental basis and the activity-based approach emphasises the co-ordination of such performance measures across the organisation. In effect the activity-based approach looks at processes and activity performance measures horizontally across the organisation and the *tableaux de bord* system involves links via sub-departmental performance measures vertically up the organisation. This gives a matrix approach to performance measurement within the organisation.

SUMMARY AND CONCLUSIONS

The activity-based approach began with the objective of unit product costing but has developed into a cost-management technique. This involves analysing activities into core/support/diversionary activities or value added/non-valued added categories. Some of the cost drivers for the activity cost pools, such as cost per material movement, have been used as activity performance measures.

As with much of British accounting, the activity-based approach has been influenced by developments in the USA. In contrast, as a broad generalisation, accounting developments in Europe have tended to be ignored by British accountants. One approach which has been followed since the beginning of this century in France is that of the *tableaux de bord*. In France *sections homogènes* (homogeneous cost pools based on sub-departments) have been identified, particularly on the factory floor, and each sub-department has developed its own *tableau de bord*.

These *tableaux de bord* involve each sub-department choosing its own initial success factors such as quality or delivery time and deciding upon appropriate performance measures for those factors. It is important to emphasise that the *tableaux de bord* are established by these sub-departments themselves and involve self-control with their own reports; they are *not* part of the formal reporting process. Usually the performance measures in the *tableaux de bord* are non-financial – such as the number of late deliveries.

With the *tableaux de bord* being on a sub-departmental basis, their non-financial performance measures tend to be linked vertically within a department. In contrast, the activity-based approach emphasises the co-ordination of overhead performance measures horizontally across departmental boundaries. This is why a few French organisations have found recently that the *tableaux de bord* and the activity-based approach are complementary and give a matrix approach to the organisation's performance measurement system. This combination of the activity-based approach and the *tableaux de bord* may also give better integration of the non-financial and financial overhead performance measures. Just as French organisations are finding it helpful to combine *tableaux de bord* and the activity-based approach, so British organisations may find it worthwhile to explore the French performance measurement system of *tableaux de bord*.

References

Bellis-Jones R. (1992) Activity-based cost management, in C. Drury (ed.), *Management Accounting Handbook*, Butterworth–Heinemann and CIMA, Oxford, pp. 100–27.

Brimson, J. A. (1992) The basics of activity-based management, in C. Drury (ed.), *Management Accounting Handbook*, Butterworth–Heinemann and CIMA, Oxford, pp. 64–99.

Cooper, R. (1985) *Schrader-Bellows*, Harvard Business School Cases, HBS, Boston, Mass.

Cooper, R. (1992) Activity-based costing for improved product costing, in B. J. Brinker (ed.), *Handbook of Cost Management*, Warren Gorham and Lamont, Boston, Mass., pp. B1–1 to B1–50.

Cooper, R. and Kaplan, R. S. (1987) *Winchell Lighting Inc*, Harvard Business School Cases, HBS, Boston, Mass.

Cooper, R. and Kaplan, R. S. (1988) How cost accounting systematically distorts product costs, *Management Accounting (US)* (April), pp. 20–7.

Gray, L. and Pesqueux, S. (1993) Evolutions actuelles de systèmes de tableaux de bord, *Revue Française de Comptabilité* (February), pp. 30–32.

Greif, M. (1993) Le déploiement du tableau de bord dans les ateliers, *Revue Française de Comptabilité* (March), pp. 15–18.

Horngren, C. T. (1990) First discussant on contribution margin analysis no longer relevant/strategic cost management: the new paradigm, *Journal of Management Accounting Research* (Fall), pp. 2–24.

Innes, J. and Mitchell, F. (1990) *Activity-Based Costing: A Review with Case Studies*, Chartered Institute of Management Accountants, London.

Innes, J. and Mitchell, F. (1991) *Activity-Based Cost Management*, Chartered Institute of Management Accountants, London.

Innes, J. and Mitchell, F. (1995) A survey of activity-based costing in the UK's largest companies, *Management Accounting Research*, Vol. 6, no. 2, pp. 137–53.

Kaplan, R. S. (1987) *American Bank*, Harvard Business School Cases, HBS, Boston, Mass.

Lebas, M. (1993) 'Tableau de bord' and performance measurement. Paper presented at MARG Conference at the LSE on 22 April.

Saulou, T. (1982), Le tableau de bord du décideur: méthodologie de mise en place, *Travail et Méthodes* (November).

Staubus, G. (1990) Activity costing: 20 years on, *Management Accounting Research*, Vol. 1, no. 4, pp. 249–64.

9

The Theory of Constraints and Performance Measurement

CHRIS SALAFATINOS

INTRODUCTION

The theory of constraints (TOC) is an approach which changes the way in which management views the organisation by reordering their priorities. Traditional management accounting focuses on the allocation of costs to various products and the control and reduction of these costs. It places first priority on reducing operating costs, followed by increasing throughput and, finally, the reduction of inventory (Burch, 1994). In contrast, TOC considers throughput as the first priority of management. Only after throughput is increased can inventory be reduced. Achieving these aims will ultimately provide the context in which operating expense can be effectively reduced. This reordering of priorities changes management's view of what is important, and consequently alters the performance measurement tools used to monitor, control and improve the organisation.)

This chapter introduces the TOC concept of management, and outlines the performance measurements which may be used to support it. In addition, the objectives and priorities of TOC are compared against traditional performance measures to determine which measures support and which conflict with TOC.

The theory of constraints

TOC is primarily a manufacturing theory which attempts to focus management's attention on three basic objectives. The first priority is to increase throughput. Throughput is defined as the rate at which sales margin is created. Sales margin is the difference between sales and the cost of materials sold. The second priority is to reduce the level of inventory, particularly work-in-process. The final priority is to reduce operating expenses.

Goldratt and Cox (1984, p. 59) related these objectives to the basic theme of making money. They defined inventory broadly as 'the money still in the system'. Throughput is defined as 'the money on its way it': this is the rate at which money is generated transforming materials into sales revenue.

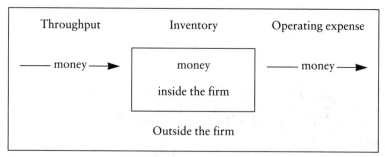

Figure 9.1   *The TOC framework*

Operating expense is defined as 'The money on its way out': this is all the money spent to create throughput (Goldratt and Cox, 1984, p. 59). This is illustrated in Figure 9.1.

One of the most important objectives for TOC is to reduce the level of inventory, because it has such a significant impact on profitability. For example, Garrett Automotive (Darlington *et al.*, 1992) has considered the impact that TOC could have on its operation and performed a sensitivity analysis of processing costs. It found that material costs ranked as the highest percentage of total costs. Garrett concluded that improvements not only in the cost of materials but in inventory levels possessed the greatest potential for long-term cost reduction and profit improvement. It therefore adopted TOC as a means of achieving these aims.

A manufacturing company is profitable only if the rate at which money is earned exceeds the rate at which money is spent (Galloway and Waldron, 1988). Success, as indicated by profitability, is influenced by the rate at which a business contributes money relative to the rate at which money is consumed through expenses. Therefore, according to TOC, profitability is a function of 'time' and 'inventory'. Moreover, profitability is inversely related to 'time' and 'inventory' (Bromwich and Bhimani, 1994). Reducing the time required to pass a product through a production system reduces inventory and increases profitability.

All things held equal, increasing the rate at which a product travels from receiving to shipping would have the effect of reducing inventory and consequently reducing money tied up in the system. Process constraints hinder this rate. A bottleneck or constraint is some factor which inhibits the rate at which products can move through the system. They represent a resource that is pressed near or beyond its capacity. Throughput can therefore be increased by reducing the effects of bottlenecks in the chain of production processes.

A resource can be pressed beyond its capacity when the term 'capacity' is meant to express the optimal level of operation rather than a theoretical maximum as McNair (1994) describes. A resource which is used beyond this optimal point begins to exhibit overload problems such as breakdowns and defective outputs. Other resources, which precede a bottleneck, begin to 'pile up' inventory in front of the bottleneck resource. In addition, as the constrained resource is pressed beyond practical capacity, management tends to increase inventory stocks as a buffer to accommodate expected breakdowns and defective output.

TRADITIONAL SYSTEM DIFFICULTIES

Traditional cost management accounting leads to the build up of unreal inventory profits, the use of economic order quantities (EOQs) that are not economical and the encouragement of 'local' efficiency, which is detrimental to 'global' performance (Jayson, 1987). This is because the traditional approach leads factory managers to focus their attention on the maximisation of each resource independently. The underlying logic of this is that if all resources are utilised to their capacity the entire system will yield maximum efficiency. Maximum efficiency translates into maximum profits. Measurements like 'parts produced per hour per machine' are used to measure resource utilisation. An idle worker is considered a 'bad thing' because this labour resource is being used at less than its capacity. A localised view of efficiency supports the idea that management should keep workers and machines busy producing product. This is an attempt at maximising each and every resource as if they were unrelated to one another. The managerial objective, therefore, is to balance the capacity of localised factory resources with the demand on those resources (Goldratt and Fox, 1986).

This sort of localised efficiency analysis has been supported for a long time by cost variance analysis and standard costing, a staple of cost accounting education and practice. Standard costs are developed to support the budgeting process and help control various aspects of the factory. Standards of capacity for each resource are budgeted, and variances are addressed. For example, a labour standard might be used to control the efficiency of a particular process. Management may conduct time studies to determine that an average worker in the drilling work area should be able to drill 100 holes every hour. A standard is then set to evaluate this worker to make sure that 100 holes are, in fact, drilled each hour. If the worker produces only 75 holes, a negative labour efficiency variance results and management attempts to bring the level of efficiency up to 100 holes. The aim is simply to support the idea that each resource has a predetermined capacity or standard that must be maximised in order to make more money for the company overall. Waldron and Galloway (1989a, p. 32) highlighted the motivational consequences for management: 'When we measure standard hours produced, we create an environment in which we strive to keep people busy producing.'

This is the idea that worker activation is the same as worker utilisation. The result is a policy of trying to balance capacity with demand from the marketplace. Indeed, Waldron and Galloway (1989b) suggest that balanced capacity is unattainable because organisations are constantly challenged by business fluctuations and disruptions. Even under the best of conditions absenteeism and machine breakdowns will occur, resulting in lack of productivity. As a result, 100% utilisation of resources is never a possibility (Coughlan and Darlington, 1993). TOC is based on the idea that one should not try to balance factory capacity with demand but, rather, balance the 'flow of production' with demand. The 'flow of production' refers to the rate at which product can move through the production process without leaving behind inventory residue (Jones, 1995).

THE DYNAMICS OF TOC

With TOC, there is a recognition that each factory resource has a different and unique capacity. That is, some employees work faster than others and some machines produce more parts per hour than others. Recognising that each resource does not work independently but in co-operation with other resources is the central theme of TOC. In other words, it is not important to maximise every independent resource but, rather, to maximise the flow of product through the entire system. This is the 'global' view of efficiency. Thus, from a TOC perspective, the whole company is conceptualised as a large single resource for 'making money'. TOC emphasises resource co-ordination over resource activation. What is important is not how well independent resources are used in a company but how well they work together to increase throughput. This is the reason TOC places great importance on production constraints. Bottlenecks in the production process govern the rate at which throughput can be achieved.

To illustrate this idea, assume that machine A produces subassemblies for use in machine B. Also assume that machine A produces subassemblies twice as fast as machine B can use them. If these are the only two machines in the system, it will produce final output only as fast as machine B can produce it. Hence, the bottleneck governs the speed that a product flows through the system. Now assume that machine A is underutilised. That is, it sits idle for 50% of the time while machine B is pressed to capacity. Under a traditional localised approach to efficiency, machine A must be speeded up to improve its efficiency. On the other hand, machine B is of little concern since it is being utilised to its fullest. If management is unsuccessful in bringing machine A up to 100% capacity, what would be the result? The company throughout would be unchanged since the system will still be able to produce product only as fast as machine B can process it and therefore, from a TOC perspective, no improvement would have taken place. This is because machine B can go no faster and it governs throughput. In fact, a negative result – increasing work-in-process inventory – has occurred. Machine A, working twice as fast as machine B, would begin to 'pile up' more and more unfinished product in front of machine B waiting to be processed.

The TOC approach states that it is better to leave a resource idle if this reduces work-in-process inventory and does not reduce throughput. Effort should therefore be placed on those resources that are near or over capacity rather than on resources which are underutilised. Since throughput is governed by the slowest process, it is the bottlenecks that deserve attention.

In summary, improving the 'flow of product' through the factory increases throughput and causes inventory and operating expenses to go down. The more conventional idea that each resource needs to be pressed to capacity ignores the interrelationship of resources in the system and results in an incorrect view of the organisation. Traditional management accounting control techniques like standard costing have fostered this view. Standard costing treats the company like a collection of separate and independent investments, rather than a single organism designed for making money. In contrast, the TOC approach gives emphasis to finding bottlenecks and smoothing the flow of product through the system to increase throughput, reduce inventory and increase profits. Reducing bottlenecks is therefore the path to balancing the flow of production with demand and increasing profitability.

With regard to this view of profitability, performance measurement tools have been developed to determine the impact of bottlenecks and how to reduce their effects on throughput.

TOC PERFORMANCE MEASURES

Once management subscribes to the TOC approach, increasing throughput becomes the main objective. It is argued that bottlenecks are the primary barrier to throughput and this is why TOC performance measures focus upon bottleneck reduction. Indeed, many of the performance ratios intended to inform management of the profitability and efficiency of the entire firm are, in fact, measures of bottleneck resources within the firm. Another main focus of TOC performance measures is on 'time'. Just as net income is a measure of the excess of revenue over expenses in a given period. TOC uses time as a way of providing a common denominator for comparing performance of different periods. However, TOC uses time in smaller increments than traditional methods. Many of the TOC ratios break down performance in terms of hours or even minutes as opposed to quarters or years.

Waldron and Galloway (1988), who refer to TOC as 'throughput accounting', have constructed various measures of throughput performance to ensure that every minute of operation is devoted to producing something that can be sold. The key part of the phrase here is 'that can be sold'. TOC measures differ from traditional efficiency measures because the focus is not on the maximisation of production output (which could be for sale or stock) but, rather, on the production of product which is sellable immediately finished goods are completed. TOC performance measures are based on four general principles:

(1) ensure that every minute of direct labour is spent on sellable products and not on producing inventory;
(2) any action or decision which increases inventory is bad;
(3) the shorter the lead time the better;
(4) bottlenecks govern the rate of output.

Applying these principles generate TOC performance measures that can be classified into three groups. The first group focuses on bottleneck output, the second on the rate of throughput and the third on efficiency of operations.

Bottleneck measures

Bottleneck performance measures focus on resources which constrain the flow of product through the system. Bottlenecks can be identified through observation of the plant or, more systematically, by using process activity maps (Salafatinos, 1995). Performance measures are used to determine the impact a bottleneck resource has on total output. The two key measures for this purpose are the return on bottleneck (RDP) and the cost of bottleneck (COB) ratios.

The ROB is computed by dividing the total gross profit by the amount of time used by the bottleneck resource:

$$\text{Return on bottleneck (ROB)} = \frac{\text{Total gross profit}}{\text{Bottleneck minutes used}}$$

The numerator is determined by deducting direct costs from total sales revenue. The denominator is the sum of minutes of all bottleneck resources employed to produce output. This ratio informs management of the rate of yield produced by the bottleneck resources. Since the bottleneck governs the rate of output for the entire process, management needs to monitor the profitability which results from every minute of bottleneck operation. An improvement in the yield of a bottleneck resource represents an improvement in the yield for the entire firm. In contrast, an improvement in the yield of a non-bottleneck resource returns no benefit at all to the firm and instead increases inventory.

The COB ratio is computed by dividing total factory costs, excluding materials, by the practical capacity of the bottleneck resource. The capacity of a bottleneck resource is normally measured in number of minutes available for production in a given period.

$$\text{Cost of bottleneck (COB)} = \frac{\text{Total factory costs}}{\text{Capacity of bottleneck}}$$

This ratio indicates the total cost for every minute of bottleneck operation. This is important because management must recognise that every minute saved on a bottleneck resource is a saving, not only for the costs of the resource, but for the entire conversion cost of the firm. Total factory costs per unit decrease when output volume increases. Since bottlenecks control the rate of output for the entire firm, every minute saved translates into increased output for the firm and a reduction to the cost of each unit of product.

Throughput measures

The primary measure of TOC is the level of throughput compared with the cost of achieving it. This is accomplished by dividing throughput by total factory costs (Waldron and Galloway, 1989a).

$$\text{Primary measure (Pl)} = \frac{\text{Throughput}}{\text{Total factory costs}}$$

Throughput for the firm is total sales revenues less total material costs of goods sold in a given period. Total factory costs are the firm's total expenses other than direct material costs within the same period. This ratio informs management as to how well it is managing the flow of production. The calculation implies that only material costs are variable and that all other costs, including direct labour and variable overhead, are fixed in the relative short term. This is the basis upon which TOC is criticised as a short-term approach to management. TOC advocates argue that all costs, except materials, are largely predetermined in the short to medium term. In addition, it is more useful and infinitely simpler to consider these costs in a single classification as 'total factory costs'. The Pl measure is an 'overall' indicator to gauge the entire operation similar to the way net income is used with traditional performance measures. However, net income equally focuses on the reduction of all costs, while the Pl measure focuses particularly on the reduction of material inventory costs. The difference between the Pl and net income measures reflects the relative importance that management places on throughput, inventory and operating costs.

Throughput measures can also be used to evaluate the profitability of individual products (Yoshikawa *et al.*, 1993). Products are evaluated in terms of their relative contribution per minute of bottleneck resource. In other words, the process constraint, which governs the rate of output, serves as the primary indicator for determining a product's profitability. This is computed by dividing the gross margin of a product by the bottleneck minutes required to produce it.

$$\text{Product profitability ratio (PPR)} = \frac{\text{Gross margin per unit}}{\text{Bottleneck minutes used per unit}}$$

Gross margin is the difference between the unit sale price and the unit material cost of the product. The bottleneck minutes are the number of minutes of the constrained resource required to produce each product. Therefore, products which require more of a bottleneck resource will have to generate comparable higher sales revenues than products which require less usage of bottleneck resource time.

The PPR measure contrasts with the traditional approach to product profitability evaluation. Traditional product performance measures frequently consider the contribution margin of each product without regard to process constraints. The higher the contribution margin per unit the more profitable the product. TOC argues that this simplistic view can result in incorrect decisions with regard to product profitability. For example if product A has a contribution margin of 0.95 per unit and product B of 0.65, the conventional conclusion is that product A is more profitable. However, if product A requires four minutes of bottleneck resources and product B requires only two minutes, then from a TOC perspective, product B is more profitable than product A. This is calculated by using the PPR measures of profitability as follows:

PPR of product A is $0.95 \div 4 = 0.237$
PPR of product B is $0.65 \div 2 = 0.325$

Since bottleneck resources govern the rate of production, the product which yields the higher throughput per minute of constraint contributes greater income to the firm.

Efficiency measures

Efficiency measures are used to support primarily the efficient use of labour and inventory. The labour efficiency measure can be calculated by dividing the throughput of the firm by total direct labour costs.

$$\text{Labour efficiency ratio (LER)} = \frac{\text{Throughput}}{\text{Total direct labour costs}}$$

The LER measure reflects TOC's 'global' approach to production optimisation. TOC argues that what matters is using direct labour for every minute of production on products that can be 'sold'. Traditional measures of labour efficiency are based on goods 'produced'. This results in the view that utilising labour to its capacity results in maximum productivity for the firm. This 'localised' approach to production optimisation leads to the build up of work-in-process inventory and ultimately to an increase in operating expense. The LER measure increases when labour costs result in sales revenue but actually decreases when labour is used to build up inventory. TOC supports the idea that it may be better to leave a worker idle if it helps to reduce inventory and does not reduce throughput.

Another TOC performance measure focuses on the level of inventory stock itself. Inventory reduction is a central objective of TOC. Inventory stock efficiency can be computed by dividing throughput by the total inventory stock value.

$$\text{Stock efficiency ratio (SER)} = \frac{\text{Throughput}}{\text{Total stock value}}$$

The SER measure informs management about the relationship between 'the money still in the system' and 'the money on its way in'. It encourages management to reduce the amount of money tied up in the company (inventory) by reducing lead times and increasing throughput.

TRADITIONAL MEASURES AND TOC

Traditional performance measurement tools can both support and conflict with the TOC approach to management. Those measurement tools that encourage the increase of throughput and the reduction of inventory and operating expense are considered to support TOC. The problem is that parts of the traditional measurement tools may support TOC while other parts may conflict with it. In this section some traditional performance measures are considered and assessed against the objective of TOC.

TOC is not a unique approach with respect to reducing inventory and operating expense. The novel aspect of TOC comes from the recognition that throughput is the most important short-term criterion by which to judge performance. Traditional cost management has, for a long time, supported similar ideas with regard to inventory and operating costs. This is evidenced by a number of established performance measures that support aspects of the TOC approach. For example, the inventory turnover ratio compares the level of inventory with the costs of goods sold. This ratio supports TOC in two ways. First, it considers 'goods sold' rather than 'goods produced' in the numerator. This focuses management on throughput rather than on production volume. Second, it places importance on the level of inventory stock as a measure of performance which can motivate management to try to reduce inventory levels. However, the inventory turnover ratio possesses some underlying problems which conflict with TOC. The problem with this ratio, and indeed any ratio which uses inventory as a component of the measurement, is in the way inventory is valued. Most companies are required to use some form of absorption costing for reporting. Consequently, the inventory figure is composed of not only material costs but conversion costs as well. Combining production costs with material costs conflicts with TOC in two ways. First, TOC argues that only material costs are truly variable in the short and medium term. Second, management is encouraged to produce inventory in its quest to be efficient and to maximise resource potential.

Another widely used traditional performance measure which supports TOC, to some extent, is the return on investment (ROI) ratio (net income ÷ total assets). This ratio supports the idea that the 'money still in the system' (assets) must be compared to the 'money on its way in' (throughput) as a measure of performance. The ratio encourages management to reflect on the investment required to produce the current level of earnings. However, the problem with the ROI measure is that it does not directly connect the reduction of inventory to an increase in performance. The ROI only considers the reduction of the inventory investment in the denominator (assets) while the numerator (income) is not directly affected. Although the reduction of inventory is likely to lead indirectly to reduced expenses and thus an increase in income, it is not directly expressed in the ROI ratio. TOC advocates argue that reducing inventory directly increases income and is therefore expressed in the TOC ratios. Income is increased by the reduction in material handling costs, interest charges, storage costs, scrap costs and obsolescence costs. In addition, reducing inventory increases product quality by allowing for defects to be found faster and for engineering improvements to be implemented sooner.

CONCLUSION

Performance measurements help to determine if the firm is operating in accordance with management's concept of a successful company. Management philosophy determines the characteristic of the management approach and hence defines the tools of performance measurement. If management believes that overhead costs should be the focus for a successful firm then activity-based costing (ABC) systems may be employed. In this instance, performance indicators would involve the concentration on cost drivers and resource allocation. If reduction of inventory and lead times is the main focus then a just-in-time (JIT) system may be introduced. Performance indicators such as lead times, product delivery rates and the level of inventory are employed. Finally, if quality is considered to be the key success factor, then total quality management (TQM) programmes might be put in place. Indicators such as the number of defects and the level of customer satisfaction would be used to guide management's efforts.

There are clearly many aspects of profitability. To focus on only one or a few leaves other important issues unaddressed. If management concentrates too much on product quality, without adequate consideration of overhead costs, profitability may be jeopardised. The TOC approach to management does not and should not exclude other important views of performance such as TQM and JIT. In fact, there exists a synergy in which all three approaches to management complement one another. Therefore, the performance measures used in a TOC environment could be and should be used with TQM and JIT performance measures. The connection between these management approaches is summarised by Goldratt (1990, pp. 8–9) as follows:

> It is about time to realize that JIT's primary focus is not the reduction of inventory on the shop floor. It is not just mechanical 'kanban' technique. It is definitely a new overall management philosophy.
>
> It is about time to realize that TQM's primary focus is not the quality of the products. It is not just a mechanical statistical process control technique. It is definitely a new overall management philosophy.
>
> It is about time to realize that TOC's primary focus is not bottlenecks on the shop floor. It is not just a mechanical optimized production technique. It is definitely a new overall management philosophy.

The three management philosophies could be regarded as complementary. For each to succeed, however, key different performance measurement tools must be used.

References

Bromwich, M. and Bhimani, A. (1994) *Pathways to Progress*, CIMA, London.
Burch, J. (1994) *Cost and Management Accounting, A Modern Approach*, West Publishing, Saint Paul, MN.
Coughlan, P. and Darlington, J. (1993) As fast as the slowest operation: the theory of constraints, *Management Accounting (UK)* (June), pp. 14–17.

Darlington, J., Innes, J., Mitchell, F. and Woodward, J. (1992) Throughput accounting: the Garrett Automotive experience, *Management Accounting (UK)* (April), pp. 32–8.

Galloway, D. and Waldron, D. (1988) Throughput accounting: the need for a new language for manufacturing, *Management Accounting (UK)* (November), pp. 34–5.

Goldratt, E. (1990) *The Haystack Syndrome: Sifting Information Out of the Data Ocean*, Northriver Press, Great Barrington, Mass.

Goldratt, E. and Cox, J. (1984) *The Goal*, Gower, Aldershot.

Goldratt, E. and Fox, R. (1986) *The Race*, Gower, Aldershot.

Jayson, S. (1987) Goldratt & Fox: revolutionizing the factor floor, *Management Accounting (USA)* (May), pp. 18–22.

Jones, T. C. (1994) *Social Organization of Intellectual Knowledge: Theory of Constraints and the Goldratt Institute*, Interdisciplinary Approaches to Accounting Workshop, Manchester Business School, January.

McNair, C. (1994) The hidden costs of capacity, *Journal of Cost Management* (Spring), pp. 12–24.

Salafatinos, C. (1995) Integrating the theory of constraints and throughput accounting with activity-based costing, *Journal of Cost Management* (Fall), pp. 56–61.

Waldron, D. and Galloway, D. (1988) Throughput accounting part 2: Ranking products profitability, *Management Accounting (UK)* (December), pp. 24–5.

Waldron, D. and Galloway, D. (1989a) Throughput accounting part 3: A better way to control labour costs, *Management Accounting (UK)* (January), pp. 32–3.

Waldron, D. and Galloway, D. (1989b) Throughput accounting part 4: Moving on to complex products, *Management Accounting (UK)* (February), pp. 40–1.

Yoshikawa, T., Innes, J., Mitchell, F. and Tanaka, M. (1993) *Contemporary Cost Management*, Chapman & Hall, London.

PART II
The Public Sector

10

Reflections on Performance Measurement in the Public Sector

IRVINE LAPSLEY

INTRODUCTION

There is now a voluminous literature on the issue of performance measurement in the public sector. Much of this is addressed to the mechanisms of measuring the performance of specific segments of the public sector, with an emphasis on possible performance indicators and guidelines for management action. An exception to this is Jones (1993, p. 43), who describes the current preoccupation with public sector performance measurement as an infatuation and, more particularly, an infatuation which has seized the imagination of auditors and the accounting profession. A major aspect of Jones's reservations rests on the integrity of numbers used in the construction of performance indicators. This issue, and the managerialist perspective mentioned above, are both examined in later sections of this chapter, but first there is an appraisal of the context in which such measures of performance are used in the public sector. The chapter addresses these in five stages:

(1) an examination of the *rationale* of performance measurement in the public sector;
(2) performance measurement *in action* – a discussion of alternative models of implementation;
(3) performance measurement as a *management process* – a discussion of the managerialist perspective alluded to above;
(4) performance measurement as it affects *specific* industries; and, finally,
(5) performance measurement in the *future*.

Each of these stages is examined below.

W/H M ?

THE RATIONALE OF PERFORMANCE MEASUREMENT IN THE PUBLIC SECTOR

There are four major strands to the emergence of performance measures as a central feature of the UK's public sector:

(1) fiscal pressures;
(2) the perceived inefficiency of the public sector;
(3) the absence of managerial incentives and clearly defined commercial objectives; and
(4) the dependency culture of a nation too reliant on the public purse.

While this set of arguments is most closely aligned to the ideas of the Thatcher government of 1979 (and indeed subsequent Conservative governments), it is important to note that the move to performance indicators precedes the change of government in 1979. Examples of pre-1979 central government guidance to public sector institutions on the need for performance indicators can be found in the White Papers on the nationalised industries (notably Cmnd 3437 (Treasury, 1967) and Cmnd 7131 (Treasury, 1978)). In part, this can be attributed to the need to ensure the efficiency of state industries against a background of slow economic growth, an increasing public sector borrowing requirement and consequent pressure on public expenditure. Thus poor post-war (macro) economic performance can be seen as a continuing theme behind the attempts of administrations of differing political complexions to improve the efficiency of state industries – a precursor of the drive for performance indicators. But part of the rationale for this push towards performance indicators for state industries can be seen (pre-1979) as a demonstration effect, in which the nationalised industries could demonstrate their efficiency in the face of criticisms of their performance (see, for example, Polanyi and Polanyi, 1974). Similarly, as opponents of the policy of nationalisations, the incoming Conservative administration in 1979 shared the perceptions of critics of state industries that they were inefficient, and sought to scrutinise their performance and, indeed, this is further reflected in the more recent announcement of the Citizens' Charter.

While the above debate can be seen as a convergence from different parts of the political spectrum, the remaining arguments cited above are most closely associated with the Right and, most importantly in any appraisal of the effectiveness and eventual fate of such measures, they represent only part of a total picture of reforms of the public sector. Thus, previous reliance on the public service tradition of the *administration* of public services (usually with policy or political input at national level) contrasts sharply with the model of devolved *management*, favoured by the reformers of the public sector. In this context, performance indicators had a major role to play as tools by which these new public service managers could discharge their responsibilities. But the final argument cited above for performance indicators – the existence of the dependency culture – is a more fundamental attack on the concept of a public sector. This stems from the ideas of property rights theorists who see the existence of state ownership as inconsistent with the efficiency of service delivery. In this case, performance indicators (expected to be adverse) can be seen as a prelude to the demise of state industries.

The principal mechanisms by which the radical reformers of the 1980s and 1990s sought to change the public sector were the privatisation of industries and services and the introduction of more commercial, accountable management. The impact of the former mechanism is taken up further in the concluding part of this chapter, which seeks to chart the likely future of performance measures. But the second of these mechanisms presents a powerful rationale for the implementation of performance indicators. The extension of these indicators can be seen as a recognition of the need for intervening variables of public services performance given the difficulties posed by the absence of the market-place. These issues are taken up further in the following section.

PERFORMANCE MEASUREMENT IN ACTION

In this section we examine attempts at global performance measurement models, specifically those of:

(1) economy, efficiency and effectiveness (the three Es), as espoused by the National Audit Office;
(2) the Fédération des Experts Comptables Européens (FEE); and
(3) Mayston's (1985) model of performance measurement.

The desire for such global measures of performance measurement can be seen in the light of a desire to impose order, economic logic and tidiness on an apparent 'disorderly', 'fragmentary', fuzzy picture. In this way, these models provide a construct or overall yardstick against which the success of public service organisations can be tested.

The three Es

The search for a market surrogate for the public sector can be seen in the frequently used construct of 'efficiency, economy and effectiveness'. An interesting illustration of this can be seen in Figure 10.1, which sets out the National Audit Office's interpretation of the three Es.

This can be seen to be simultaneously non-controversial (in the sense that proponents of 'value for money' (VFM) would be likely to agree with their contents) and contentious (in the sense that the use of the terms spending *well* and *wisely* demonstrates the ambiguity inherent in the VFM approach). A closer examination of the difficulties of implementing VFM can be seen by considering an NAO illustration of its application. This is shown in Figure 10.2. Here the implications of VFM implementation are evident: as we move from the *general* to the *specific*, we also move from the *simple* to the *complex*. In Figure 10.2 there is nothing contentious in the definition of 'economy', but this cannot also be said

---

Economy is concerned with minimising the cost of resources acquired or used, having regard to appropriate quality.

(in short, spending less)

Efficiency is concerned with the relationship between the output of goods, services or other results and the resources used to produce them. How far is maximum output achieved for a given input, or minimum input used for a given output?

(in short, spending well)

Effectiveness is concerned with the relationship between the intended results and the actual results of projects, programmes or other activities. How successfully do outputs of goods, services or other results achieve policy objectives, operational goals and other intended effects?

(in short, spending wisely)

Source: National Audit Office (1988).

Figure 10.1   *The National Audit Office definition of the three Es*

For example, a VFM examination of a hospital building programme might cover any or all of the following aspects:

– the tendering, contract and project control procedures to establish how far the hospital and associated facilities had been built to specification, on time and at lowest achieveable cost or within approved cost limits (**Economy**)
– utilisation of wards, beds, theatres and equipment; medical and administrative staff allocations and mix; integration of services; maintenance; management and resource allocation systems; etc. (**Efficiency**)
– results in terms of – for example – reductions in patient waiting lists, increases in operations performed, improved diagnostic and treatment rates and (ultimately) improvements in health and quality of life, reduced mortality rates, etc. (**Effectiveness**)

Source: National Audit Office (1988).

Figure 10.2   *The VFM approach: an exemplification*

of the definitions of 'efficiency' and 'effectiveness'. The definition of efficiency in the context of a hospital building programme is broadbrush and fragmentary. There is no indication of the connections between the various service components and no hint of the mapping of an optimally available set of resources. In sum, this portrays a highly judgemental assessment of efficiency. Similarly, the definition of effectiveness poses questions. For example, the capacity measures referred to give indications of productive efficiency, rather than effectiveness. There is also the piecemeal nature of the aspects of service delivery identified. More fundamental, however, is the nebulous nature of criteria such as 'improvements in health and quality of life' – which in themselves are extremely slippery concepts for which operational measures are not readily available. The major message from this is the *complexity* of implementing the three Es or VFM approach. This issue is taken up further, below.

The FEE model

The FEE model is shown in Figure 10.3.

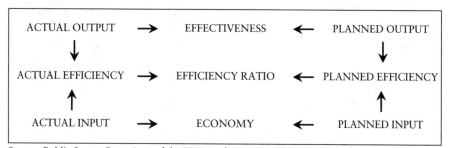

Source: Public Sector Committee of the FEE, *Performance and Financial Management* (undated).

Figure 10.3   *The FEE model of performance measurement*

This model builds on accounting notions of control and variance analysis, in the comparison of actual and planned inputs and outputs. This is allied to the concepts of effectiveness, efficiency and economy, as discussed in the context of the NAO's approach to value for money audits. Thus, in this model, *economy* is measured by the ratio of actual input to planned input; *efficiency* by the ratio of actual efficiency to planned efficiency; and *effectiveness* by the ratio of actual output to planned output. But this construct, while of interest at a general level, begs the question of how both 'output' and 'efficiency' are to be defined. The industrial or production model implicit in the FEE approach does not translate well to the public sector context. While it may be meaningful for certain organisations in the public sector (for example, trading activities, such as transport, housing construction), it is of less relevance to non-market-orientated public agencies, such as the police and fire services, libraries, the Houses of Parliament. This is another indication of the difficulties posed by the move from the general to the specific, and from the simple to the complex. This is *prima facie* an argument for the use of partial, rather than global, performance measures. This issue also emerges in the following discussion of Mayston's (1985) model.

The Mayston (1985) model

The model of performance measurement (labelled as the 'stages to policy optimisation') proposed by Mayston (1985) is shown in Figure 10.4. This model is evidently more complex than that of the FEE. Like the FEE model, it too seeks to build on the concepts of economy, efficiency and effectiveness, by integrating them more explicitly with policy evaluation, rather than the basic accounting control model. But this model has its own set of difficulties, which can be categorised as (1) implementation issues and (2) the related, but

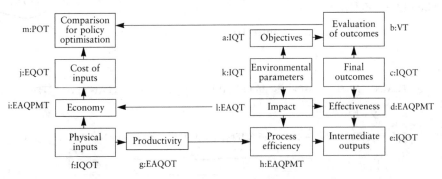

Key to individual steps: A = Assess, E = Examine, I = Identify, M = Maximise, O = Optimise, P = Improve, Q = Quantify, T = Monitor, V = Evaluate.

Source: Mayston (1985).

Figure 10.4 *Mayston's model of performance measurement*

particularly significant, problem of 'noise' included by variation in accounting practices. Examples of such difficulties can be demonstrated, as follows.

(1) *Implementation*

  (a) In a: IQT (in Figure 10.4) there is a need to identify, quantify and monitor the objectives of the focus under study. But this implies ease of quantification and that the interrelationships (particularly cause and effect) can be demonstrated. There are particular difficulties, here, not so much in identifying inputs but in the use of intermediate outputs (e.g. numbers and schoolchildren taught) instead of final outputs (e.g. quality of education received).

  (b) In h:EAQPMT, i.e. examine, assess, quantify, improve, maximise and monitor for economy, efficiency and effectiveness, there are similar implicit assumptions about known functional relationships to operationalise these procedures.

(2) *Accounting noise*

  Also implicit in this model is the assumption that accounting numbers are available in a manner which permits comparisons to be made. But there is evidence within the public sector that this is not the case, particularly on:

  (a) the treatment of capital assets (where these might be regarded as 'free goods'), or recorded at different bases of valuation (historical or current cost), or may be influenced by the nature of capital financing);

  (b) the treatment of overheads (which may be defined inconsistently over time and between organisational units, allocated wholly or partly, or allocated on an inconsistent basis); and, finally,

  (c) the differences between cash-based and accruals information.

These kinds of reservations undermine the general validity of these global models. A consequence of this is the reliance on partial indicators (e.g. with either/or labour or capital as inputs; with descriptions of service levels, rather than quantification). A concomitant practice is the adoption of management checklists as mechanisms by which the three Es are pursued. This is taken up further, in the next section.

PERFORMANCE MEASUREMENT AS A MANAGEMENT PROCESS

The problems posed by the absence of a comprehensive operational model of performance measurement and the need to rely on partial indicators of service delivery have resulted in the emergence of checklists as points of reference for managers of public services. This phenomenon is explored below, in two stages: (1) an overview of models of performance measurement as 'checklist management' and (2) a discussion of associated implementation problems.

Performance measurement – management checklists

Examples of the kinds of management checklists available for managers of public services are shown in Table 10.1. These are both by highly respected and knowledgeable figures on the public sector scene – Peter Jackson (1988) and Andrew Likierman (1993). This serves to underline the inherent difficulty in teasing out solutions to the public sector performance measurement problem. This can be seen on two levels: the specific nature of the guidance offered, and more general observations on the context in which such checklists are intended to be implemented.

An examination of these models reveals the difficulties. For example, Jackson's nine concepts of consistency, comparability, clarity, controllability, contingency, comprehensive, bounded, relevance and feasibility have intuitive appeal. Indeed a number of these concepts (consistency, comparability, controllability, relevance) are well entrenched in the language of accountancy. But a major difficulty with this set of concepts is that of dealing with issues of capturing the reality of the situation and portraying this in shorthand form. Thus, the call for *clarity* (simple, well-defined, easily understood, etc.) cannot be questioned *per se* but it need not sit well with 'contingency, comprehensive and bounded'. More specifically, these criteria can be seen as internally inconsistent: the model calls for 'consistency' but also advocates 'comprehensiveness' ('all important indicators') and 'bounded' (i.e. select a 'limited number of key performance indicators') (Jackson, 1988, p. 12).

Also within this model there is a picture of equivalence, but there is a case for recognising different orders of difficulty attaching to these different concepts, notably what Jackson (1988) calls 'contingency'. In this concept Jackson observes that management style, the organisation structure and the internal and external environment are important variables and performance measurement is not independent of these. As discussed further below, these are critical dimensions of the management process, which cannot (should not) be contained as a side-issue.

Table 10.1　*Performance measurement: checklists for management*

Jackson (1988)	Likierman (1993)	
1. Consistency	1.	*Concept*
	1.1	All elements
2. Comparability	1.2	Appropriate numbers
	1.3	Safeguards
3. Clarity	1.4	Accountability issues
4. Controllability	2.	*Preparation*
	2.1	Ownership
	2.2	Avoid short-termism
5. Contingency	2.3	Reflect effort
	2.4	Uncontrollables?
6. Comprehensive	3.	*Implementation*
7. Bounded	3.1	Revision
	3.2	Linkages
8. Relevance	3.3	Understandable
	3.4	Proxies
9. Feasibility	3.5	Reassess
	4.	*Use*
	4.1	Trusted data
	4.2	Guidance
	4.3	Feedback
	4.4	Trade-off
	4.5	User-friendly

Source: Jackson (1988) and Likierman (1993).

The second checklist in Table 10.1 has been compiled by Andrew Likierman (1993) as lessons from the early use of performance indicators. This presents a more dynamic picture of the process than the other checklist by, for example, its guidance on the need to revise performance indicators and to reassess their use in the context of internal and external relationships (see 3.1 and 3.5). The tension created by the simultaneous need to take cognisance of the wider picture *and* to focus on specific aspects of performance measurement is also evident in this model (see 1.1 and 1.2). There are also several cautionary notes to be found in this checklist: the recognition of the potential for 'uncontrollables'; caveats on the use of 'proxies'; the need for users of performance measures to feel 'ownership' of them. But there remains, nevertheless, the implicit assumption within this guidance that there exist functional deterministic relationships in service delivery, for example managerial efforts can be reflected in accomplishments. This issue is taken up further, next.

The previous discussion of two specific management checklists for performance management has touched on a general observation on the context in which such checklists are intended to be implemented – the importance of different models of management. A contrast can be drawn between rational, logical systems and cultural models of management control. This rather sharp dichotomy obscures all shades of grey in between these alternatives. But, at one end of the spectrum – in which management can be characterised as rationalist, in which organisations are mechanistic, not organic, where formal relationships are regarded somewhat rigidly, organisational events are predictable, and means–end relationships are known – we find the management model implicit in these checklists.

But there is a competing view of management in the public services. This characterises management scenarios which may be chaotic, rather than orderly, and in which there may be considerable ambiguities over the determination of 'success' or 'failure'. Such organisations may also exhibit other characteristics, such as political controls and more intuitive/judgemental management styles. Indeed, these different models can be seen as representing competing modes and between which there is a collision of values. An example of the circumstances can be gleaned from Bourn and Ezzamel's (1986, p. 213) observations on the NHS:

> clinical freedom (is) . . . a vehicle for attaining medical care. It has two main elements: freedom of medical practices and caring, trust-based personal relationships between clinicians and their patients. These elements are harmonised and controlled essentially through self-regulation by the medical profession as reflected in the ethos and professional training of its members, rather than by hierarchic systems of financial control and accountability.

These observations could also be made of other public service professionals, such as academics and social workers. This picture is one of potential collision of a 'public service ethos' and a move to 'commercialisation' associated with the adoption and use of performance measures and indicators. This layer of complexity can lead to unintended consequences in embarking upon a programme of performance indicators. This issue is taken up further below, in a discussion of implementation problems.

Management checklists – implementation problems

The problems associated with a management checklist approach to performance measurement can be broadly categorised as follows:

(1) ambiguity;
(2) displacement;
(3) omission;
(4) conflicts.

Each of these is considered below.

The *ambiguous* nature of performance measurement in public services is demonstrated in the particular case of health care. There is no satisfactory definition of the outputs of health care. A major difficulty in disentangling cause and effect associated with medical interventions is the way in which medical outcomes are embedded in the whole fabric of society and not just related to a given medical treatment. Age, diet, residential location, form of work and other facets of lifestyle and the quality of the environment in which individuals live can all impinge on medical outcome. Thus recent visible improvements in the population's physical condition (greater life expectancy, for example) cannot be attributed solely to medical practices. Also, the phenomenon of medical innovation, in which sophistication of new developments may exceed medical need, distorts assessments of performance. This inability to disentangle the effects of service provision also extends to other parts of the public sector, e.g. education and social work.

The *displacement* effect created by performance measurement is a function of the need to quantify service delivery processes and outcomes in the construction of performance indicators. This has the consequence that managers focus on performance indicators. In this way, the *quantifiable* aspects of service delivery receive most attention and, in so doing, managers may drive out or displace consideration of the intangibles in service delivery. There are a number of examples of this where the elusive nature of 'quality of service' could have this effect: the quality of care received by the terminally ill in palliative care; emotional and social support for the elderly and the disabled; counselling provided by social work services.

On *omission*, this is the effect of the targeting ('bounded' numbers, advocated by Jackson (1988), and the 'appropriate numbers', advocated by Likierman (1993)) of performance indicators in management checklists. These suggestions of targeting a few key indicators may have the unintended consequence of the possible omission of other significant indicators.

Finally, on *conflict*, reference has been made above to the collision of the public service ethos and the new accountable/commercial management. These tensions between professions may undermine the benefits of performance measurement. In particular, this may arise because the values of the professional codes are not readily conducive to measurement. There is the point of view that such conflicts and tensions can be positive and creative forces within organisational life. But the real issue here is whether the clumsy use of numbers inadequately addresses the subtleties of professional value systems and adversely, and unnecessarily, threaten or destabilise such social controls within organisations.

PERFORMANCE MEASUREMENT IN SPECIFIC INDUSTRIES

So far, we have examined general considerations in performance measurement. This section takes a closer look at two specific settings (state industries and the NHS) to explore further the impact of performance measurement practices.

Hesitancy and refinement: the case of nationalised industries

The initial thrust in the demand for performance indicators at nationalised industries in the UK was directed at the familiar accounting numbers: target returns on capital employed; breaking even on revenue account; self-financing ratios. An alternative model of regulation is that of having a financial objective, subject to a specified volume constraint. This imposes financial discipline, but also leaves discretion to management on how to manage the services offered. It may apply to a subsidised service (to mitigate the possible proliferation of expenditure without regard to financial constraints and adequacy of services) or to a profitable monopolist (to prevent the restriction of output and increases in prices). This model can have weights assigned to prevent cross-subsidisation of services. An illustration of this model is set out below, after Glaister and Collings (1978).

(1) Maximisation of passenger miles, subject to a budget constraint:

$$\text{Max. } \Sigma f_i(g_i)$$

$$\text{s.t. } \Sigma[p_i f_i(g_i) - C_i\{f_i(g_i)\}] \geq \pi$$

$$0 \leq g_i \leq \alpha_i \qquad i = 1, 2 \ldots n$$

where f_i = no. of passenger miles per annum
$\quad g_i$ = pence per passenger mile at fare level, g
$\quad p_i$ = money fare
$\quad \alpha_i$ = an upper limit on fares
$\quad C_i$ = operating costs
$\quad \pi$ = contribution to fixed costs

(2) Maximisation of profit, subject to a passenger miles constraint:

$$\text{Max. } \Sigma[p_i f_i(g_i) - C_i\{f_i(g_i)\}]$$

$$\text{s.t. } \Sigma f_i(g_i) \geq M$$

$$0 \leq g_i \leq \alpha_i \qquad i = 1, 2 \ldots n$$

where $f_i, g_i, p_i, \alpha_i, C_i$ as before
$\quad M$ = minimum passenger miles

In this model, expressed as a non-linear programme, formulation (1) depicts a scheme of regulation in which the non-financial indicator, passenger mile (for freight traffic this could be substituted by net tonne miles), is maximised, subject to a financial constraint. In this formulation g_i are weights, with which the Minister of Transport (or other relevant policy-maker) indicates the amount by which he or she is prepared to subsidise different services. Under this arrangement, the contribution margin, π, required from railway operations might be positive or negative, dependent on the size of the subsidy payable. Formulation (2) presents the situation for a profitable monopolist and here the constraint M specifies a minimum level of passenger miles (or net tonne miles) to be provided.

This second formulation is the dual of formulation (1). Thus, if the lower limit on passenger miles, M, in formulation (2) is set at the maximum value of the passenger miles in the passenger-miles maximising problem; and if the contribution margin constraint, π, in formulation (1) is set at the maximum value of the constrained profit-maximising formulation, identical solutions to (1) and (2) will result. (This also assumes that the same weights, g_i, would be attached to the various segments of the volume of services to be attained in both versions of the model.) While this model had been applied successfully at London Transport, it was never (despite the declared interest of British Rail (BR)) applied at BR. It may have been that this particular form of regulation and performance measurement left too much discretion to existing cadres of managers with a public service tradition, rather than supporting new-style business managers who were introduced to bring about change within BR (see Dent, 1991). In any event, BR was pointed firmly in the direction of batteries of performance indicators as, with the 1978 White Paper on the nationalised industries (Treasury, 1978), there came the requirement that all state industries compile and publish comprehensive performance indicators.

BR is an interesting illustration of the response to the 1978 White Paper which demonstrates why this development can be characterised as one of hesitancy and refinement. BR's first attempt at the production of performance indicators produced a block of 12 such indicators: loaded train miles per train crew member; loaded train miles per route mile; passenger miles per loaded passenger track mile; average wagon load; net tonne miles per loaded freight train mile; passenger miles/net tonne miles per member of staff; average fare per passenger mile; revenue per £1,000 of paybill; freight revenue per wagon; Public Service Obligation (i.e. government subsidy) contract payments per passenger mile; Public Service Obligation contract payments as a percentage of GDP; passenger trains arriving on time, or less than five minutes late, as a percentage of total passenger trains. These indicators were presented for a five-year period. While those familiar with the railway industry will recognise at least some of these indicators as long-established statistics on activity within the railways, there is, nevertheless, no evident pattern which can be discerned from this initial attempt at performance indicators. Also, the presentation is as an addendum – yet another schedule among the supporting information for the annual accounts.

Lapsley (1984) suggested a restructuring of this information to highlight these performance indicators analysed across financial and non-financial aspects of their operations and by operating services (distinguishing between passenger and freight services) and infrastructure (or permanent way). And, indeed, as discussed further below, there has been refinement of these measures. But the major thrust of these indicators has been on the *inputs* of service provision. In part this is a consequence of the fact that, while there is a market in transport services, this market operates imperfectly. From the perspective of performance indicators, a result of this is that public services are quickly driven into partial indicators, with an emphasis on service inputs.

This is not to say that BR was unaware of the quality of service ('outputs') dimension. For example, in 1979 it published its report on quality of service (BR, 1979) which identified six components of passenger services: (1) a punctual and reliable service as timetabled; (2) clean, bright and cheerful trains; (3) reasonably comfortable seats for all passengers except on short journeys of 10 to 15 minutes; (4) information and advice in case of disruption; (5) adequate staffing and environment at stations; and (6) free movement between coaches to increase personal security, reduce vandalism and improve ticket control. But there was evident hesitation in including these dimensions of service as performance indicators in BR's annual report. Nevertheless, there was subsequent refinement of the performance indicators in BR's annual report and accounts. The 1986/87 report and accounts for BR won the CIPFA annual accounts award for public sector organisations. In these accounts, the performance indicators of the late 1970s have been expanded, but, more important, they have been related to specific segments of BR's activity (for example, freight, rail workshops).

This development was reinforced by the publication in 1991 of the Citizens' Charter, which sought to improve the quality of public services, to increase choice over service delivery, to charge public services with the duty of specifying their standards and compensating users where these standards are not reached – all of this in the context of providing 'value for money'. The BR response to this is interesting, on a number of counts. The Passengers' Charter was published in 1992. With the significant difference of compensation schemes, this charter has a close resemblance to BR's 1979 effort. It includes (1) a fair and satisfactory response if things go wrong; (2) clear and up-to-date information; (3) friendly and efficient service; (4) clean stations and clean trains; and (5) a safe, punctual and reliable train service. On (5), for example, the intercity services' standards are punctuality (90% of trains to arrive within ten minutes of scheduled time) and reliability (99% of services to run). While the acceptance of the Citizens' Charter initiative, with its explicit focus on service outcomes, can be seen as yet another refinement of BR's performance indicators, there is a need to distinguish between the fact of assembling and disclosing this information, on the one hand, and the actual implications of such policies, on the other.

In this regard there are important lessons from the USA in the measurement of quality of service of Amtrak. Lapsley (1984) gives an account of these issues. Of particular relevance to the UK situation is that of the timeliness of services. The Amtrak system was based on schedule adherence (a base standard for timeliness, plus marginal incentive bonuses), excessive delay (i.e. actual time of trip less scheduled time less 'excess delay' tolerance parameter) and schedule improvements. There are two difficulties with such a scheme as a basis for the compensation of passengers. The first is the extent to which results are contingent upon factors beyond the control of railway management. For example, the frequency of the cleaning of trains can be regarded as controllable, but adverse weather conditions are not. Second, management can manipulate key performance indicators, specifically by the inclusion of built-in organisational slack in target-setting. So by modifying timetables it made them easier to achieve, thereby avoiding the penalties of a 'poor performance'.

Indeed, this phenomenon has been observed within the UK. Harlow (1994) reports on numerous instances of this: Waterloo to Folkestone was scheduled at 89 minutes in 1994, but took 77 minutes in 1963; Euston to Glasgow was scheduled at 5 hours 38 minutes in 1994, but only 5 hours 8 minutes in 1974; Paddington to Bristol was 100 minutes in 1994, but only 85 minutes in 1979. Harlow also reports on the use of two timetables printed by BR for the east coast main line between King's Cross and Edinburgh, one for the public and one for the drivers, the latter several minutes ahead of the public schedule. This allows station managers to report arrivals as being ahead of (their public) schedule. But this should not be unexpected. This is a story of the fragile nature of these measures of performance. The major thrust of introducing these performance indicators is the public accountability of management, but they are open to misinterpretation and manipulation.

Need, confusion and turbulence: the National Health Service

Until the 1980s the major control devices in the NHS were cash limits and annual accounts of expenditure for both revenue and capital. These were aggregate figures for containing expenditure and 'balancing the books'. Hospital activity statistics (HAA returns) were gathered from the 1970s but it is not certain that these informed the administration of the NHS – they appear to have assumed the token significance of being an end in themselves. In part, this can be seen as a product of the fact that health authorities were able to balance their books (which, in turn, is attributable partly to the NHS enjoying annual increases in expenditure, albeit in the face of continually increasing demand for its services). Another major constraining factor on the development of performance measurement in the NHS was the inherent difficulty of the task. This has been alluded to above, in earlier discussion.

The generality of NHS objectives (the improvement of health care of the population) challenges the conventional assumption of measuring achievement against objectives set. If the focus is shifted from the service, in its totality, to its constituent parts, the difficulty remains. By focusing on specific sets of activities, such as acute hospitals, or client groups, such as the mentally ill, the identification of cause and effect which results in a given medical outcome is not readily demonstrated. In the face of such fundamental difficulties, it is evident why coarse aggregate financial figures would suffice – in the absence of something more refined the implicit assumption could be made that, as long as the books were balanced, value for money was being obtained. But that cosy assumption was shattered by the probing of Yates (see e.g. 1978), which demonstrated the considerable variation which existed in statistics of health care across the country. Whether this was a matter of the quality of the statistics, or of inherent variations, was not known, but the Department of Health and Social Security was unable to provide an explanation to the nation at large, and the Public Accounts Committee in particular. The climate of continuing annual increases in health-care expenditure was being challenged by a government set to probe the very nature of public expenditure, root and branch. The *need* for performance indicators in the NHS had been established.

The response of the DHSS was that which had served it well in many other contexts: establish a pilot study at one part of the service, with the aim of extending the results to the rest of the service. The pilot was conducted at the Northern RHA (see Smith, 1983, for an account of this). Smith's account reveals the enormity of the task facing the Performance Indicators Group (PIG) – the difficulties of measuring health-care outcomes, mentioned above, quickly forcing the group to acknowledge that it would have to work with intermediate data, and those data which were already available. This latter constraint was necessary because there was considerable statistical information which was routinely collected within the NHS.

This pilot work focused on four areas: clinical activity, financial indicators, manpower indicators and estate management indicators. An example of the kinds of indicator developed is given in Table 10.2. It is evident that the preoccupation within these indicators is with activity, with input and through-put, and not with performance, as measured against outcomes and quality of service.

Table 10.2 *Selected performance indicators*

---

(1) *Costing information*
    1.1 Average total costs per in-patient
    1.2 Average costs of direct treatment, services and supplies per in-patient
    1.3 Average costs of medical and paramedical support services per in-patient
    1.4 Average costs of general (non- clinical) services per in-patient

(2) *Admissions policy*
    2.1 % of all admissions classified *immediate*
    2.2 % of all admissions classified *urgent* involving a delay of more than one month before admission
    2.3 % of all admissions classified as *non-urgent* involving a delay of more than one year before admission

(3) *Use of facilities*
    3.1 Average length of stay for hospital in-patients
    3.2 Average number of in-patients per bed per year
    3.3 % of all in-patients and day patients treated as day cases
    3.4 Average number of out-patients seen in each clinic session
    3.5 Ratio between new and returning out-patients

(4) *Staffing*
    4.1 Number of health visitors and district nurses per head of population
    4.2 Number of administrative and clerical staff per head of population

---

Source: DHSS (1983).

It is important to note that this is a distillation of the NHS performance indicators, purely to serve as an illustration. An appraisal of the effectiveness of the DHSS package of indicators by a senior government official sets out the problems and pitfalls of this (Morison, 1987, p. 84):

The first DHSS package of PIs issued in 1983 had 2 major drawbacks. Firstly, it contained 1981 data, and was thus substantially out of date and of limited value. Secondly, it was issued in hard copy, of telephone directory dimensions and was just as difficult to read and interpret. The need for something more up to date, more useful and more readily accessible to managers was recognised. DHSS accordingly set up a Joint Group on Performance Indicators. As a result of their recommendations a micro computer-based PI package was developed based on a BBC micro. 1983/84 data was issued in October 1985; and 1984/85 data issued in January 1986. This represents a significant improvement on the 'telephone directories' but the criticisms remain. The system is large (over 450 PIs) cumbersome and inflexible – data can be analysed only in certain predetermined ways – and there is no facility to manipulate the data.

This trenchant criticism captures the description of this phase of the development of performance measures for the NHS – *confusion*. This was a confusion created not only by the inherent defects of the data collected but also by the sheer number of performance indicators collected, and their diffuse nature. The purpose of much of this information was not evident. This is an issue of decision relevance and also of the need to relate different kinds of indicators to different levels of the organisation, such that there is a common purpose. And here is the rub – if the overall goals are vague and not readily translated into operational goals, and there are significant variations in medical care (which may be for a variety of reasons – historical, regional variations in the incidence of sickness, different ranges of medical services on offer in different hospitals, different hospital facilities, and so on) which may be unrelated to management performance, by relying on batteries of low-level (and conflicting) indicators, you create confusion.

The next phrase of the development of performance indicators in the NHS can be characterised as being one of 'turbulence'. Here, limited though it was, their development has to be seen against a background of some considerable upheaval within health care, as the following list (not exhaustive) indicates:

(1) the introduction, and extension, of general management (from 1983 onwards);
(2) the implementation of management budgeting (1985) and resource management (1986);
(3) the use of options appraisal in capital programmes (from 1982 onwards);
(4) competitive tendering for support services (from 1983 onwards);
(5) the introduction of the annual efficiency savings initiative, which continues to date;
(6) the demise of district health authorities, the introduction of the purchaser/provider split with self-governing hospital trusts, fund-holding GPs, new roles for regional health authorities.

The perspective from within was once expressed to me, by a beleaguered general manager, as 'death by 1,000 initiatives'. This anecdotal evidence does not *per se* justify the description of turbulence, but, given the limited success of the performance indicators initiative, it can be seen as having lost its way as successive, substantive change was forced on the NHS.

Currently, performance indicators are undergoing something of a revival in the NHS. In the wake of the Citizens' Charter there is a Patients' Charter. But the focus of this is on a particular kind of performance, i.e. responsiveness to patients in health-care settings. This reports on the incidence of cancelled operations, response rates of ambulance services, proportion of day care as opposed to in-patient surgery and waiting times. On this last, for example, reports are made on the percentage of out-patients seen within 30 minutes of appointment and also the percentage of patients assessed within five minutes of arrival at accident and emergency. These 'quality' of service (not care delivered) indicators were first published in 1994, on a hospital by hospital basis. Laurance (1994) sets out the key finding – *there is considerable variation across these hospitals.* This, of course, is where we came in. The fact that there is variation is one thing, but the ability to achieve uniformity or, at least, less variation is another. And here, we are dealing with issues of controllability, of management influence, of resource availability, but also of quality of information. As Williams (1985, p. 5) put it, in his appraisal of waiting list data, we need to know answers to the following questions before we can interpret this information:

(1) By what criteria do people get on to such lists?
(2) Are these criteria uniform across consultants, and across districts?
(3) What internal prioritising goes on within a list?
(4) How frequently are they updated?
(5) What happens to a patient who is called up, but does not come, cannot come, or is turned away at the last minute due to bed shortages?
(6) Do people who are given 'booked admissions' (i.e. promised admission on a definite date, maybe six to twelve months ahead) count as being on a waiting list?
(7) Are the data compiled from who is on the list at some point in time, or from the length of time that recently treated patients had actually waited prior to treatment?

It is evident from the above that these various dimensions offer the potential for considerable bias to be introduced into such 'performance indicators'.

However, there has been continuing research into the measurement of health state outcomes. The most significant advance in recent years has been the advocacy of 'quality-adjusted life years' (QALYs). These scores range from zero (dead) to one (perfect health). For a given individual the QALY score is calculated by weighting each remaining year of his or her life by the expected quality of life (EQF) in the year in question. EQF is computed as a probability-weighted average of the quality-of-life scores for each of the possible health states in which he or she might find himself or herself. The summation of all these individual QALYs gives society or community QALYs. One advocate of QALYs, Williams (1985) has argued that health-care procedures should be ranked, such that activities which generate more gains to health for every £1 of resources should take precedence over those which yield less and, in this way, the overall standard of health in the community would increase. Williams has even specified particular procedures which would gain (heart pacemakers, hip replacement, replacement of valves for aortic stenosis) and those which would lose (kidney transplants, coronary artery bypass grafting for severe angina with one vessel disease). But QALYs have not resolved the dilemma of health-care output measurement. They stand as instruments of efficiency, at the expense of equity; problems with the stability of the values of QALYs are compounded by different values being obtained by different estimation methods; there are implicit assumptions of risk aversion in the case of patients, clinicians or planners which may not be justified in practice, and the model is based on significant ignorance of decision-making practices by such key factors (see Mooney and Olsen, 1991).

Thus, there remains the fundamental difficulty of (1) deriving global measures of health-care outcomes and (2) decomposing the constituent elements of such global measures in such a way that meaningful information is made available to all levels of management, in different kinds of organisations, which co-ordinates responses in pursuit of the global measure of improving health care. This in itself represents a difficulty – at once conjuring up a substantive challenge and, at the same time, presenting too functional and mechanistic a view of a very complex process.

PERFORMANCE MEASUREMENT IN THE FUTURE

Crystal-ball-gazing is always a hazardous business and no more so than in the case of public sector performance measurement, where the complexity of the strands of influence (pressures for change; difficulties of measurement; ambiguity of intentions (and of consequences); massive implementation problems; lack of consensus on the way forward) is so profound. It has been shown above that global performance measures are not sufficiently robust to translate into operational practice. The subsequent reliance on performance indicators which are partial measures of performance paves the way for inconsistencies, tensions and contradictions, particularly because these tend not to articulate the aims and activities of lower and higher levels of the organisation.

The analysis above may seem overly negative, but it should be seen for what it is – reflections on a decade and a half of providing performance measurement initiatives in the public sector which have had, at best, mixed experiences rather than outright success. Also, these developments should be seen as mechanisms which were put in place to assist both managers of public services and the examination of, or public accountability of, such managers to oversight bodies, users and the general public. But that vision has been replaced by another. The emergence of the performance measurement industry in the public sector can be attributed to market imperfections and the need to determine surrogates to inform managers, policy-makers and public service financiers. But now we have the creation of new forms of markets within the public services. At one end of the spectrum, the privatised utilities face increased competition, which is fostered by their regulators; at the other end we have the creation of quasi-markets for public services, such as health care and social care. Furthermore, we have a change in prospect for British Rail, which has been restructured and is being privatised. (Indeed this trend seems to be continually expanding with the market testing of civil servants' jobs and the outsourcing of in-house finance departments in health and local authorities.)

This change of scenario may ease the pressures for large chunks of public services to have performance indicators, as new forms of market are brought into play. This may result in an attenuation of the need for market surrogate measures of success or failure in these organisations. Thus, hospital trusts now have explicit profit targets (to break even on revenue account, earn a target return on capital employed and remain within their external financing limits). In this way, the performance indicators initiative could be seen as redundant. Indeed, the Patients' Charter and the performance indicators initiative in the NHS can be seen as merely recycling ideas which have been within the NHS for many years. The real advances have been on the accounting front. It is important not to overstate the case for this line of argument. There are still ragged edges – there is no seamless transition to markets in public services. At these points of convergence of the new markets and the old services (where strategic positioning, as in health authorities, is undertaken), there may yet remain a role for performance indicators.

An alternative view is that espoused by management theorists within the private sector, who focus on the need for quality management and non-financial data in support of profit and other financial indicators. This may set up a continuing agenda for the refinement of performance indicators, to benefit management. This accords with Griffiths' view of health service management i.e. the need for financial and non-financial measures of performance which are different for different levels and complement each other. But there is a contradiction here. As the above analysis of performance indicators in the public sector shows, a major concern with such measures has not been with management decision-making and control, but with issues of public accountability, and with efficiency of service provision, to contain costs and to lay the myth of the 'inefficient' public sector. But will or can the existing performance indicators within the public sector fit the new, market-orientated public sector? Will radical changes be necessary in their composition and use? Or will this continue to be a story of the relentless pursuit of a policy which is no longer necessary? All of this remains to be seen.

References

Bourn, M. and Ezzamel, M. (1986) Organisational culture in hospitals in the National Health Service, *Financial Accountability and Management*, Vol. 2, no. 3, pp. 203–26.
British Rail (1979) *Towards a Commuter's Charter*, British Railways Board, London.

Dent, J. (1991) Accounting and organisational cultures: a field study of the emergence of a new organisational reality, *Accounting, Organisations and Society*, Vol. 16, no. 8, pp. 705–32.

Department of Health and Social Security (1983) *Performance Indicators*, DHSS, London.

Glaister, S. and Collings, J. J. (1978) Maximisation of passenger miles in theory and in practice, *Journal of Transport Economics and Policy* (September), pp. 304–21.

Griffiths, R. (1983) *The NHS Management Inquiry*, DHSS, London.

Harlow, J. (1994) BR 'getting there': it just takes longer, *Sunday Times* (10 July), p. 7.

HM Treasury (1967) *Nationalised Industries, A Review of Economic and Financial Objectives*, Cmnd 3437, HMSO, London.

HM Treasury (1978) *The Nationalised Industries*, Cmnd 7131, HMSO, London.

Jackson, P. (1988) The management of performance in the public sector, *Public Money and Management* (Winter), pp. 11–16.

Jones, R. (1993) An indictment of performance measurement in the public sector, in E. Buschor and K. Schedler (eds.), *Perspectives on Performance Measurement and Public Sector Accounting*, Haupt, Stuttgart, pp. 43–57.

Lapsley, I. (1984) Financial objectives, productive efficiency and the regulation of a subsidised state monopoly, *Accounting and Business Research*, Vol. 14, no. 55, pp. 217–28.

Laurance, J. (1994) Tables show suitable cases for treatment, *The Times* (30 June), pp. 8–9.

Likierman, A. (1993) Performance indicators: 20 early lessons from managerial use, *Public Money and Management* (October), pp. 15–22.

Mayston, D. J. (1985) Non-profit performance indicators in the public sector, *Financial Accountability and Management*, Vol. 1, no. 1, pp. 51–74.

Mooney, G. and Olsen, J. A. (1991) QALYs: where next?, in A. McGuire, P. Fenn and K. Mayhew (eds.), *Providing Health Care: The Economics of Alternative Systems of Finance and Delivery*, Oxford University Press, Oxford, pp. 120–40.

Morison, H. (1987) Performance measurement: the case of the Health Service, pp. 83–7, in ICAS and CIPFA, *Research in Action: Performance Measurement*, ICAS, Edinburgh and CIPFA, London.

National Audit Office (1988) *A Framework for Value for Money Audits*, NAO, London.

Polanyi, G. and Polanyi, P. (1974) *Failing the Nation: The Record of the Nationalised Industries*, Fraser and Ansbacher, London.

Smith, G. (1983) National Health Service performance indicators, *Public Finance and Accountancy* (April), pp. 17–19.

Williams, A. (1985) Performance measurement in the public sector: paving the road to hell? Arthur Young Lecture No. 7, University of Glasgow.

Yates, J. M. (1978) *In-patient Waiting Lists Statistics – Handle with Care*, Health Service Management Centre, University of Birmingham.

11

Effectiveness – The Holy Grail of Accounting Measures of Performance

JOHN SMALL

'Effectiveness' is perhaps the most important and challenging aspect of what is generally described as 'value for money, i.e. the search for economy, efficiency and effectiveness'. Although much of this will be drawn from my experience when I was Chairman of the Accounts Commission in Scotland I would not wish it to be thought that all my observations relate specifically to that organisation or to the work which it has done.

VALUE FOR MONEY AND PROFIT

'Value for money' is regarded as a concept which applies almost exclusively to the public sector. We should ask ourselves why, not only this, but also a host of other performance indicators including, e.g. the Citizens' Charter, have been imposed on this sector which now spends not inconsiderable sums seeking to show the world at large that it has taken steps to try to achieve value for money – particularly when as yet we have no methodology for checking that indeed it has. In some public sector institutions, e.g. local authorities, there is a statutory requirement for the auditor to attest that the authority is taking steps or has procedures which seek to achieve value for money but they do not attest that they have actually done so. Just because you spend a lot of money getting consultants to advise you does not demonstrate that you have achieved either value for money in general or effectiveness in particular.

For some time there has been a generally accepted presumption that the public sector would be improved if it adopted private sector practices. At its most charitable it finds expression in the belief that because the public sector lacks the profit motive and the discipline of the market-place, as a substitute for these it is necessary to impose upon it the requirement to seek economy, efficiency and effectiveness. There is the less charitable view that the public sector is always incompetent and inefficient when compared with the private sector and that those who participate in its direction and management are almost by definition of a lower standard than their private sector counterparts, and therefore you must continually, and in a variety of ways, check what is being done. This latter view is, of course, nonsensical and stems simply from ignorance. There are many examples where the quality of management and the exercise of duties in the public sector stand comparison with the best elsewhere.

PROFIT ALONE IS NOT AN ADEQUATE MEASURE OF EFFECTIVENESS

The profit measure – while perhaps necessary for judging effectiveness in the private sector – is certainly not sufficient by itself. It can be argued that to rely solely on the profit measure will be at best misleading and at worst totally unreliable. Despite the attempts of the accounting profession to narrow the accounting options available there still exists a range of dubious – sometimes rather euphemistically called creative – accounting practices which can be applied to the same economic event with, of course, totally different impacts upon profit. The problems, for example, of accounting for goodwill, acquisitions and mergers, off-balance sheet financing and foreign currency translation have been tackled but not entirely resolved. It is not surprising that a fairly cynical view of accounting numbers still persists and that there is still a belief that to improve your profit you need not change your productivity, your investment or your management practices; rather, you simply change your accountant and hire a lawyer!

In addition, there is growing concern that profit is essentially a short-term measure and does not necessarily serve the best long-term interests of the firm and the economy in terms of investment and national strategy. In order to serve a meal that satisfies the dietary needs of the City, firms are often forced to cook and eat their seed potatoes. This is one, if not *the*, reason that there is much concern about investment in training, investment in research and development, investment in quality.

The audit expectation gap – what the auditor can and does do as opposed to what the public *thinks* the auditor does – has also dented faith in the profit measure and those who certify it. Finally, even the most ardent supporter of the 'let the market take care of it' club has begun to recognise that, in using profit as a measure of value for money, the most important factor is not whether we are dealing with the private or the public sector but the type of market within which the organisation trades. The degree of competition and the source of revenue for the output provided are much more significant than whether the business is located within the private or the public sector. Monopoly in the private sector is no less dangerous or inefficient than monopoly in the public sector. Privatisation has demonstrated that where market position and the resultant economic and social influence are dominant it is necessary to put in place some other regulatory and monitoring arrangements and performance measures to consider value for money.

I am not, of course, minimising the powerful role of profit in keeping organisations alert, lean and hungry or attempting to disregard it or reduce its importance in favour of something else. By and large it is the best motivator and measure we have yet managed to find; in the private sector, however, we need also look at other measures. If the public sector succeeds in measuring value for money, some of this success will doubtless be transferred to the private sector irrespective of the political colour of the government of the day.

WHAT IS VALUE FOR MONEY?

In the technical accounting sense we are all aware of the definition of value for money: the achievement of economy, efficiency and effectiveness. I say 'accounting sense' because we must not assume that others – ratepayers, politicians, the general public, and so on – will apply anything other than the language and meaning of everyday usage, and take it for granted that 'efficiency' embraces all three concepts.

The terms 'economy', 'efficiency' and 'effectiveness' are, or course, non-contentious – who would *not* wish to be economic, efficient and effective? Unfortunately, however, the context in which they are discussed is often felt to be uneconomic, inefficient and ineffective, which does not create a favourable climate for their adoption. I used to ask my private sector colleagues how they would view a right for independent people to audit, for example, their transport or maintenance policy and then publish the report for the public in general and shareholders in particular to read. The thought horrified them. But this is what we do in the public sector so why not in the private sector too?

Economy and efficiency are really opposite sides of the same coin – with economy we seek to minimise input for a given output and with efficiency we maximise output for given input. These are relatively easy concepts to grasp, particularly when dealing with apparently mechanistic matters such as miles per gallon, bad debts per £1,000 due, and so on. We are all familiar with their use in time and motion studies, work studies, organisation and methods, and so on.

THE MEASUREMENT OF EFFECTIVENESS

When we turn to effectiveness, that is, the achievement of objectives or goals, we find it much more elusive, problematic and politically sensitive, and progress in measuring it – if indeed it *can* be measured – has (for understandable reasons) been slowest. I say '*can*' because ultimately effectiveness, particularly when it encompasses political and social issues, can only be judged. Perhaps the best we will ever develop are a few measures which will aid in this judgement, and highlight areas worthy of further investigation, but even this is a long way off.

Because we have not moved far along the way toward developing indicators or measures of performance relating to effectiveness (and I suspect that progress will continue to be slow), economy and efficiency have been and continue to be used as surrogates for effectiveness. The question which is asked is: 'How can you be effective if you are inefficient?' ('Therefore in testing your effectiveness we will first measure your economy and efficiency.')

There are a number of technical problems in trying to relate inputs (economy, efficiency) to outputs (effectiveness), particularly when the output is of a social nature. It is not only difficult to quantify the output but it is even more difficult to put a price or value on it. This is accentuated because there will rarely be a single output, and with every increase in the number of different outputs comes an almost exponential increase in the number of indicators which can be used. This offers great scope for value judgements and statistical creativity. How do you determine the output of a university? Is it the number and/or quality of graduates, the number of graduates in specific disciplines (such as science, engineering or the arts) or the number within specific subject areas (e.g. physics, accountancy)? What about research, what about consultancy? Even when you have this information how do you process it? Do you use straightforward multiple regression – where, for example, the output of the university (or school or hospital) can be compared to the average output for its size – or do you use data envelope analysis where the input can be compared to the maximum possible output given the inputs which are available? In addition, any analysis requires some judgement about the relative weights (prices) which have to be given to different activities. It will never be possible to put precise figures to these and this is why effectiveness will always involve some form of personal value judgement.

Purposeful goals/objectives are not easy to establish, particularly when they are required to be publicly stated. Neither can priorities and rankings be attributed easily to them. Life is not like that and in any event 'political man' is not so mechanistic, single-minded and robot-like as 'economic man'. Goals and their relative priorities change over time according to many factors, and expediency is no mean one. This is not to say that the question cannot be asked, but that it must not be posed in a way that simply generates numbers which are capable of statistical processing.

Although the measurement problem with effectiveness is difficult, one thing has become abundantly clear: you cannot judge effectiveness solely in terms of financial statistics. This applies even to profit in the private sector. Financial indicators have to be complemented with demographic, social and other economic data. Neither of course must these be divorced from financial indicators. Much work has been done on the client-need approach for the allocation of central government grants to local authorities. I would be surprised if this could not be used in developing VFM audit yardsticks for local authorities, and also for the type of financial reporting which will be a natural concomitant of it.

We are very far away from measurements of outputs (effectiveness) compared to inputs (economy and efficiency) and it is not surprising that many of the current assessment factors in effectiveness, e.g. style of leadership, are qualitative and ones where opinion is likely to differ substantially. This is another reason leading me to the conclusion that, in the short term at least, economy and efficiency will continue to be used as surrogates for effectiveness – despite the flaws in so doing. If effectiveness is the achievement of objectives in an economic and efficient manner the argument that lack of economy and efficiency means that you have not been effective is of course completely valid. However, it does not necessarily follow that if there *are* economy and efficiency there must be effectiveness. Many services are provided in an efficient and economic manner, but this does not mean that they are achieving their intended purpose (objectives). This soon becomes clear in any debate or discussion about the National Health Service. The dilemma facing us is that, given our inability to audit effectiveness in any purposeful fashion, the vast majority of work and activity in the whole area of value for money is, and will continue to be, centred around economy and efficiency. How then can we move forward? A first step would be to consider the policy audit.

THE AUDIT OF POLICY

The first step in an audit of policy is to set objectives plus any constraint that is or will be applied in seeking to achieve these. It is a dynamic programming operation. Even a simplistic objective for a private sector organisation, such as maximise profits or increase annual earnings or share price by a factor above inflation, has constraints (often implicit) such as 'not breaking the law' or 'not allowing failure in any one project to force the organisation into liquidation'. Any way forward must allow for the statement of multi-objectives, the social as well as the economic. Any stakeholder may seek to influence and change the objectives and the constraints of a particular body. This is of course the political dimension to effectiveness. But once the objectives have been set policies must be established which are consistent with their achievement.

Effectiveness is about the achievement of objectives and there is therefore a need for policy-makers – directors, elected members – to be much more explicit about their objectives and, equally important, their policies if we are to audit effectiveness. The setting out of objectives is not always greeted with great enthusiasm. Perhaps not doing so avoids the embarrassment of checking (auditing) to see whether or not they have been achieved, and at what cost. Not specifying objectives also affords the opportunity to confuse them with activities. The supply of a service is an activity; it should not be an objective in itself but a means of achieving an objective. But how often do we hear claims for more resource input, e.g. more doctors or teachers, without an adequate explanation of what is to be achieved with them?

You cannot divorce policies from objectives and sometimes it is difficult to distinguish between the two. To understand objectives requires an examination of policy and vice versa. By way of illustration, I read recently a statement that the policy should be to provide one teacher for every ten students at university. Now is this part of an objective to increase employment opportunities for university teachers? Is it an activity-maximising objective, i.e. the type that usually finds favour with the supplier of the service in question? Or is it part of a policy whose objective is to improve the quality of education students receive and, if so, how will this achieve it and how will we measure and judge success? Or is it a policy/objective to reduce the opportunities for students to study at university – student/staff ratios can always be improved by reducing the number of students!

AUDITOR AND POLICY

~~Immediately policy is examined the auditor will be criticised.~~ It is readily accepted that there is no role for the auditor – state or private – to play in the determination of policy. This is a matter for those who are appointed to do so – elected representatives in the case of government, boards of directors of private sector companies, and so on. However, non-involvement in policy determination does not mean that it cannot be questioned or the information upon which it is based be examined. It is difficult to see how effectiveness can be assessed unless both policy and objectives are examined. I repeat: not questioned but examined. We have to understand the objectives of any policy. The value for money audit is concerned not with the determination of policy but with its execution.

We should not be hyper-sensitive when we hear the word 'policy' or be put off by contentions that what is being investigated is a matter of policy and therefore not for audit. We must ask ourselves what claims that something is a matter of policy entail. What 'policy' certainly does not cover is every decision of the ruling body, be they elected representatives or boards of directors. Policy is certainly not synonymous with political sensitivity and thus not all politically sensitive issues can be deemed to be matters of policy; otherwise it would provide an opportunity to prevent any matter being audited. It is all too easy for policy-makers to convince themselves that anything which is politically sensitive must be a matter of policy. Decisions which are held out to be implementation of policy are often simply administrative decisions that should be judged only on their economy and efficiency.

One of the weaker characteristics of traditional budgetary planning techniques in the public sector ~~(and in the private sector)~~ is that they concentrate on incremental changes at the margin and often little attention is paid to the objectives of existing policies, particularly if they have been around for a long time. The question 'Why are we doing this?' should be asked about existing as well as proposed activities. In addition, irrespective of how policy is defined, the information upon which it was based can certainly be examined and an opinion expressed on the results which have been achieved in the light of the objectives that the application of the policy was meant to achieve.

THE INDIGNATION FACTOR

Study of the application of state audit in various countries highlights that one of the most powerful weapons auditors have is the publication and dissemination of their findings. To report without fear or favour is undoubtedly one of the auditor's most important rights. However, this means that the auditor must deal with the indignation factor, i.e. the chorus of comments, protests and criticisms which almost invariably follow the publication of his or her report. Indignation is a reaction, not a primary emotion. The causes of this reaction have interested behavioural scientists for many years and various reasons have been put forward for it such as guilt, protection, and so on. Be that as it may, it is a factor with which the auditor has to contend. Audit reports are of interest to journalists, politicians, pressure groups and other users of financial statements. Each of these acts as a further publicist but after filtering the report to suit a particular purpose. This in turn increases the indignation factor, which is expressed in a variety of ways: hurt innocence, 'Why bother with small issues?', 'Why wait until the battle is over then come along to kill off the wounded?', 'It's all water under the bridge' – and so on. Hurt innocence then gives way to outraged indignation, with attacks on the independence and/or competence of the auditing body. There is, of course, nothing new about this. It is a fact of life which those who are concerned in this area have to accept and learn to live with. In carrying out the responsibilities and obligations placed upon them and exercising these with the independence and firmness of action and neutrality in reporting, one measure of performance which is not applicable to auditors is popularity.

When the indignation factor is at its loudest one is reminded of Edmond Burke's famous essay 'Reflections on the Revolution in France', where he wrote:

> Because half a dozen grasshoppers under the fern make the field ring with their importunate chink, whilst thousands of great cattle, reposed beneath the shadow of the British oak, chew the cud and are silent, pray do not imagine that those who make the noise are the only inhabitants of the field.

Although the grasshoppers do not bother me, there is another dimension to the publicising of reports which is of concern. It has long been accepted that financial accounting is about reporting on management whereas management accounting is reporting for management. The former is for public dissemination, the latter for internal consumption. In the public domain that distinction is much less clear. There is a greater likelihood of a report becoming publicly available and, even if intended to be a report for management, it becomes a report on management and the whole scenario is changed. The actual publication of VFM assessments may partly defeat their very own purpose, and may have a counterproductive effect. When you extend this to policy execution and the role of management and the like the dilemma becomes apparent.

Lest I be misunderstood let me hasten to say I am not suggesting that the policy audit should be undertaken by the accounting profession as it stands today. It has neither the skills nor the people to do so at present but it would not be impossible both to incorporate other skills into it and to train some of its own in what is required.

CONCLUSION: THE HOLY GRAIL – IS IT WORTH PURSUING?

There is virtually no evidence for the existence of the Holy Grail, the chalice used by Christ at the Last Supper. Yet the remotest possibility that it might exist and might be found has inspired, and will continue to inspire, many to search for it. The prize is enormous and well worth the effort. In addition, the search cannot be measured in terms of cost alone – value concerns more than just price. So too with effectiveness: if worthwhile attestable measures can be developed which improve our understanding of and ability to judge effectiveness and enable us better to answer the question 'Have we achieved value for money?' the prize will also be enormous – not only for the public at large but also for our profession.

12

Governance in the National Health Service

MICHAEL MUMFORD

INTRODUCTION

This chapter considers three contrasting views of governance in the National Health Service (NHS) in the context of the 'market reforms'. The first applies neo-classical economic analysis as moderated by transaction cost economics (TCE). The second takes a more critical view, rejecting TCE as an inadequate instrument of analysis. The third, advanced here, takes a different interpretation of TCE, and stresses the need for innovation as the prime means to attain higher productivity in the NHS.

The three main features of the market reforms are matters of common ground, whichever view of governance is taken:

(1) the separation of purchasing authorities (mainly health authorities) from providers (acute hospitals, community services and others);
(2) the imminent move towards replacing 'block contracts' for the purchase of health care with more detailed 'cost per case contracts'; and
(3) shifts in the culture of the NHS, so that some of the power formerly exercised by clinical consultants has moved towards purchasers and some towards a new cohort of administrators appointed within the NHS to set up and monitor contracts.

The analysis of corporate governance in the NHS begins with theories of governance more generally, as applied in both the public and private sectors. The three alternative views are contrasted in terms of the theoretical positions that they adopt and in the way that they each view the NHS.

In Lapsley (1993) the NHS is analysed from the perspective of TCE, and more specifically within the framework of 'markets and hierarchies'. He argues that the agenda for reform in the NHS has had the effect of shifting the typical mode of control: the dominant mode of governance was formerly through clans and culture, but this has progressively been giving way first to governance by hierarchies and thence towards the discipline of competitive markets. By contrast, says Lapsley, a movement in the opposite direction is observable (albeit over a much longer time scale) in the private sector. The movement is far from complete in either direction. To Lapsley, contracting processes work to minimise costs of conducting business relations and confer market advantage on those organisations that optimise their contracting relationships. Meanwhile, as a matter of recent NHS history, new competitive pressures force higher levels of performance from the organisations involved and from the individuals who work for them.

Ezzamel and Willmott (1993) apply a more critical view of the reform process. In contrast to Lapsley, they argue that the current changes in the NHS have less to do with lowering transaction costs or raising productivity than with the political struggle for power over the NHS labour force and the distribution of benefits. The reforms are essentially a political process, of which political dialogue and strategic alliances form an integral part. Talk of minimising transaction costs, according to Ezzamel and Willmott, is merely the rhetoric used to rationalise changes in power relations. The aim of the reforms is to secure higher output from fewer resources by forcing reduced security of employment and lower unit labour costs, plausibly as part of a more general attack on public services. What is needed, in their view, is greater democratic control.

The third viewpoint, advanced in this chapter, stresses the role of technical change as a source of higher productivity. Many of the lessons of TCE are accepted as valuable, but (following Lazonick, 1991) the significance of the theory lies in its power to explain how organisational design can achieve not cost reductions but new products and processes by means of innovation and technical change. Under the former version of TCE, technical transformation functions are taken as exogenously given in a static equilibrium framework: in the latter version, they are endogenous parts of a dynamic economic growth process.

THREE COMPETING CORPORATE GOVERNANCE THEORIES

Explanations of governance structures intertwine politics with economics. One extreme model of political economy, the 'pure' neo-classical equilibrium market model, claims that overt political intervention is otiose since the operation of free markets can produce conditions for optimal social welfare. The opposite extreme model, of a complete command economy, would claim that individual bargaining is redundant in a system which can meet the need of each citizen through central planning and co-ordination. In the absence of either in the real world, theorists and policy-makers have to assess the benefits of centrally imposed regulation against the autonomy of the individual.

Classical economic theory (including the Paretian optimality conditions often assumed in welfare analysis) relies on trades in all commodities in well-behaved markets. Contractual relations are completely captured by a sale in which both the price and the quality of the purchase are known to all parties: once the sale is completed, no further commitments exist on either side.

These conditions are often not fulfilled in the real world, and neo-classical economics has developed the idea of more complex forms of contract to capture many more bargaining situations. Thus warranties may cover the possibility that goods are not of the quality they claim to be (and statutory 'sale of goods' provisions further redress the information asymmetry between buyer and seller). These more complex contracting arrangements allow future performance to be anticipated, over long periods of time. The development of the concept of 'rational expectations' adds to the theoretical completeness of the economics. The possibility that contracts can fully specify complete sets of relations revives the prospect of free markets producing optimal welfare outcomes throughout the economy. But this itself imposes important conditions on the contracting process. In particular, the provision of appropriate information is needed for monitoring and enforcement.[1]

In practice, there are many contracts whose outcomes cannot be fully specified in advance, and which therefore need to include provisions for renegotiation. The admission that full information may not be available at the time the contract is formed also raises questions about precisely what needs to be known at that time and what remains to be disclosed at later stages. It is still possible to form contracts that are essentially complete even though they do not specify what happens in every possible outcome. However, such contracts lay down processes (for example, arbitration mechanisms) rather than precise terms of redress.[2]

Issues of governance arise only when complete contracts cannot fully specify and enforce bargaining relations. As Baiman (1990) points out:

> In essence, governance procedures set the rules of the *renegotiation game* which must be played when a contingency which is not covered by the *ex ante* contract arises . . . transaction cost economics is especially interested in situations in which the role of competition as a disciplining device is reduced. One such situation occurs in the presence of asset specificity. This condition arises when the value of an asset within an ongoing relationship exceeds the value of the asset outside of the relationship; that is, there are quasi-rents to be gained by continuing the asset-specific relationship.
>
> (Baiman, 1990, p. 347, original emphasis)

Neo-classical economics has until recently had little to say about governance since it has taken the nature and existence of the firm for granted. As long as market forces are assumed to determine economic relations in society, every pair of interactions between members of that society are viewed as independent bargaining outcomes between willing actors. The firm as an institution has little distinctive contribution to make.

The rise of the 'New Institutional Economics' (Williamson, 1975) gave more reason to modify this view within neo-classical economics, since it explains not merely the existence of the firm as a form of organisation but also the boundaries set around firms and the operating divisions within them.

Three classes of transaction cost are distinguished in TCE. Where goods and services of known quality are actively traded in competitive markets, there is relatively little difficulty in making purchases from day to day (and there is conversely little benefit to be gained from supplying them). All the information needed to complete a bargain is available at the time of purchase. This is the type of trade contemplated in classical economics. Characteristics and prices of all commodities are known at little or no cost, and competition drives the system.

The second class of transactions involves contractual relations for repeated trades – or 'ongoing relationships', to quote Baiman. This goes beyond the scope of day-to-day bargains because the sellers or the buyers (or both) require more information than observable quality and known price. Acquiring and using this extra information is costly. The quality of goods or services involved may be difficult to specify in advance (so that the seller knows what is needed) and to observe at the time of supply (so that the buyer knows what is on offer). Delivery may be only part of the bargain: there may also be warranty provisions, ancillary services, redesign and modification terms, deferred payment, trade-in conditions, and so on. It is common in establishing such ongoing relationships that the supplier needs assurance of an adequate market before undertaking asset-specific commitments, and buyers need to know they can obtain a sustained flow of supplies. Having found each other, buyers and sellers often have an incentive to form a persisting contractual relationship, to allay further search costs and reduce market uncertainties.

The third class of transaction is for the supply of still more specialised items – those that constitute the 'core' assets of the firm. TCE explains the very existence of firms in terms of their specific core assets (human as well as physical). It requires particular knowledge first to define, then to obtain, and finally to use these assets effectively. Often they will be generated by the firm itself, for its own use (for example, by training its own staff). Where they take the form of large pieces of equipment, these will typically be bought externally from specialist suppliers. There will be few suppliers with the relevant knowledge, and few purchasers: deals will be rare.

The extreme case of interdependence leads to takeover. But one of the lessons of TCE has been that ownership is not necessarily the best way to secure co-ordination and integration. It is too complicated. Other, more effective, forms of network can be achieved by appropriate forms of contract, and 'demergers' may produce this result. In effect, the NHS reforms represent just such a demerger.

While both Lapsley (1993) and Ezzamel and Willmott (1993) find TCE valuable as analysis, they differ as to its validity. Both conclude that, as a matter of fact, the NHS will increasingly come to be moulded by market forces, but they differ over the damage this causes. The third view, presented below, suggested that the outcome of the reforms is far less certain to be mediated by market forces. Neither of the 1993 studies acknowledges that all three classes of transaction exist alongside one another, and are likely to persist in future within the NHS. Rather than a general movement towards day-to-day purchasing and complete contracts, there is likely to be, at most, a shift in the mix of transactions. There are not many supplies or services that can sensibly be bought day to day from external suppliers. Moreover, at the other extreme, control over core assets seems also to have become fairly well established. New NHS trusts have taken over existing assets, the overwhelming bulk of which have remained with the acute hospital trusts as 'core' assets. These cannot easily be used on their own without expert knowledge.

However, instead of the former unitary health authorities running hospitals as directly managed units, there is now the split between purchasers and providers. The real question is whether the forms of service contact that will develop between them will be complete, so as to permit a market (or 'quasi-market') solution, or incomplete so that the system will have to rely on a common culture to sustain it.

Reliance on suppliers under long-term contacts constitutes the key feature of the market reforms. It is intended to focus attention on costs and service quality. But this goal can be attained by formal contracting only to the extent that complete contracts can be specified, with adequate opportunities for monitoring and third-party verification (Baiman, 1990, p. 342, fn. 4). But, as Lapsley (1993, p. 389) notes, the purchaser/provider split in the NHS 'reveals favourable conditions for opportunistic behaviour; major uncertainties (particularly in the contracting process); bounded rationality and, to some extent, the negative impact of small numbers on the functioning of the market'. Together with incomplete knowledge of the transformation process and inability to measure outputs accurately (despite attempts to make cost allocations in increasing detail), the environment is still far more suited to clan control than to market deals.

All three theoretical views in this chapter can accept most of the analysis of TCE. This points out that reducing transaction costs can materially affect the shape and boundaries of the organisation. But, of course, these boundaries within the NHS are not decided by their management: they have been imposed by the Department of Health as a matter of political strategy. The trusts have little autonomy when it comes to reshaping internal or external boundaries. Moreover, as noted below, there are several other ways in which they are constrained from acting as market entities.

Lapsley's analysis

Lapsley (1993) offers an 'orthodox' version of TCE, drawing on Williamson (1975, 1978, 1991) and the analysis of clan relations by Ouchi (1977, 1979, 1980).

Lapsley recognises that governance falls into two types, based on hierarchical (or bureaucratic rule-based) controls and on clan (or culture-based) control systems. Clan control is important 'where knowledge of the transformation process is imperfect and the ability to measure outputs is low' (1993, p. 386). It implies 'a reliance on shared values and beliefs – common agreement on appropriate behaviour and high commitment to this code of behaviour' (ibid.). This is important where market failure prevents prices giving reliable signals and the formal rules offered by bureaucracy are inadequate to deal with real-world complexities and subtleties, such as opportunism. He cites Bourn and Ezzamel (1986) that a medical clan used formerly to dominate within a system of administrative and financial controls. They predicted that attempts at the time to impose new, accounting-based rules to constrain the power of the medical clan would prove no more than a ritual. 'Indeed,' says Lapsley (1993, p. 388), 'there is evidence to support this view.' However, 'while the new style hierarchical controls do not yet appear to have weakened the influence of health care professionals, the advent of a market solution to the regulation of the NHS may yet do so'.

There are two possible ways to privatise public services. The first of these, the adoption of the 'pure property rights approach', rejects as a matter of principle the concept of state ownership. However, the government has apparently rejected this option, which implies converting the NHS into private corporations.

Lapsley (1993, p. 388) observes: 'An alternative approach to privatisation is the gradualist one which draws on the theory of contestable markets . . . in which markets for public services are opened up to *potential* entrants.' This has been used in several areas of public service, for example with the introduction of compulsory competitive tendering. Lapsley notes that this 'has generated substantial savings for the tendering of domestic services', but there has been evidence of 'loss leaders' and contractor failure. As far as the NHS is concerned, he identifies the key features of the market solution as being the purchaser/provider split, which relies on general practitioner fund-holders as purchasers and NHS self-governing trusts as providers, 'both of which are novel organisational forms introduced as part of the NHS reforms and which are pivotal elements of the internal market' (ibid., p. 389).

Trust status offers financial attractions not previously available to NHS organisations. Lapsley notes that in principle they can now determine local pay, employment conditions and employment structure, keep surpluses, borrow funds, and employ public dividend capital. However, in practice some of these powers are constrained. For example, borrowing still forms part of the Public Sector Borrowing Requirement, and is subject to government consent. He conjectures (1993, p. 392) that some trust managements may try to arrange buyouts, particularly to acquire the more successful acute hospitals. He implies that private status will offer significant competitive advantages, which will be denied to trusts that stay within the NHS.

The use of 'cost per case' contracts for the purchase of services in place of the former 'block contracts' will, says Lapsley (1993), stimulate the development of new measures of clinical output, offering better information on the performance of medical specialties. This ability to measure output removes one of the conditions that support medical clan control, even though information on the transformation process remains imperfect. In short, despite many opportunities for opportunism and obfuscation, Lapsley sees cost per case contracting advancing the market in health care, together with the consequent shift in power for consultants towards purchasers and administrators.

Such a conclusion has to involve considerable conjecture. As for empirical evidence, Lapsley cites at least as much that prevents the operation of a market in health care as he offers in support of it. He notes repeatedly that the transaction costs of operating such a market are exceptionally high. He refers (1993, p. 389) to several causes of high costs of this kind:

> considerable uncertainty, not only over cause and effect of particular treatments, but also because of the unpredictable nature of much non-elective medical care; the sheer scale of the number of contracts which would require to be placed on a 'cost per case' contracting system . . . ; . . . scope for opportunistic behaviour [including adverse selection]; . . . [and] major difficulties for providers in generating sufficiently precise costing information to enable such contracts to be made.

He warns that 'attenuation of the traditional position of the hospital consultant . . . may prove to be inappropriate' (ibid.). Moreover, he comments on limits on self-governing hospital trusts to compete 'because of the specialised nature of some facilities (e.g. heart surgery)' as well as the tendency of spatial monopoly to lead to bilateral dependencies (ibid., p. 391).

Moreover, Lapsley rather overstates the current attractions of NHS trust status. The rules in force at present not only place limits on borrowings as well as requiring a 6 per cent return on capital employed (both of which Lapsley (1993) notes): they also place a ceiling on the amount of profit that can be carried forward from one year to the next, and include a general rule that prohibits cross-subsidisation, between clinical directorates, between treatments and between patients. This makes it virtually impossible for providers to take risks. Not only do NHS reward mechanisms inhibit risk-taking, but successful developments cannot be used to compensate for failures. It is impossible to develop a portfolio of activities in which risk is diversified. By comparison with private sector companies, the NHS is functioning at a serious disadvantage.[3]

In spite of these criticisms, Lapsley (1993) may well be right that further moves towards cost per case contracts will exert pressure for tighter clinical controls. But because of the joint nature of so many inputs and outputs, it is impossible to define costs accurately, unless hospitals try to make their costs variable rather than fixed. It might well be possible in theory to do this, for example by hiring staff and equipment on short-term contracts. It will be argued below, however, that this would be impossibly inefficient: it runs directly counter to the need to raise productivity by means of innovation, which implies high fixed costs.

Ezzamel and Willmott's analysis

According to Ezzamel and Willmott, market economics needed the advent of institutional economics to legitimise its analysis. Policy goals rationalised on the basis of economic theory were simply incredible otherwise. The 'markets and hierarchies' (M&H) framework was an important development of institutional economics. They comment (1993, p. 110) that:

M&H is [also] seen as providing a powerful analytical framework which builds on the interplay between historical conditions and economic processes to generate apparently unambiguous but, as we wish to argue later, problematical, statements concerning the most economically efficient means of organizing transactions.

A major deficiency of M&H analysis (just like Paretian optimality conditions, one might add) is its acceptance that the existing distribution of wealth and power in society is to be taken for granted.

[But] institutional economists' appreciation of the social and organizational dimensions of contractual relationships is constrained by a failure to understand how 'market' relations are routinely predicated on a hierarchical structure of domination.

(Ezzamel and Willmott, 1993, p. 110)

Instead of understanding hierarchies as something that arises from market failures, it is more plausible to view hierarchy as a significant condition of market-based transactions. The very development and institutionalization of markets is based on hierarchical relations of exchange.

(ibid., p. 113)[4]

If Ezzamel and Willmott see the root cause of the economic problem as being unequal bargaining power, this suggests they would accept the welfare implications of market economics if only the initial distribution of wealth were equalised. However, they do not refer to this. Instead, they write of a historical movement towards domination, bolstered by arguments that rationalise the process by reference to economic 'laws'.

They comment (ibid., p. 111) that, in contrast with the introduction of greater market pressures, 'It is only by developing more substantially democratic forms of governance that there is any prospect of removing the irrational consequences attributed to markets and hierarchies.' They are not very specific about how they would characterise 'more substantially democratic forms of governance', although they note that 'such a mode of resource allocation would begin by opening up channels of communication between those who pay for, those who receive and those who provide public services' (ibid., p. 128).

It is not clear how this improves resource allocation. Keat (1991, p. 216) contrasts a system which maximises 'want-satisfaction' (i.e. a competitive market economy) with one that meets some set of broader criteria that 'might loosely be described as cultural'. In a market system, he observes (ibid., p. 217),

The satisfaction of people's wishes is taken to be intrinsically desirable, whatever the character or content of those wishes may happen to be: one is not permitted to discriminate between more-or-less valuable, desirable or acceptable forms of satisfaction. To do so would involve adopting instead what may be termed an 'ideal-regarding' standpoint.

The ideal-regarding pattern of activities in society requires outcomes to be monitored and, where necessary, adjusted by expertise and culture (by implication, supplied by some sub-set of society). Keat points out that the two may not produce the same outcome.

On the other hand, it is not impossible to suppose, in contrast both to Ezzamel and Willmott (1993) and to Keat (1991), that the two may coincide. Moreover, this might not simply be a matter of chance. It is usually assumed in welfare economics that individuals in society are 'rational economic men' (*sic*), with independent utility functions, and irresponsible patterns of individualistic 'consumer' behaviour. Fortunately, this is merely a convenient simplifying assumption that aids economic analysis – it is not a description of, or a pre-scription for, human behaviour. It is just as plausible that individual demand patterns are not independent, but are culturally dependent. Concepts of culture can exist among consumers as well as producers: indeed, most consumers *are* producers. Moreover, ideal-regarding consumption may be seen as the mark of a civilised society just as irresponsible consumption is the mark of a debased society which denies the existence of social obligations.[5]

Problems tend to arise when there are conflicts to resolve. Ezzamel and Willmott (1993) object, reasonably, that in a market economy it is the wealth-iest that always prevail. But, just as plausibly, in a democratic system it is the most articulate that prevail. Is that necessarily more just? Keat (1991) explores the conditions that produce well-informed judgements, whose authority is based upon expertise. He does not define the proper membership of that expert group, or justify the criteria that would lead to exclusion. Without such guides, or some process that arrives at them (such, perhaps, as the 'reflective equil-ibrium' of Rawls, 1973), we are left without a way to proceed. Democratic rights imply access to information, including access to the processes by which ideals are formulated. At some stage criteria must be posited, from which a culture can emerge.

The NHS reforms themselves seem to be predicated upon uncertain principles or criteria. Lapsley (1993, p. 389) claims that the 'aim of [this] inter-nal market is to increase the efficiency of health care provision and, thereby, to increase the overall level of patient care (without concomitant additional resources)'. By contrast, Ezzamel and Willmott (1993, p. 116) comment that the 'express purpose of all these developments is to achieve greater economies in the mediation of public sector activities by promoting highly calculative and rationalistic regimes of competitiveness and financial accountability'. They are concerned with the high costs of the reforms, not so much in terms of the administrative expenses involved but in the declining quality, range and delivery of care to those 'who are assumed to be the recipients of market/ hierarchic regulated services' (ibid., p. 119). 'These visible costs demonstrate the failure of governance modes rooted in economic rationality, such as M&H, to promote both the development and delivery of high quality public service' (ibid., p. 120).

It has been a claim of thinkers of the right during the 1980s that welfare problems in practice tend to reflect not an excess of market intervention but a dearth of it. My point is not to argue for market economics, but to suggest that

Ezzamel and Willmott's (1993) rejection of it appears to raise problems that are also unresolved – the key problem being to define authority.

Ezzamel and Willmott identify two forms of argument adduced by market advocates to support hierarchy as a step on the route away from clan control and towards market forces. The reforms are intended either 'to improve efficiency by gaining more output from a similar amount of input – often by introducing market disciplines into "bureaucratic" organisations' (1993, p. 120) (basically the claim made above by Lapsley, 1993); or they are designed to reduce the 'burden' of the public sector. They observe that this misses the point behind the diversity of economic institutions – the public sector thrives because it offers 'the sense of purpose and *service* that is more difficult to generate and sustain in for-profit organizations' (ibid., original emphasis). This sense of service is embodied in the clan culture, but as 'market disciplines have been introduced into the public sector, established forms of clan control have been subverted by the disciplines of financial accountability' (ibid., p. 123).

Ezzamel and Willmott (1993, p. 126) suggest that members of the 'clans' may yet be able to capture control of the new bureaucracies, but it is also just as likely that individual professionals may act 'as the unwitting destroyers of their clan culture as they become surrogate managers and administrators'. They conclude (ibid.) that 'Despite the difficulty, and perhaps the absurdity, of deriving meaningful prices for goods and services in situations of high task interdependence – a common characteristic of public sector organizations – the primacy of the market forms of governance is being rapidly established.'

An alternative analysis

If the prime aim of the NHS reforms is to raise productivity, this may be achieved by

(1) forcing people to work harder;
(2) making systems more adaptable (perhaps with no need to work harder); or
(3) innovation in better equipment, clinical practices, staff, organisation and management.

These factors are not necessarily mutually exclusive, but they need further consideration. The first will not offer much scope for raising productivity, but some form of motivation is essential to induce staff to accept changes and the uncertainties that these will bring. The second and third cases can be identified, respectively, with short-term tactical changes and long-term strategic planning. A firm can decide as a matter of policy either to pursue adaptability, which means keeping open as many of its options as possible, or innovation, defined as building up long-term competitive advantage by committing itself to high levels of fixed investment in specific assets, used intensively to yield very high quality at very low unit costs (Lazonick, 1991). The adaptive firm, by contrast, is prepared to change its product range, its methods, suppliers and output markets immediately it sees any opportunity to cut costs or make a sale.

Adaptability was allegedly the hallmark of 'proprietorial capitalism' in the first industrial revolution in the nineteenth century, supported by the ideology of classical economics. The scale of operations was usually small enough to allow new investment plans to be implemented and amended quickly. But even this relatively small-scale revolution was not achieved by unrestrained market competition. According to Lazonick (1991, p. 5), whilst British advocates of *laissez-faire* extolled to the world the virtues of market competition, British companies were actually enjoying state protection of a massive order. Much of their success was due to this. Yet the rhetoric was to become a major barrier to innovation, and still is:

> the propensity of mainstream economists to look first and foremost to market coordination to allocate resources serves as an intellectual barrier to perceiving the changing institutional reality of successful capitalist development; for as history shows, the changing institutional reality is characterized by the growing importance of planned coordination within the business organization and the growing dominance of the business organization over the determination of economic outcomes. Through the process of innovation, particular business organizations gain competitive advantage, thus driving the development process. Mainstream economics contains no theory of innovation and no theory of competitive advantage.
>
> (Lazonick, 1991, p. 7)

The rise of 'managerial capitalism' in America between 1880 and 1950 produced the second industrial revolution, with very much larger companies and a larger scale of industrial innovation. The third industrial revolution, based on 'collective capitalism', has centred on Japan since the middle of the present century, and requires co-ordination and specialised investment on a much vaster scale, led by high technology.

> What is needed to understand technological and economic change is a theory that asks what determines the differences in the technological and economic capabilities of competing enterprises. Yet to assume away all technological and economic differences among enterprises is precisely what neoclassical microeconomic theory – what I have labelled the 'theory of the market economy' – not only does but is *designed* to do.
>
> (Lazonick, 1991, p. 287, emphasis in original)

According to Lazonick, three factors are necessary for successful innovation:

(1) the commitment of the firm to investment in highly specialised plant, processes, staff, management and organisation;
(2) well-developed links with the markets for the supply of inputs and the sale of outputs, since high levels of fixed cost are too risky to undertake unless the technical uncertainties of production are minimised (by excellent research and development) and trading uncertainties are minimised (by networks that ensure vertical co-ordination); and, finally,
(3) strategic support must be assured by the state, which is responsible for

providing the infrastructure and clear strategic goals, well co-ordinated across firms and industries.

The firm has a strategic choice to make: either to be adaptive and keep its capacity to change direction at a moment's notice, or to take a long-term view and innovate despite the high fixed costs this necessitates. Innovation requires a high volume of throughput to achieve low unit costs (indeed, very low marginal costs since so much input is now in the form of fixed costs).

Evidence of the importance of innovation and technical change abounds in economic and business history. Lazonick draws heavily on the work of Alfred D. Chandler Jr (1977), but he recognises that many neo-classical economists do so too, including Oliver Williamson. Lazonick credits Nelson and Winter (1982) for reviving interest in Joseph Schumpeter's work on the dynamics of innovation. Despite their major contribution, Nelson and Winter miss the full significance of Chandler's work on the relationships between investment strategy and organisational structure.

> In their brief discussion of 'analysts of firm organization and strategy', they recognized the strategy–structure connection but treated as an afterthought Chandler's argument that structure follows strategy – that is, that a firm builds an organization to plan and coordinate a high-fixed-cost strategy. Although they referred to the work of Oliver Williamson and Alfred Chandler, they did not distinguish Williamson's transaction cost framework, which, as we have seen, neglects the analysis of technological change from Chandler's strategy–structure framework, which focuses on the issue of how organizations generate new cost structures.
>
> (Lazonick, 1991, pp. 287–8)

Applying innovation theory to the NHS in Britain, new forms of clinical treatment may be divided into minor adaptations that offer some limited progress and major changes that potentially transform whole processes. Minimally invasive surgery has already reduced recuperation times and reduced bed occupancy. Indeed, innovation has probably done more to raise productivity than the entire market reform programme. If Lazonick is right, the movement towards market competition is in diametrically the opposite direction from the development of long-term relationships that support innovation.

Investment in highly specific innovation does not always mean expensive equipment in medical care. Magnetic resonance imagers are expensive, but much of the innovation needed in the NHS is a matter of the diffusion of best new practice, for example in diagnostics and prescription by general practitioners. Innovation often needs high levels of training for complete teams of staff, as in laparoscopic ('keyhole') surgery. Production risk must be minimised, by research and development and training, as well as market risk. The new techniques must work properly, but there must also be patients in sufficient number to justify the investment – and it is also necessary nowadays that purchasers will be able and willing to pay.

The new problem for acute providers is the replacement of block contracts by cost per case contracts which specify particular numbers of treatments within particular clinical directorates. The difficulty is that, even with very large health authorities serving large populations, it is often not possible to predict the case mix with accuracy. Rarer, and often more expensive, forms of treatment like organ transplants are not only difficult to foresee, but they typically cross clinical boundaries. Given the need to incur high fixed costs to train teams of specialist staffs, added to other forms of joint costs that arise from cross-specialty care, the problems of defining an episode of care and of costing it with any precision become very great indeed. This is why it was suggested earlier, at the end of the discussion of Lapsley's (1993) analysis, that keeping all inputs flexible might make for easier definition of costs (and prices), even though it would be economically absurd to let this drive the strategic decision as between adaptation and innovation.

The third condition that Lazonick (1991) specifies for successful innovation throughout an economy is state support and co-ordination. It is more controversial whether the state is the only possible way to achieve co-ordination. Arguably it is not necessary if only industries can form their own coherent strategies. The NHS in Britain may well not receive such support, given the British government's commitment to market economics of the very kind that Lazonick claims is obsolescent, wilfully blind, and damaging to national competitiveness. Indeed, one might see the NHS market reforms as designed to get health authorities locally to make the very strategic decisions without co-ordination that the government is not able or prepared to make on the basis of an informed strategy.

Arguably, there is a need both for competition, to induce the motivation to accept change, and long-term strategic commitment, to permit innovation. Even the longest-term contracts are renegotiated from time to time. As Lapsley (1993) notes, contestable markets only need to be *potentially* open to competition. But the more specialised and effective new techniques are, and the more difficult to acquire and master, the greater the protection they offer from competitors by way of 'first mover advantage'.[6]

Research into innovation is potentially important to the national economy, but it is not highly regarded in Britain. Ironically, there would appear to be scope within the numerous NHS health authorities for an important experiment. If actively competitive markets are successful in inducing the best available forms of health care, it should be possible to demonstrate the fact. Conversely, if close and collaborative relations are more conducive (as Lazonick (1991) predicts), then health authorities that form long-term agreements could prove their point.[7] Unfortunately, the time horizon is likely to be too short for such an experiment to run its course. Hospital trusts that fail to survive short-term financial pressures may well be closed down without the opportunity to demonstrate the long-run advantages of innovative care. Ministers seem unable to resist intervening between general elections.

On the other hand, successful long-term contracting strategy is likely to encourage innovation, albeit on a modest scale. Even if the size of hospital trusts is restricted by the Department of Health, there will still be benefits in obtaining long-term contracts for innovative care.

Strictly speaking, under present rules NHS organisations cannot form legally enforceable contracts – any breach of the present yearly 'block contracts' is resolved by internal arbitration rather than the courts. Moreover, budgets are set only annually and announced to health authorities after the start of the financial year, so they have little authority to make binding agreements for several years ahead, even though these would probably secure better quality care at lower prices.[8]

The argument of this chapter is that long-term agreements resulting in innovation will limit the operation of market forces in the NHS. Both Lapsley (1993) and Ezzamel and Willmott (1993) explain how free market competition is inappropriate to public services which use significant specialised resources. But they conclude that the driving force of market competition may produce higher productivity, implying that trusts with the lowest costs will survive. In this chapter I quote a different view of TCE. Innovation is the key to competitive advantage and economic success, at national level and also at the level of individual industries and firms, but it operates more by expanding markets and processes than by cutting costs.

The success of exporting manufacturers in the north-central part of Italy is explained largely by the benefits of networking among many small firms (Best, 1990, especially chapter 7, pp. 203–26). The future economic success of American manufacturing is predicated upon investment banking rather than the relatively poorly informed short-term processes of governance by stockholders (Porter, 1992). On a far more modest scale, the survival of individual NHS purchasers and providers may depend on their ability to hang on to as rich as possible a set of long-term contractual relations, sustained by supportive clan relations. While these may be expressed in terms of the demands of particular clinical directorates or treatments, the scope for this will be limited by the tendency of patients to suffer from multiple conditions, and require an unpredictable mix of treatments.

The very reasons that Lapsley (1993) offers as limits to the scope of market competition in the NHS within a relatively short time scale are reinforced powerfully when considering the advantages of long-term strategic agreements. Such an agenda offers the best chances of achieving the higher productivity needed to serve an ageing population with progressively better standards of care.

Notes

1. What information this might be is of some importance (especially to accountants), but it goes beyond the scope of this chapter. Clearly, the answer depends on the nature of the contract. TCE shows that keeping that scope of contracts limited and specific saves costs. Thus it benefits NHS trusts that they are not generally answerable to an amorphous body of shareholders for the use of capital. Conversely, public sector institutions have wider, less precise, social obligations than private firms.

2 Defining when a contract is complete and when it is not is mainly a matter of

whether the parties can predict at the outset all outcomes that they will regard as material if only the information becomes known to them, directly or indirectly. It may not be possible for one party to infer what the other would see as objectionable (e.g. bribery).

3. There is currently a serious shortage of secure accommodation for potentially dangerous mental patients. The cost is too great, and the demand too unpredictable, for any individual health district to build one. A nationwide series of such secure hospitals may well prove profitable, since break-even levels of occupancy can be predicted for large populations. No NHS trust can currently borrow enough for such a large project, even if profits from high occupancies could be used to subsidise low occupancies. The private sector is currently seeking long-term purchase contracts from health authorities.

4. Ezzamel and Willmott (1993) appear to be using the term 'hierarchy' in a different, broader sense than the institutional economics literature.

5. Or, maybe, even the existence of society. 'There is no such thing as society: there are only individual men and women, and there are families' (Margaret Thatcher, *Woman's Own*, 31 October 1987).

6. NHS innovations are typically very much smaller in scale and cost than similar technical R&D in advanced manufacturing industries. The scale of R&D in electronics and aerospace is so great that there is scope for only half a dozen firms in each industry worldwide.

7. I am working at present on a study which seeks to test this point empirically, by a mail survey of all health authority purchasers.

8. Of the health authorities I am currently surveying (see note 7), the majority are contracting over more than one year, and most directors of public health regard this as important for securing good quality treatment.

References

Baiman, S. (1990) Agency research in managerial accounting: a second look, *Accounting, Organizations and Society*, Vol. 15, no. 4, pp. 341–71.

Best, M. (1990) *The New Competition: Institutions of Industrial Restructuring*, Harvard University Press, Cambridge, Mass.

Bourn, M. and Ezzamel, M. (1986) Organisational culture in hospitals in the National Health Service, *Financial Accountability and Management*, Vol. 2, no. 3, pp. 203–26.

Chandler, A. D. Jr (1977) *The Visible Hand*, Belknap Press, Cambridge, Mass.

Ezzamel, M. and Willmott, H. (1993) Corporate governance and financial accountability: recent reforms in the UK public sector, *Accounting, Auditing and Accountability Journal*, Vol. 6, no. 3, pp. 109–32.

Keat, R. (1991) Consumer sovereignty and the integrity of practices, in R. Keat and N. Abercrombie (eds.), *Enterprise Culture*, Routledge, London, pp. 216–30.

Lapsley, I. (1993) Markets, hierarchies and the regulation of the National Health Service, *Accounting and Business Research*, Corporate Governance Special Issue, pp. 384–94.

Lazonick, W. (1991) *Business Organization and the Myth of the Market Economy*, Cambridge University Press, Cambridge.

Nelson, R. R. and Winter, S. G. (1982) *An Evolutionary Theory of Economic Change*, Harvard University Press, Cambridge, Mass.

Ouchi, W. G. (1977) The relationship between organizational structure and organizational control, *Administrative Science Quarterly*, Vol. 22, pp. 95–113.

Ouchi, W. G. (1979) A conceptual framework for the design of organizational control mechanisms, *Management Science*, Vol. 25, no. 9, pp. 833–48.

Ouchi, W. G. (1980) Markets, bureaucracies and clans, *Administrative Science Quarterly*, Vol. 25, pp. 129–41.

Porter, M. E. (1992) *Capital Choices: Changing the Way America Invests in Industry*, Council on Competitiveness and Harvard Business School, Cambridge, Mass.

Rawls, J. (973) *A Theory of Justice*, Oxford University Press,Oxford.

Williamson, O. E. (1975) *Markets and Hierarchies*, Free Press, New York.

Williamson, O. E. (1978) The modern corporation: origins, evolution and attributes, *Journal of Economic Literature*, Vol. XIX, pp. 1537–68.

Williamson, O. E. (1991) The logic of economic organisations, in O. E. Williamson and S. G. Winter (eds.), *The Nature of the Firm, Evolution and Development*, Oxford University Press, Oxford, pp. 90–116.

13

Pragmatic Considerations and the Joint Cost Dilemma

FALCONER MITCHELL

INTRODUCTION

This chapter examines the issues pertinent to the selection of a basis for joint cost allocation in a not-for-profit organisation located in the UK public sector. The organisation is unusual in that it is a manufacturing facility within the National Health Service and does not operate on a commercial or quasi-commercial basis. Its prime function is to process the plasma content of whole blood donations to produce a wide range of blood products required to meet clinical demand within the UK.

Its varied product output, derived by splitting a common raw material into numerous component parts, subsequent to further individual processing, created the requirement for multiple joint cost allocations to be made in order to cost individual product outputs. The need to address this costing issue was initiated by the growth in private sector health care in the UK. This trend had initiated a significant blood product supply to private hospitals by the national blood transfusion service. As a result a concern over the pricing of blood product supplies had emerged among various interested parties including the donors, the staff trade unions and the service's management. From these constituencies, a strong demand for knowledge of individual product cost as a basis for both price setting and price justification quickly became apparent.

The combination of blood products and financial considerations was particularly problematic in a UK setting where blood donations are made on a wholly voluntary basis. Indeed, as a strong altruistic motive underlies its supply (Titmuss, 1970) this has led to some debate on the relevance of conventional economic analysis to its supply function (Solow, 1971; Stewart, 1992). The arrangement of a financial gain for donors may not, in fact, lead to an increase in donations as the motives underlying supply reflect donors' concern with the well-being of others and their wishes to contribute to those in need of medical treatment involving blood or blood products. In other words, the utility which they obtain from the mere act of giving blood is distinct from but no less real than that obtained from receiving financial income. The provision of a payment to donors for blood would, in fact, reduce that utility and would therefore adversely affect supply. One danger of the underlying altruistic drive to donate is that it may well be susceptible to decay not only as a result of financial payment for the gift donation but also as a result of the linking of blood and blood products with financial reward to the collecting agency through the sale of its outputs. Donors would feel belittled if others were to gain financially from their gift. Convention, culture and care for others are thus the dominant underlying influences on blood supply in the UK (Stewart, 1992) and sensitivity to them is a key factor for those involved in obtaining and using the donations.

Against this background of donor sensitivity to financial considerations the use of cost-recovery-based charging became an attractive option for the blood transfusion service management as it was considered that it would allay donor fears that profits were being made by a government institution from their freely donated blood. Moreover, this type of charge would ensure that the National Health Service could not be viewed as subsidising private sector health care through the provision of products either freely or at below cost prices. The pursuit and adoption of this policy, however, required that the technical accounting problem of joint cost allocation be confronted and a means of dealing with it selected and implemented in order to produce individual unit product cost information as a basis for pricing the private sector supplies.

THE JOINT COST DILEMMA

Joint costs exist where 'production costs are a non-separable function of the outputs of two or more products' (Biddle and Steinberg, 1984, p. 1). In these situations the derivation of full unit costs for individual products has a high degree of arbitrariness. Indeed Thomas (1978) has described them as incorrigible and invited refutation of this description. The lack of any theoretically appropriate basis for joint cost attachment to outputs creates not only an embarrassment but also a particular challenge to accountants. The opportunity for flexibility in practice exists and indeed is apparent in empirical private sector studies (e.g. Slater and Wootton, 1984), where petroleum refining and chemical extraction are pervaded by joint costs. However, there is no theoretical reference point to justify any particular practice. The absence of theoretical justification has not deterred academic involvement and in recent years a number of novel approaches to the joint cost problem have been suggested.

In practice, manufacturing firms have had to deal with the joint cost problem for stock valuation and profit measurement, if for no other reason, and a number of methods to be found in use are designed primarily to address this issue. The first applies to joint product situations where scale and importance allow one product to be characterised as the main output and any others as by-products. No attempt is made to attach a portion of joint costs (presumably on grounds of immateriality) to the by-products although their income is either shown as a separate revenue source or treated as a reduction in the main product's cost. The second involves using a physical characteristic of the joint products (e.g. size, weight, fluid volume, etc.) as a common denominator which will provide a basis for computing the relative proportions of the joint cost to attach to each output. This approach takes no account of the relative values of the joint products and is dependent on there actually being a common physical measure of product outputs. Where they are different in nature (e.g. solid, liquid, gas) it will be problematic to apply. The third practical approach bases the joint cost allocation on the sales value of the outputs. Preferably this involves sale values at the split-off point (the point at which the joint products first emerge in separate form). Where the products at this stage are intermediate or novel and market prices are not available for them, the final product selling price less any further processing costs can be used as a best available approximation of sales value at the split-off point. Using a sales value approach allocates joint cost in proportion to the product's ability to generate revenue. Its effect is therefore to equalise the profit margin of all the joint products and thereby ensure each product is profitable when the process as a whole is profitable.

At an academic level the concept of opportunity cost has been employed to develop alternative means of common cost allocation which are also applicable to joint cost allocation (Shubick, 1962; Jensen, 1974; Moriarity, 1975; Louderback, 1976). This approach, at its simplest level, involves the identi-fication of the cost of alternative means (to that of the existing joint processing) of acquiring each of the joint products. Alternatives could involve different processing methods, different product output mixes or simply the buy-in of the product from external suppliers. The cost of the most economical alternative means of obtaining each joint product provides the basis for the actual joint cost allocation. In multi-joint product situations the options are extensive and solu-tions require considerable computational power. The estimation and computa-tion involved tend to reduce the practicality of the approach.

These alternative treatments simply allocate the total joint cost in different ways to final products. However, their application has the potential to generate individual product costs which are substantially different depending on the allo-cation basis used. Any use of these costs for stock valuation or indeed for less appropriate purposes (Thomas, 1969, 1974; Mepham, 1978) such as in manage-rial decision-making would therefore have the potential to influence behaviour and outcomes artificially. In this instance their use in a key pricing decision was under serious consideration by management and thereby the choice of alloca-tion basis could impact directly on the results of the protein fractionation centre and the actions of its managers. In other words, joint cost allocations may be incorrigible but if they are undertaken their results (product costs) may influ-ence behaviour. Moreover as different allocation approaches produce different cost splits they may therefore have different behavioural impacts (Thomas, 1977). In consequence, the particular situation in which the choice of method is to be made merits examination in order to ascertain the potential effects of an accounting practice decision as these are pertinent to a full assessment of the accounting choice to be made. This study is based on an examination of the situational factors which the managerial team involved considered relevant to the resolution of the joint cost dilemma in their organisation.

THE STUDY: SETTING AND METHOD

The study was set in one of the UK's protein fractionation centres (PFCs), essentially a highly clinically controlled manufacturing facility which produces up to 40 different therapeutic products from the plasma content of whole blood donations. The PFC's production process constitutes a classic example of the joint cost problem (see Figure 13.1). At the time of this study no individual cost information on final product outputs was available for management. All elements of production cost were joint up to the point where the three major products emerge, through the fractionation of the blood

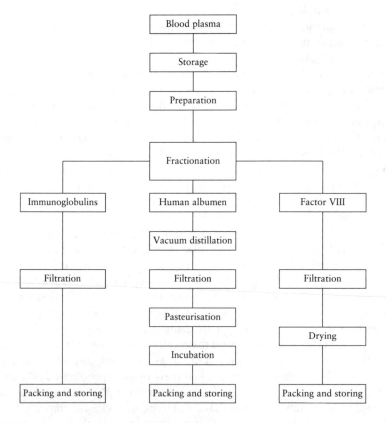

Note: This is a simplified outline of the actual production process. It does not reflect all of the complexities of the process, e.g. multiple types of blood plasma inputs, various types of immunoglobulins produced, the recycling of albumen to produce purer grades of the product, etc.

Figure 13.1   *An outline of the blood protein fractionation process*

plasma, for further individual processing. The joint costs are a substantial part of total product cost and their treatment was therefore a significant factor influencing full final product costs. As previously stated progress towards obtaining a cost recovery charge for each of these products required an allocation of all joint costs to them, outlined in the preceding section, provided different means of achieving this cost allocation. The by-product alternative could not be applied as there were at least three products considered major in each production run. Consequently, the use of a physical measure (weight), of sale values (adjusted for further processing costs) and alternative costs (computed by the researchers) were used.

As there is no correct means of dealing with the joint cost problem the choice among alternatives cannot be resolved by reference to any general costing theory. Situational factors and, in particular, the consequences, both economic and behavioural, of adopting a particular approach are therefore even more important elements of the selection process (e.g. Thomas, 1977). An appreciation of the consequences of alternatives is dependent on a familiarity with the relevant production and market situation. Those with senior work experience of blood product manufacture and use are one key group who possess this knowledge. This study is based on an investigation of whether or not the managerial team perceived any significant implications relating to the selection of particular accounting techniques for allocating joint production costs within the PFC. Their views were obtained by giving each of the 14-member management team (see Figure 13.2) at the PFC a document containing the following items:

(1) a two-product, simplified abstract example of how joint product costs could be separated and unitised using the three methods of joint cost allocation described above (i.e. physical weight, sales value at split-off and alternative cost);
(2) a table of approximate unit costs for the three major PFC products (normal immunoglobulin, albumen, Factor VIII) based on the application of these three joint cost alternatives to the PFC's processing activity;
(3) a short set of questions dealing with:
    (a) their general views and preferences for one of the alternative allocation techniques;

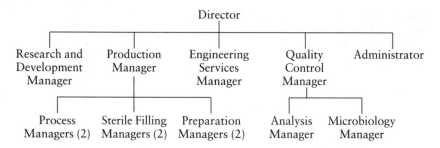

Figure 13.2 *The Protein Fractionation Centre management team*

(b) their views and preferences for one alternative technique given the sample costs of blood products derived from the application of the three joint costing alternatives; and

(c) their views and preferences for the joint costing techniques when considered as the basis for cost recovery charges being made for private sector hospital supplies.

Each manager was allowed to study and consider this document in his or her own time for one week and requested not to discuss it with colleagues. At the end of this time the managers were then interviewed by the researcher for approximately 30 minutes on the basis of the questions posed in the document.

THE RESULTS

The managerial interviews were structured to allow a focus both on general managerial preferences for particular joint cost allocation techniques and on the changes which occur in these views as managers were exposed to the impact of these techniques in their own work situation. Table 13.1 summarises the choices made by the PFC managers on the three scenarios listed above and, in addition, highlights the changes of view which occurred as the use of the joint cost allocation was made more specific to their situation. The managers' stated preferences, the changes therein and their justifications are reviewed below.

Table 13.1   *Managerial choice of alternative joint product cost allocation bases*

	Physical measures	Market values	Alternative cost	Other suggestions	No preference given
As a solution to the problem of joint costs in abstract	3	3	5	1	2
Opinion changes	−1	−1	+2		
	+1		−1		
Selection in view of their impact on the derivation of PFC product costs	3	2	6	1	2
Opinion changes	−1	+6	−3	−1	−1
	−1			+1	
			−1	+1	
Selection as a basis of cost recovery charges for supplies to the private sector	1	8	2	2	1

Managerial views on solutions to the general problem of joint cost

Views among the management team were mixed on this topic. After considering, in abstract, the three methods (see above) of dealing with joint costs and the general problem of attaching joint costs to products, two managers were of the opinion that the individual costs of joint products were subject to a high degree of inaccuracy and arbitrariness whatever method was employed. On these grounds they would not express a preference for any of the three alternatives demonstrated to them. All of the 12 other managers were prepared to express a preference. However, one of them did not consider any of the three approaches described to be appropriate. He felt that an equal split of costs to all joint products would represent the most suitable answer to a problem which precluded any definitive solution. His reasoning was based upon the notion that *all* joint products cause joint costs to be incurred and therefore all should be equally burdened with the joint cost. The 11 remaining managers each chose one of the three given approaches. Just under half (five) selected the 'academic' option, alternative cost. Three of these managers justified their choice by reference to the fact that this method was particularly appropriate for cost allocation because it was based upon a set of cost measurements relating to the joint products. They thought it logical for the prevailing cost conditions, determined as a basis for the application of this method, to provide a basis for the individual product cost ascertainment procedure. One of the others supporting this approach did so on the basis of the usefulness of the alternative cost information to management. The benefit of having this information was its relevance to managerial reviews of production policies. For example, the regular procurement of wholesale prices and alternative manufacturing costs was necessary and this ensured that information relevant to 'make or buy' or process modification screening of PFC operations would be routinely available. This would facilitate monitoring of these options. The last manager favouring the alternative cost basis could provide no positive argument to back his selection, stating only that the method did not suffer from the disadvantages which he perceived in the others.

Three managers decided that sales values were the most appropriate choice. They all substantiated their view in terms of the ready availability of the necessary data and their objectivity. In addition, two of these managers felt that there should be a relationship between cost and selling price and therefore sales values would be the fairest available reflection of the underlying costs of the individual products. The third manager considered that joint processing was undertaken only because the resultant products were valuable. Cost should reflect this underlying motive and so the allocation of cost on the basis of the best available measure of individual product values (their sales prices) seemed logical.

The final three managers selected the physical measure basis of joint cost allocation. Two of them considered that product size could be related to cost as, for example, bulkier material would require larger and more expensive processing equipment and costlier handling. The third simply found it the most comprehensible method and one which would also be easy to apply in practice.

Several of the managers made critical comments about each of the approaches which they did not select. The physical measure basis was viewed as lacking any rationale because the relative value of products might bear little or no relationship to this characteristic. Doubts about the sales value basis comprised its generation of a consistent correlation between cost and price for all products which was seen as unrealistic. In addition, the problem of product comparability with others in the market could in some circumstances (of product differentiation) complicate and cast doubt on the validity of using available sales values. Alternative costs were considered difficult to understand and highly notional in the sense of the considerable subjective estimates of the costs of alternative production or procurement policies which were required to apply the approach.

Managerial views on the results of applying alternative approaches to the joint cost problem to blood products

The managers were provided with a set of sample costs for the three major blood products derived by applying the physical measure, sales value and alternative cost bases of allocation (as can be seen from Table 13.2 the application of different methods produced considerable variation in unit costs). The managers were required to state again their preference for a method in the light of this information. Only three of the fourteen managers decided to change from the method which they had selected as, in abstract, being preferable. Two changed to alternative cost from respectively, sales value and physical measure. Both, however, justified their switch by reference to the intuitively alien pattern of costs which, they perceived, had resulted from the application of their original choice of approach to the blood product cost allocation. The importance of obtaining costs which were intuitively acceptable was supported by the other managers who had chosen alternative cost. These two managers, who had consistently selected alternative cost, considered that the technique had produced costs which confirmed their own prior perception of the relative pattern of blood product costs.

Table 13.2   *Specimen joint cost allocation results*

	Allocation method		
Product	Physical weights £	Sales values £	Alternative cost £
Normal immunoglobulin (cost per 5.2 ml vial)	0.88	3.82	5.10
Factor VIII (cost per international unit)	0.07	0.03	0.31
Albumen (cost per 400 ml bottle)	20.27	17.01	7.82

Note: The cost figures have been disguised on grounds of confidentiality although relativities have been approximately preserved.

However, certain other factors, particular to the blood products, were now also mentioned by managers as important in the selection or rejection of particular approaches. The physical measure basis received additional criticism. One manager questioned its applicability to the full range of blood products as a sensible common denominator would be hard to find due to the different nature of many of the products not included in the costing experiment. Within the full range of products, some were in the form of crystals, some pastes, some powders and some liquids. These outputs were not routinely measured in terms of any one physical attribute. Moreover, the potency (and thus clinical utility) of products could increase with their concentration. While this enhanced their worth and caused extra joint processing cost, paradoxically it reduced their physical weight and thereby the amount of joint cost attributed to the product. The relative pattern of product costs generated by this approach resulted in further managerial criticism of it. Five managers observed that the bulkiest product, human albumen, had been costed at a level which far exceeded its market value while the Factor VIII and immunoglobulin had a cost far below the prices of commercial equivalents. These managers felt that such a set of costs was simply too unrealistic in relation to both the clinical and market value of the products to be tenable.

Sales values evoked consistent support from two managers who considered that it had resulted in costs which could be considered reasonable as they were in accord with their preconceptions of the relative economic value of the products. In addition, the use of sales values would ensure that the PFC's costs would match the pattern of prevailing market prices and so should maintain the attractiveness of PFC products to clinicians should any cost-based charges have to be made for them in the future. However, three main problems were associated with the use of sales values as a basis for the joint cost allocation of blood plasma. First, the market price of many of the products was extremely variable (it could in extreme cases double almost overnight) and this type of extreme variation would be reflected in PFC unit costs. Second, commercial firms in this sector did not necessarily set price in relation to cost due to the use of loss leaders and other price-related marketing devices. These policies would negate the idea that the use of sales values would reflect commercial cost patterns. Third, the existence of comparable products to those of the PFC (particularly with respect to quality levels) was questionable for some of the product range. The manager who had initially advocated equal cost allocations suggested that the actual costings of the blood products lent weight to his argument. He felt that the unit costs computed on the suggested bases could vary as a result of the measurement technique used as opposed to operational factors, e.g. changes in external technology and market prices would directly influence internal product costs. Thus the resultant product cost information could give a misleading impression of PFC performance.

Finally, several managers expressed the feeling that product costing was simply not a crucial issue for blood product supply. This view was encapsulated in the comment of one of the managers who would not select any specific costing approach as most appropriate. He considered clinical and behavioural rather than financial criteria applied to the issue of blood supply. He stated: 'Blood products are different from pots of jam. Charges and costs are irrelevant here. We must simply supply all who are in need with the highest quality clinical products.'

Managerial views on the use of joint cost allocation alternatives to generate cost recovery charges

The managerial responses to the possible application of the costs shown in Table 13.2 as a basis for cost recovery charges for the PFC products supplied to the private sector exhibited a marked alteration from the previously expressed preferences. Six managers changed from their prior selections (half from alternative cost and one each from physical measure, equal allocation and no stated preference). They were motivated to do so by two dominant reasons (which were also shared by the three managers who retained the sale value preference). First, it was felt that the PFC cost-based charges would allow hospital buyers (there was some expectation that this could eventually extend to both private and public hospitals) to compare commercial prices directly with the transfer price of PFC products. PFC charges which exceeded commercial prices could then lead to a quick curtailment of demand for the relevant PFC output. Second, the cost-based charging system would provide an external exposure of the PFC manufacturing operations. Not only would this influence product demand but the pricing comparisons would reflect directly on the economic performance of the PFC. Being in the public domain the product costs (and their comparison with substitute products) would represent an important new high-profile performance measure for the PFC. It was recognised that cost-based charges which were above those of commercial equivalents for any products could lead to criticism of the PFC work. The following managerial comments reflect this latter view:

> If people look critically at us then they will be judging us against commercial prices.

> We can't afford to overprice the market for any of these products given that we don't have a profit objective.

> Given that we obtain the raw material free our costs must stay below the market price.

> Using sales value will ensure we stay below their [commercial supplier] prices.

The sales value alternative which reduced the likelihood of these problems thus became the first preference for a majority of the 14 managers.

Two other managers changed their respective selections of physical measures and alternative cost to a new proposal for supply charging. They both felt that any private sector supplies should be charged at the full prevailing market price. This would have the advantage of negating the need for internal product costing at the PFC and would, in all probability, also produce a profit from the transactions.

CONCLUSIONS

The joint cost problem is commonly encountered in manufacturing industry and within this sphere firms are compelled to establish means of coping with it as they require unit costs for stock valuation and profit measurement. However, the compensating effects of opening and closing stocks on profit and the absence of disclosure requirements relating to the individual product costs reduce the significance and contentiousness of a joint cost allocation method selection for these purposes. This chapter examines joint cost allocation within a context where the purpose of the allocation is different and possibly more significant, i.e. the derivation of cost recovery charges for joint products.

In this situation PFC managers were prepared to express definite and differing opinions on alternative methods of joint cost allocation. These views were fairly consistent with regard to the technical application of alternative techniques (abstract consideration versus illustrative in-house application) but exhibited considerable change when the purpose of the application was specifically linked to cost recovery charges for their products. Their justification for this reflects the fact that unit product costs were perceived by many of the managers as potentially important indicators of performance which could be used to assess the viability of their operations *vis-à-vis* the commercial sector. The results of this comparison would also become widely available outside the PFC and lead to judgement of them by donors, trade unions, the public and government funders. Implicit in these views is the notion that the technical limitations of unit cost information involving joint cost allocations would not be appreciated and/or would be ignored by those making the performance comparisons. In this their intuition may be reliable as functional fixation has been a detrimental characteristic of accounting information use, even by those knowledgeable in the syntax of accounting, when reliance is placed on accounting measures as a basis for judging performance (e.g. Abdel-Khalik and Keller, 1979; Barnes and Webb, 1986). The selection of the cost allocation alternative which would positively and most consistently reflect PFC costs in comparison with those of commercial alternatives thus became the most popular choice of the PFC managers.

The formal or informal use of particular measures to assess performance is likely to impact on the behaviour (possibly dysfunctionally) of those subject to them (Ridgeway, 1956). Where there is flexibility in the selection of a computational technique which systematically influences the nature and pattern of a performance then the possible behavioural impact of the alternatives impinges more forceably on the selection process. Where accounting theory provides little or no normative guidance on the choice of accounting method the effect of the resultant financial information on participants' behaviour becomes all the more significant as the accounting practice decision lacks any foundation in the domain of the information producers' technical expertise. This case illustrates how doubts were cast by managerial participants on the nature of cost allocation methods which produced results which could be at odds with the market and with the clinical values of products. It also demonstrates how they were sensitive to the performance assessment implications of the choice of joint cost allocation method. The potential economic significance of ignoring this cost accounting issue (e.g. the potential loss of specific product line business) was also viewed by many of the managers as a key aspect of accounting method choice.

Particularly in a health sector context, where the joint cost problem is extensive (Perrin, 1987) and where attempts to deal with it may be motivated by more than the need to cost stocks, the processes of information production and use should be examined closely by the accountant with ultimate responsibility for generating information and for determining accounting practices. The absence of any theoretical accounting basis for a technical solution to this problem does not imply that selection of a joint cost allocation basis can be made at random. The choice of method can have behavioural (particularly where performance measurement is one purpose of the information generated) and economic (particularly where decisions on the use of resources are contingent upon product costs) consequences. These merit identification and analysis in order to assess and determine the most suitable costing practice in any given circumstances. The organisational situation and the views of managerial participants will provide a rich source of the many pragmatic considerations which can beneficially inform and guide the accountant's practice in this area of arbitrary flexibility in the technicalities of costing.

References

Abdel-Khalik A. R. and Keller, T. F. (1979) Earnings or cash flows: an experiment on functional fixation and the valuation of the firm, *Studies in Accounting Research*, no. 16, American Accounting Association, Sarasota, Florida.

Barnes, P. and Webb, J. (1986) Management information changes and functional fixation: some experimental evidence from the public sector, *Accounting, Organizations and Society*, Vol. 11, no. 1, pp. 1–15.

Biddle, G. and Steinberg, R. (1984) Allocations of joint common costs, *Journal of Accounting Literature*, Vol. 3, pp. 1–46.

Jensen, D. L. (1974) The role of cost in pricing joint products: a case of production in fixed proportions, *The Accounting Review* (June), pp. 465–76.

Louderback, J. G. (1976) Another approach to allocating joint costs: a comment, *The Accounting Review* (July), pp. 683–5.

Mepham, M. J. (1978) Joint production costs – a re-appraisal of sales value apportionment, *Management Accounting* (February), pp. 64–8.

Moriarity, S. (1975) Another approach to allocating joint costs, *The Accounting Review* (October), pp. 791–5.

Perrin, J. (1987) The costs and joint products of English teaching hospitals, *Financial Accountability and Management* (Summer), pp. 209–30.

Ridgeway, V. F. (1956) Dysfunctional consequences of performance measurements, *Administrative Science Quarterly* (September), pp. 240–7.

Shubick, M. (1962) Incentives, dencentralised control, the assignment of joint costs and interim pricing, *Management Science* (April), pp. 325–43.

Slater, K. and Wootton, C. (1984) *Joint and By Product Costing in the UK*, CIMA Research Studies, London.

Solow, R. M. (1971) Blood and thunder, *Yale Law Review*, no. 80, pp. 1696–711.

Stewart, H. (1992) Rationality and the market for human blood, *Journal of Economic Behaviour and Organisation*, Vol. 19, pp. 125–43.

Titmuss, R. M. (1970) *The Gift Relationship*, Allen & Unwin, London.

Thomas, A. L. (1969) *The Allocation Problem in Financial Accounting Theory*, American Accounting Association, Sarasota, Florida.

Thomas, A. L. (1974) On joint cost allocations, *Cost and Management* (September/October), pp. 14–21.

Thomas, A. L. (1977) *A Behavioural Analysis of Joint Cost Allocation and Transfer Pricing*, International Centre for Research in Accounting, University of Lancaster, Stupes, Champaign, Illinois.

Thomas, A. L. (1978) Arbitrary and incorrigible allocations: a comment, *The Accounting Review* (January), pp. 263–9.

14

Performance Management in the Social Services: Its Meaning and Measurement

SUE LLEWELLYN

INTRODUCTION

The performance of the social services has come under scrutiny across a diversity of perspectives. There have been criticisms emanating from the three Es discourse of the 'new right', challenges from radical community workers on 'empowerment', user dissatisfaction with social work interventions and generalised suspicions of welfare empire-building. But despite the performance of the social services coming under the public gaze, the meaning of performance in this domain and its measurement remain problematic. This chapter explores issues around the meaning and measurement of performance in the social services and argues that the inherent difficulties of performance evaluation in this domain are fostering the use of efficiency rather than effectiveness measures. A focus on efficiency rather than effectiveness is linked with the 'depoliticising' of the social services and this issue is also discussed.

There are two major criticisms of the performance of the social services which derive from discourses on the three Es. First, there is a charge that the social services are failing to use resources economically and, second, they are said to be inefficient in terms of providing an optimal level of services from a given level of resources. The charge of wastefulness is based on evidence, such as that gathered by the Audit Commission (1986), that resources have been directed towards expensive institutional care rather than being deployed towards supporting the lower-cost domiciliary care which clients want. The charge of inefficiency flows from data which demonstrate wide variations in the services provided by different local authorities from similar levels of expenditure (Langan and Clarke, 1994). Such charges, when allied with perceptions that value for money can be secured by 'improving the performance of public sector providers, rather than the mechanisms of public expenditure planning and control' (Beeton, 1988, p. 99), have fostered a powerful 'new right' political rhetoric for the introduction of performance measurement in the social services.

Challenges to social work performance and practice have also been launched from the left of the political spectrum. Doubts have been voiced over the care/control dynamic of social work. Community workers advocate an agenda based on citizens' rights rather than clients' needs and argue for empowerment as the key concept in service delivery. There are also wider public concerns that the social services operate as part of a welfare empire run more to further the interests of the professionals who administer them than to serve the needs of 'consumers'. Such claims are buttressed by media reports which consistently portray the failures rather than the successes of social work interventions. These criticisms, from across the political spectrum, have converged to form a consensus on social work failure. Social services are seen to have produced services which are simultaneously costly, ineffective and disempowering to consumers (Langan and Clarke, 1994). Yet, despite this consensus on low performance, the pursuit of performance 'measures' for social work professionals is fraught with difficulty for the fundamental reasons that, first, the 'outputs' of the social services are not directly determined by professional inputs (hence, in the social services, the concept of 'performance' can never be reduced to that of 'productivity') and, second, the overall objectives of the service are ambiguous and, sometimes, conflicting.

Social service professionals work with people rather than products; therefore the 'outcomes' of their interventions reflect not only the resources deployed by social service departments but also the contributions and characteristics of the clients with whom they work. Thus, in the social services, the processes of 'production' and 'consumption' are interwoven and the user is an inherent part of service production (Stewart and Walsh, 1989). That social work activities reflect the contributions of both the professional and the client renders the exercise of discretion and the management of risk inescapable elements of social work practice.

There are also underlying tensions in the purpose of the social services; social work professionals perform both caring and controlling tasks. Social work clients have needs which are consequent upon various forms of disadvantage and welfare professionals within social service departments work to alleviate the needs which disadvantage produces, rather than directly tackling the causes of that disadvantage. On this interpretation, society as a whole commonly expresses concern about the outcomes of the distribution of resources (e.g. poverty), but apparently prefers to set up services which will diffuse discontent, rather than change the existing pattern of resource distribution (Wilson, 1993). Social workers diffuse discontent through such caring activities as the disbursement of relief to emergency applicants but they have also to a large extent taken control of the lives of many vulnerable sections of society (Perkin, 1989, p. 349). This duality of care/control within social work tasks has created multiple and sometimes conflicting objectives for welfare professionals.

Social service professionals face ambiguity in the purpose of objectives they are working towards (which encompass both care and control) and uncertainty in the processes through which they work (which involve engagements between both the professional and the client). Such ambiguity renders the standards of performance (the overall cost of the service, the amount of service provided, the extent of the use made of it by the public, the quality or effectiveness of the service and its value for money (Stewart and Walsh, 1994)) inherently both politically contested and technically difficult to measure. Moreover, the enhanced role of performance measurement in the field of welfare introduces greater means–end rationalities into this domain and, therefore, has the potential to change the inherent values of the social services. The acceptance of the need for performance measurement in the social services legitimises the concept of quantitative control for welfare and brings the values of financial accountability and personal responsibility to the heart of social service departments. Whether programmatic discourses which express financial and managerial values will induce substantive change in the social service is not yet clear, but there are circumstances surrounding the development of social work professionalism which indicate that such discourses may be more readily taken up in social work than in health and education. In order to explicate the potential permeability of social work to managerialism in general, and accounting performance measures in particular, the tasks of welfare professionals in the social services will now be explored in greater detail. The chapter will then offer critiques on the meaning and measurement of performance in this area.

THE DEVELOPMENT OF SOCIAL WORK PROFESSIONALISM

The origins of social work lie in the attempt by the Charity Organisation Society in late Victorian England to discriminate between the 'deserving' and the 'undeserving' poor. This categorisation was later modified to one which distinguished 'helpable' from 'hopeless' cases. These attempts to categorise were subsequently formalised and a training course for 'case workers' was established at Southwark in 1892, which, when transferred to the new London School of Economics in 1912, formed the foundation for the social work profession. 'Professional social work was [therefore] invented by social workers' (Perkin, 1989, p. 348). Concern that the profession was developed to serve the interests of the providers of the 'service' rather than to meet the needs of vulnerable sections of the community was voiced by Titmuss in 1958 in his classic *Essays on 'The Welfare State'*, where he questioned whether the social services were 'being artificially developed by the professional, administrative and technical interests upon whose skills the services depend' (quoted in Perkin, 1989, p. 344).

The establishment of training in case work marked the beginning of a more scientific model of social work practice. Specialised functions – child care, adoption and fostering, the elderly and the mentally handicapped – gradually emerged and the pursuit of these specialisms was backed by training in three areas: social studies, case work theory and supervised practical experience (Abbott and Wallace, 1990). It was not, however, until the Seebohm Report (1968) led to the creation of social service departments within the local authorities and the British Association of Social Workers was formed in 1970 that social work professionalism clearly advanced (Sibeon, 1990). However, the period since the early 1970s has not been marked by further rationalisation through continuing professionalisation; indeed de-professionalisation themes gained credence during the 1980s as some of the inherent contradictions in social work practice failed to be resolved.

The ambiguity produced by the care/control dynamic inherent in social work practice has generated intellectual critiques within social work's professional knowledge base. Acknowledgement of the 'ideological paradox which stems from the claim to be people-helping and to be providing "therapy" yet being employed by organisations in the interests of creating additional rationality and control' (Esland, 1980a, p. 255) lies at the roots of various critiques of social work such as the 'labelling' perspective (see Becker, 1963, for this perspective on deviant behaviour). The claims of social work professionals to be able to diagnose and treat pathological behaviour rest upon public recognition that they can identify various social 'problems' – social workers are, therefore, 'reality definers' (Esland, 1980a, p. 262) for social pathologies. This power to categorise individuals as problematic (from the perspective of 'normal' social relations) has been criticised as having very negative consequences for those who are so diagnosed (Goffman, 1963). Being 'labelled' as a prostitute or a criminal or accepting the descriptive categories of abusive, damaged or disturbed will result in social stigma and, as Goffman argues, may, through internalisation of the 'labelling', perpetuate rather than attenuate the problematic behaviour. Frequently, however, there are material incentives for clients to take on the professionals' categorisation. As social workers perform a 'gatekeeper' role for access to welfare resources, the acceptance of the assigned label may underlie the 'treatment' which will include material benefits for the client. The professional labelling critique forms part of an internal critical perspective which may inform the practice of the more radical sections of the social work profession and which results in social work being characterised by a fragmented and internally contested knowledge base.

Social work practice is also being questioned by community workers who are outside the profession. Grassroots community-based initiatives have sought to raise public awareness of structural inequalities and to recognise that workers in people-centred occupations may have as much or more to contribute through work experience than from formal qualifications. Rather than employing the care/control dynamic of social work, the approach of many community workers has been to tackle the causes of clients' disadvantage through empowerment. The problematising of the client (as in labelling) shifts focus towards the problematisation of the client's circumstances. This more radical approach holds out the promise of a service which is closer to clients' needs. As a movement, community work represents 'a powerful combination for overcoming professional elitism and challenging inequalities from the bottom up' (Issitt and Woodward, 1992, p. 41). With such an agenda community workers would work directly with clients to tackle the causes of their disadvantage rather than serving their professionally defined 'needs'. Professional social workers have dealt with these threats to their dominance of practice by using both assimilation and exclusion. Whilst there has been informal recognition of community-based knowledge and methods and some assimilation of these into mainstream practices, 'access to training, paid employment and career progress has often been denied without a paper qualification' (ibid.). Community work, with its more holistic approach, continues to pose dilemmas for professional social work and, paradoxically, in view of their left-wing radicalism, the ethos of the market-place may open up more opportunities for vocationally qualified practitioners.

Social work is, therefore, incompletely professionalised; it suffers from internal critiques and the boundaries of professional practice are being breached by vocationally qualified practitioners. These circumstances reinforce the largely negative public perceptions of social work interventions. The psycho-therapeutic case work (which is the hallmark of the professionally qualified social worker) is also frequently not well received by clients in materially disadvantaged circumstances who require practical advice on welfare rights (Rees and Wallace, 1982, quoted in Sibeon, 1990, p. 104). Where social workers act on decisions such as taking a child into care they are 'brokers in lesser evils, frequently faced with the need for choice followed by action whose outcome is unpredictable . . . society is deeply ambivalent about social work . . . and quick to point harshly to its failures, especially those in relation to functions of social control' (Stevenson, 1994, p. 173).

This high level of uncertainty has fostered the traditional public service values of equity, justice, democracy, collective action and client advocacy. Such values, when allied with a lack of technical knowledge to integrate practitioners' differing perceptions of clients' 'problems', have created a social work culture which can easily become 'a breeding group for prolonged debate and discussion, but little activity or decision' (Rogers, 1994, p. 50). Thus, although the traditional values of welfare professionalism are not aligned with the accounting categories (or values) of economy, efficiency, value for money, financial accountability and personal responsibility, the relatively low status of the social services, along with their non-directive culture, offers few barriers to the discourses of accounting and managerialism.

THE MEANING OF PERFORMANCE MEASUREMENT IN THE SOCIAL SERVICES

The construct of 'performance measurement' can operationalise the concept of accountability; this accounts for the political appeal of performance measurement, particularly in the unclear domain of the social services. Accountability has many facets, however, and public accountability, as opposed to the more narrowly defined concept of financial accountability, is integral to the political intent of the public services in Western democracies. As Stewart (1992, p. 35) comments,

A public organization should monitor its own performance, but should also have its performance monitored. The first is necessary for effective management of the organization, but the second is a condition of public accountability. The dilemma of public management is that performance in the public sector is necessarily multi-dimensioned because activities in the public sector reflect not single objectives, but a balance between objectives. This means that there can rarely be simple measures of the impact of a service. Thus it may not be sufficient to know whether a service has met the needs of users: one also has to know whether it has met the public purposes underlying the service, including, for example, the distributional effect.

This view of public accountability and performance monitoring (rather than measurement) reflects the public sector values of democracy, justice, equity and responsiveness to public interests. Of significance also for public accountability is the emphasis within the public sector on the collective interest as well as individual (or user) need. Responsiveness to the public interest involves more than just choice (through 'exit') or even voice (through 'representation'): 'responsiveness' should extend to enabling public discourse 'by sustaining access to the public arena, by supporting learning through openness and by removing barriers to the public' (Stewart, 1992, p. 32).

Public accountability, in this sense, involves political debate in the public arena over whether the 'right' policies are being pursued – a broad definition of accountability which encompasses political judgement. This broad definition of accountability is not easy to translate into measurement terms 'as it assumes assessment of the inputs consumed, the outputs produced, and the impacts associated with those policies pursued against the inputs, outputs and impacts of all those alternative policies which were not' (Lapsley, Llewellyn and Mitchell, 1994, p. 35). Such policy analysis will be wide-ranging. When policy is driven solely by financial considerations, however, 'policy' accountability will equate with financial accountability. These narrower definitions of accountability may be formulated so as to make reference to standards rather than judgements. Stewart (1984) portrays a 'ladder' of accountability which ascends from accountability for probity and legality (the traditional territory for financial accountability) through process, performance and programme accountabilities to the final 'rung' of policy accountability. Standards are possible for probity and legality and also possible (although more problematic) for process and performance accountabilities. Whether 'standards' can be applied to programme accountability (which questions whether policy goals are being met) will depend upon whether standards for policy goals can be agreed upon. Thus the meanings attached to performance measurement in the social services will depend on how broadly (or how narrowly) accountability is being defined. When broad definitions of accountability are used, measurement, as opposed to monitoring, is hardly possible. Only when narrower definitions of accountability are applied can the processes of standardisation and quantification work to produce performance 'measures'.

Narrower definitions of accountability will exclude debate on the policy objectives of the social services. Such debate has always been integral to the role of local government – as a political institution – and the exclusion of accountability for policy will effectively disempower social service agencies. The distancing of the social services from policy formation effectively depoliticises their role and, arguably, this is integral to the government's intent. The Deputy

Director of the Citizens' Charter Unit said: 'Long-term success in improving public services depends in my view in maintaining impetus over a long period; this means "de-politicising" it' (Goldsworthy, 1992, p. 1, quoted in Pollitt, 1994). As Pollitt (1994, p. 11) points out, 'de-politicisation' can be construed as 'detachment from adversarial party politics' or as 'the emptying of public service delivery from all political content'. It is also possible that the pursuit of the latter may be carried out in the name of the former. The 'de-politicisation' of the local authorities then masks the centralisation of political decisions along with the devolution of responsibility for their implementation. Political issues are thereby removed from the provider/client interface and open political debate is stifled.[1] Governmental reform of local government through the creation of quangos has contributed to the depoliticising of their role by transferring out many policy decisions from the local authorities. The transfer of responsibilities for policy formation to quangos (and quangocrats) has fostered 'concentrations of power that are not accountable to the electorate and a huge increase in central government patronage' (*The Economist*, 1994, p. 19). Where public discourse on policy is marginalised the values of the social services remain unexpressed – for it is through policy decisions that public sector values are revealed. Yet debate on values and striking a balance between differing values in policy formation has been integral to the tasks of various departments within the local authorities. The operationalisation of performance measurement, as opposed to performance monitoring, will, therefore, exclude examination of one of the most important functions of the social services as political institutions – the constitution and the expression of the values of society.

THE MEASUREMENT OF PERFORMANCE IN THE SOCIAL SERVICES

Before performance can be measured it must first be standardised – for only homogeneous categories of things can be counted and compared. 'Once rationalisation has standardised and tamed the social meaning of the components of activity – actors, objects and action – accounting become easier' (Meyer, 1994, p. 124). It can be seen from the preceding section that this standardisation actually involves not just the 'components of activity' but the social meaning of the theoretical concepts which inform this activity. Only when the meaning of 'public accountability' has also been 'standardised and tamed' to that of 'financial accountability' rather than 'policy accountability' can performance measurement (as opposed to performance monitoring or policy analysis) be carried out.

The primary organisational task, before performance measurement can be accomplished, is one of bringing costs and 'outputs' into alignment. Dunleavy and Hood (1994, p. 9) express this in the following terms: 'Reworking budgets to be transparent in accounting terms, with costs attributed to outputs not inputs, and outputs measured by quantitative performance indicators.' Such a juxtaposition (re)presents the social services as an economic system which transforms inputs into outputs, heightening the relevance of both costs and financial (or distributive) effects, and creating causal chains between inputs, activities and consequences, thereby ensuring that events happen in a sequence rather than being disconnected in time/space. If this (re)presentation is achieved the productive capacity (or efficiency) of this realigned system can then be captured by accounting measures. The matching of inputs and outputs (or costs and activities) is, however, problematic: before inputs and outputs can be compared they must first be identified and standardised.

The standardisation of activities involves the definition of 'outputs' (and, also, possibly 'outcomes') in the social services. The simplest category of 'output' in the social services is the 'referred client'. Thus counting the numbers of 'counselled' or 'treated' social work clients constitutes a crude output (or throughput) measure. Alternatively, 'referred clients' could simply be viewed as a measure of activity (on the assumption that 'outputs' should make reference to the services offered or the benefits accrued – see the discussion below). Counting clients as outputs, although advantageous in terms of simplicity, will immediately raise some objections (even absurdities) from the perspective of social work practice. Clients differ greatly in the demands they make on social work time – hence the client/session (where the 'session' is also a standardised time period) must be substituted for 'clients' as an output measure. However, this measure remains inadequate: first, it does not reflect the complexity and difficulty of the client's problems – those clients whose circumstances are particularly grave will usually require more time – not just in terms of counselling but in order to provide practical help involving interactions with other agencies (health, housing, welfare rights, and so on). Second, the measure does not take account of the effectiveness of social work practice – hence if numbers of client/sessions per social worker were used as an output measure those social workers whose counselling was ineffective (to the extent that clients were constantly referred back) would be more efficient than those whose clients were more effectively helped. The first difficulty (over the differing levels of complexity in clients' presenting problems) can be addressed by the construction of a client 'typology'. Such a client typology could take a number of different forms but, basically, it would acknowledge that clients present with problems of differing severity and complexity – hence they consume differing amounts of professional time and, therefore, will be varied in terms of their demands on resources. The second issue (over the measurement of the effectiveness of social work practice) is more difficult to deal with and involves more complex measurement problems.

Measures of social work effectiveness could either be built around assessing the quality of the service provided to clients or, more ambitiously, measure the impact (or outcomes) of professional social work. Quality of service outputs when compared to costs could produce cost/quality ratios. Quality of service analyses have broken down the concept of 'quality' into component parts, e.g. the service characteristics, the physical environment, personal relationships and customer power (Skelcher, 1992). Such analyses, however, demonstrate the difficulty of integrating measures of these dimensions into a single 'quality of service score'. Can a single measurement scale capture the quality of staff–client interactions and the quality of the service surroundings? If the pursuit of single performance quality measures is accepted as unrealistic then the evaluation of performance must acknowledge the multidimensional nature of social work practice. An alternative to relating costs to quality of service would be to relate costs to activities. Thus social care 'products' such as 'care plans' or 'home visits' could be costed (Llewellyn, 1993). Social work 'products' do not, however, encompass the nature of social work interventions, which critically depend on interpersonal client/professional relationships. The links between 'products' and outcomes are also tenuous and scientific processes for tracing them through (as in treatment and results for medical interventions) are lacking.

Measuring the outcomes of social work interventions may take the form of, first, assessments of 'value or benefit' (Henderson-Stewart, 1988) or 'value-added' (Glennester, 1994) or, second, surveys of user satisfaction. The impact or outcomes of social work interventions reflect not only the quality of service processes (or outputs) but are inextricably linked to the contributions and char-acteristics of clients. 'Hard to serve' clients might be expected to have worse outcomes than more 'amenable' ones. The diversity among clients was discussed earlier when it was argued that such diversity necessitated the use of some form of client typology (if client/sessions were to be used as activity or output measures). This same difficulty, when considering outcomes, involves capturing the 'value-added' to the client. But the measurement of 'value-added', although frequently advocated, has not been tackled by its proponents (Midwinter, 1994). Although politically appealing and, hence, useful in terms of aspirations for government agencies, it seems destined to permanent failure as a practical proposition. Even if 'the measurement of value' is attempted it can be argued that the exercise is conceptually confused, as the notion of 'value' will have different meanings to different people at different times.

Surveys or interviews to assess client satisfaction can also serve as outcome measures but such measures will reflect both perceptions of service quality and individual client histories, experiences and expectations. That the balance of power between professional and client is weighted towards the professional may render clients reluctant to voice in public those negative opinions which they may recount in private (Wilson, 1993). This reluctance to criticise will be ampli-fied where professionals act as gatekeepers to resources. On the other hand, where the power wielded by social workers has resulted in actions such as the removal of a child from the family the anger engendered by such decisions may result in unduly negative opinions of social work interventions. Such circum-stances make the authenticity of public accounts of client satisfaction somewhat dubious and their interpretation problematic.

Any 'global' measures such as the increase/reduction in the occurrence of social pathologies are difficult to trace back to social work interventions. As social workers tackle symptoms, rather than causes, it can be argued that social work effectiveness is unlikely to have a major impact on a global measure such as the rise and fall in crime rates. For the domestic problems (e.g. child abuse) which are the special preserve of social work there is the added difficulty that any measured impact tends to circularity as social workers themselves function as 'reality-definers' in the construction of such social problems.

Recognition of the complexity and difficulty of performance measurement in areas such as the social services has fostered a number of responses. First, there has been the response that, although complex and difficult, performance assessment should be attempted albeit that 'performance indicators' (acting as 'alarm bells') are probably more descriptive of what is possible than are 'performance measures'. This perspective is illustrated by Jackson (1988, p. 15):

> Performance management presents a number of challenges. There are difficulties in defining performance in the public sector . . . [but]. . . enhanced efficiency and improvements in performance across a wide range of dimensions (economy, efficiency and effectiveness) are undoubtedly the substance of accountable management. Performance indicators are a means of assisting responsible management to make efficient and effective decisions.

Second, and in opposition to this view, is the idea that performance measurement in this area is basically flawed and should be abandoned or redefined. Midwinter (1994, p. 41, original emphasis) comments on performance indicators in the local authorities:

> The notion that authorities' performance can be reduced to a few simple, quantifiable indicators which can provide the basis for comparison of organisational efficiency, is fallacious . . . the data generated in the public domain should be reclassified as simply *local government statistics*. The application of the term 'performance indicator' is not justifiable given the current state of the art.

The third response involves recognition that performance measurement in the public domain necessarily involves value judgements and, hence, 'The assessment of performance will shift as political debate develops. Fully satisfactory measures of performance are unlikely ever to be discovered. There is a need to recognise the imperfections and limitations of measures, and to use them as a means of supporting politically informed judgement' (Stewart and Walsh, 1994, p. 45). This view emphasises that different performance measures will reflect differing value systems (e.g. professional, economic, democratic and legal).

These responses to the inherent difficulties of performance measurement in this domain, although varied in terms of their conclusions, share a basic assumption – that 'performance measurement', as an organisational construct, is to be discussed and evaluated in terms of how well it measures performance. The next section explores this assumption.

DISCUSSION AND CONCLUSIONS

Where the norm of participative governance operates, the interests of multiple constituencies are given recognition and outputs elude measurement; hence organisational performance will be construed broadly (Meyer and Zucker, 1989, p. 111). As argued above, the advent of financial performance measures has fostered narrower definitions of accountability, has contributed to the depoliticisation of the social services and had led to a focus on efficiency rather than effectiveness. The permeability of the social services towards efficiency-driven performance measurement is likely to be greater than in, for example, health, where clinicians are more able to capture performance measurement systems through setting their own criteria for effectiveness (by reference to medically credentialled standards for the outcomes of interventions). In social work there are no scientific evaluations of 'treatments' and therefore there are no publicly validated bases for building professionally defined effectiveness measures. Where professionally defined effectiveness criteria are lacking efficiency measures are much more likely to dominate.

Using Weber's categorisation the distinction between effectiveness and efficiency mirrors 'substantive' and 'formal' rationalities where 'substantive rationality represents the degree to which provisioning is shaped under some criterion of values . . . [and formal rationality represents the] . . . extent of quantitative calculation or accounting which is technically possible and which is actually applied' (Eisen, 1978, p. 64, quoted in Colignon and Covaleski, 1991, p. 146). The substantive rationality of performance measurement would be assessed in terms of how far its introduction had enhanced particular values (e.g. the equity of social work practice) whereas its formal rationality would be measured in terms of the feasibility and actual application of accounting techniques. The substantive rationality of accounting cannot exist without its formal rationality (Jones, 1992) as the values of accounting trade upon the adequate operationalisation (however defined) of its techniques. That substantive rationalities are considered alongside formal rationalities is crucial to the evaluation of performance measurement – yet this distinction is frequently collapsed. When substantive rationalities are ignored the assumption is that the organisation merely serves societal ends and that organisational output meets these ends in an unproblematic way (Colignon and Covaleski, 1991). Accounting then comes in as a technical artifact which, through aligning outputs and inputs, may improve their relationship and thus enhance efficiency.

As the distinction between formal and substantive rationalities is frequently collapsed the assumption of the merely formal rationality of accounting is both persuasive and prevalent. 'Indeed the functionality of public sector accounting may not be because it is a technical fix but because it offers a way of making moral choices indirectly' (Chua and Degeling, 1993, p. 312). As this chapter has argued, the introduction of performance measurement has allowed the concept of accountability to be narrowed from policy accountability to financial accountability – the substitution of one for the other is a moral choice. Yet the making of this choice has been obscured by a focus on the instrumentality of performance measures – the intervention of a technical system such as performance measurement did not directly challenge the values of equity, collective action and citizenship but, nevertheless, such values are being supplanted by those associated with performance management: targeting, personal responsibility and consumerism. Such incursions have seen the overarching managerial value of efficiency becoming 'culturally prized for its own sake, as an end in itself, as something in which we trust' (Clegg, 1990, p. 155). That these moral choices are being made indirectly negates public debate on the issues involved and diminishes resistance to the changes. It is not only that, as Stewart (1992) argues, different performance measures will be promoted by different political interests; the construct of performance measurement, when enacted, expresses and promotes particular values.

In its expression of values performance measurement provides a particular way for organisational members to understand their capacities to do their jobs and their contributions both to their clients and to wider society. Social workers have traditionally understood their occupational capabilities through the concept of competence. Such competence has comprised both a paper qualification and demonstrations of adequate practice (Issitt and Woodward, 1992). Yet, as the earlier discussion on the role of the social services brought out, professional social work is permeated with uncertainty on many different levels. Although training programmes are recognised and accredited no clearly bounded technical knowledge base exists. The effectiveness of social work interventions is difficult to establish both because client characteristics and contributions effect outcomes (hence impacts are not solely dependent upon professional inputs) and because social workers deal largely in the amelioration of symptoms and the prevention of crises rather than in treatments which effect results. Competence, under these circumstances, becomes simultaneously a flexible concept and one that is easily challenged. As argued earlier, challenges to social work competence have been mounted across a broad spectrum of political opinion from the 'new right' discourses around the three Es to the leftist community action critique emphasising empowerment rather than the care/control dynamic. Such discourses and critiques threaten the already fragile status of social work professionals, who find it more difficult to lay claim to 'sacred agendas' than do the health and educational elites. Under these circumstances (and despite the loss of professsional discretion and status involved) it might be anticipated that welfare professionals will move further towards the bureaucratic means of legitimating their activities and place less reliance on professional codes of conduct. Such shifts may indicate that managerial and financial discourses (or programmatic statements on the rational administration of activities) will encounter less resistance in the social services than they have met in the more powerfully defended realms of health and education. The impact of increased managerialism on social work practice may be, as has already been observed in the probation service, to emphasise the social control dimension (Stevenson, 1994). Allied with enhanced social control may be fragmentation (through the exit from the profession of disillusioned case workers) and ultimately a disintegration of the social services as presently constituted, such as has been seen in the USA (Schorr, 1992). Thus the assessment of the performance measurement construct in the social services, whilst linked to issues of operationalisation, should be judged in much wider terms – through encompassing an evaluation of the impact of performance measurement on the aims, processes and practices of professional social work.

Acknowledgement

The author acknowledges the constructive comments made on an earlier version of this chapter by David Cooper, Chris Humphrey, Bob Scapens and Stephen Walker. The chapter has been much improved as a result of their helpful remarks.

Notes

1.   I am indebted to Professor Robert Scapens for this particular interpretation of 'de-politicisation'.

References

Abbott, P. and Wallace, C. (1990) Social work and nursing: a history, in P. Abbott and C. Wallace (eds.), *The Sociology of the Caring Professions*, Falmer Press, London.

Audit Commission (1986) *Making a Reality of Community Care*, HMSO, London.

Becker, H. (1963) *Outsiders: Studies in the Sociology of Deviance*, Free Press, New York.

Beeton, D. (1988) Performance measurement: the state of the art, *Public Money and Management* (Spring/Summer), pp. 99–103.

Chua, W. F. and Degeling, P. (1993) Interrogating an accounting-based intervention on three axes: instrumental, moral and aesthetic, *Accounting, Organizations and Society*, Vol. 18, no. 4, pp. 291–318.

Clegg, S. R. (1990) *Modern Organizations: Organization Studies in the Post Modern World*, Sage, London.

Colignon, R. and Covaleski, M. (1991) A Weberian framework in the study of accounting, *Accounting, Organizations and Society*, Vol. 16, no. 2, pp. 141–57.

Dunleavy, P. and Hood, C. (1994) From old public administration to new public management, *Public Money and Management* (July/September), pp. 9–16.

The Economist (1994) Questions about quangos (6–12 August), pp. 19–21.

Eisen, A. (1978) The meanings of confusions of Weberian rationality, *The British Journal of Sociology*, Vol. 29, no. 1, pp. 57–69.

Esland, G. (1980) Diagnosis and therapy, in G. Esland and G. Salaman (eds.), *The Politics of Work and Occupations*, Open University Press, Milton Keynes.

Glennester, H. (1994) New challenge for management accounting: issues in health and social services, *Financial Accountability and Management*, Vol. 10, no. 2, pp. 131–41.

Goffman, E. (1963) *Stigma*, Penguin, Harmondsworth.

Goldsworthy, D. (1992) Talk to the 'Hanrahans Group', South Yorkshire Police Service. Text of speech, 4 March.

Henderson-Stewart, D. (1988) Performance measurement and review in local government, in M. Cave, M. Kogan and R. Smith (eds.), *Output and Performance Measurement in Government*, Jessica Kingsley, London.

Issitt, M. and Woodward, M. (1992) Competence and contradiction, in P. Carter, T. Jeffs and M. K. Smith (eds.), *Changing Social Work and Welfare*, Open University Press, Buckingham.

Jackson, P. (1988) The management of performance in the public sector, *Public Money and Management* (Winter), pp. 11–15.

Jones, T. C. (1992) Understanding management accountants: the rationality of social action, *Critical Perspectives on Accounting*, Vol. 3, pp. 225–57.

Langan, M. and Clarke, J. (1994) Managing in the mixed economy of care, in J. Clarke, A. Cochrane and E. McLaughlin (eds.), *Managing Social Policy*, Sage, London.

Lapsley, I., Llewellyn, S. and Mitchell, F. (1994) *Cost Management in the Public Sector*, Longman, London.

Llewellyn, S. (1993) Linking costs with quality in health and social care: new challenges for management accounting, *Financial Accountability and Management*, Vol. 9, no. 3, pp. 177–94.

Meyer, J. W. (1994) Social environments and organisational accounting, in W. R. Scott and J. W. Meyer (eds.), *Institutional Environments and Organisations*, Sage, London.

Meyer, M. W. and Zucker, L. G. (1989) *Permanently Failing Organizations*, Sage, London.

Midwinter, A. (1994) Developing performance indicators for local government: the Scottish experience, *Public Money and Management* (April–June), pp. 37–43.

Perkin, H. (1989) *The Rise of Professional Society: England since 1880*, Routledge, London.

Pollitt, C. (1994) The Citizens' Charter: a preliminary analysis, *Public Money and Management* (April–June), pp. 9–14.

Rees, S. and Wallace, A. (1982) *Verdicts on Social Work*, Edward Arnold, London.

Rogers, S. (1994) *Performance Management in Local Government*, Longman/Local Government Management Board, London.

Schorr, A. (1992) *The Personal Social Services: An Outside View*, Joseph Rowntree Foundation, York.

Seebolm, Lord F. (1968) Cmnd. 3703, *Committee on Local Authority and Allied Personal Services Report*, HMSO, London.

Sibeon, R. (1990) Social work knowledge, social actors and de-professionalization, in P. Abbott and C. Wallace (eds.), *The Sociology of the Caring Professions*, Falmer Press, London.

Skelcher, C. (1992) *Managing for Service Quality*, Managing Local Government Series, Longman, Harlow.

Stevenson, O. (1994) Social work in the 1990s: empowerment – fact or fiction?, in R. Page and J. Baldock (eds.), *Social Policy Review 6*, Social Policy Association, Canterbury.

Stewart, J. D. (1984) The role of information in public accountability, in A. Hopwood and C. Tomkins (eds.), *Issues in Public Sector Accounting*, Philip Allan, Oxford.

Stewart J. (1992) Guidelines for public service management: lessons not to be learnt from the private sector, in P. Carter, T. Jeffs and M. K. Smith (eds.), *Changing Social Work and Welfare*, Open University Press, Buckingham.

Stewart, J. and Walsh, K. (1989) *The Search for Quality*, Longman/Local Government Management Board, Essex.

Stewart, J. and Walsh, K. (1994) Performance measurement: when performance can never be finally defined, *Public Money and Management* (April–June), pp. 45–9.

Wilson, G. (1993) Uses and providers: different perspectives on community care services, *Journal of Social Policy*, Vol. 22, no. 4, pp. 507–26.

15

Accounting for the Performance of Scottish Bus Companies, 1978–1993

GEORGE HARTE

INTRODUCTION

During the 1980s the widespread commercialisation of the public sector in Britain included the deregulation of bus services (under the Transport Act 1985). This resulted in a significant reduction in the powers of the industry regulators, the Traffic Commissioners, changing their role from one of arbitrating on prices to monitoring competition. The commercialisation of the public sector is seen to have increased the role for economic calculation in the general management of corporate affairs, with greater emphasis on traditional accounting information (Hopwood, 1986). In addition, the three principles of efficiency, effectiveness and economy (overall value for money) have become increasingly important (Thomson, 1992), with performance indicators being seen as an important aspect of the value for money (VFM) idea (Midwinter, 1994).

This chapter examines the external reporting of the major Scottish bus companies over the period from 1979 to 1993. Previous research (Harte, 1993) suggested that the deregulation of the industry and the new role of the Traffic Commissioners may have brought about changes in reporting by a large Scottish bus company. It appeared that deregulation, and the resultant threat of competition, had led to a reduction in the scope of reporting of performance. However, given the case study emphasis of that study it remained to be seen whether such change was widespread.

The chapter begins with brief description of recent changes in the Scottish bus industry, before considering the changing nature of the contribution of accounting information, particularly in regulation. This is followed by a discussion of the traditional accounting model of external reporting, before we turn our attention to the external reporting practices of the major Scottish bus companies. By means of content analysis, we examine the annual reports and accounts of these companies for the 1979–93 period. The justification for this focus is the view that annual reports and accounts can be seen to be the most significant regular, external, publicly available statement of corporate performance. Although firms can and do use alternative means of communication, annual reports and accounts are seen as a regular opportunity for management to comment on an organisation's performance. Although reporting is influenced by legislation and professional accounting pronouncements, these are in fact a minimum and managers are free to report on other matters as they see fit. Annual reports and accounts have the potential to have real consequences, in setting an agenda for debate of the performance and impact of corporations, and by their focus (some would say particularly in their exclusions) have the opportunity to affect definitions of (economic and social) reality. They can 'down play, reinterpret and reconstruct a history of social and economic events' (Tinker and Neimark, 1988, p. 59). This is not to suggest that accounting reports are the sole contribution to the creation of reality; rather, that they may influence our view of reality while at the same time trying to reflect it.

THE SCOTTISH BUS INDUSTRY

Privatisation and deregulation have been major planks of economic policy of recent Conservative governments. Such policies have stressed the economic over the social, further emphasised the importance of economic calculation (Hopwood, 1986), and so perhaps not surprisingly have intensified the focus on accounting numbers and accountants as the providers of solutions to our economic and social problems. This is reflected not only in the increasing managerialism of the public sector (with its accompanying discourse) but also in the introduction of market mechanisms where privatisation of ownership is not an acceptable solution.

The original impetus for regulation of the bus industry, eventually resulting in the Road Traffic Act 1930, appears to have arisen from concerns with safety (particularly because of the use of surplus ex-army lorries after the First World War) (Savage, 1985). However, an important consequence of this regulation was consolidation of the industry (Bagwell, 1974). The fierce competition between rival bus companies using war surplus vehicles before 1930 resulted in a high accident rate caused by poor driving and maintenance of vehicles (Mulley, 1983, referred to in Savage, 1985). Bagwell (1974) refers to London County Council's problem with 'pirate' bus operators in 1922. The 1930 Act resulted in quality control (with the introduction of driver and vehicle licensing, though not operator licensing) and quantity control by route licensing (including registration of route, timetable and fare scale with the newly created regional Traffic Commissioners) (White, 1988). As a consequence, the entrance of new operators to the market was controlled. Traffic Commissioners (TCs) were appointed to cover a particular geographical area, and were expected to make decisions in the interests of their community, often leading to sanctioned cross-subsidisation of services (Button, 1988). Cut-throat competition, fare-cutting wars and the racing of vehicles was ended (Sleeman, 1953).

Following the 1930 Act a consolidation of the industry took place, with surviving operators offered greater security of tenure (Sleeman, 1953). In some cases long-standing agreements were reached with local authorities (e.g.

SMT and Edinburgh Corporation), where the agreement signed in 1920 lasted until 1954, enabling the company to offer a monopoly service in the city, with a levy per bus mile being paid to the Corporation (Hunter, 1987)).

However, like many other areas of the public sector the industry was affected by the monetarist, privatising and deregulating policies of the Thatcher government which came to power in 1979. Concern with growing subsidies (Hibbs (1991) and Hart (1984) refer to the rise in revenue support grant in Britain as a whole, from £10 million in 1972 to £520 million in 1982) and cross-subsidisation in an attempt to maintain levels of service as demand fell appears to have left the industry vulnerable. Ideologically the Thatcher government was opposed to the public interest theory of regulation which had dominated in the sector since 1930 (Gwilliam, 1989), although it has also been suggested that a preoccupation with reducing public spending was an important reason for the deregulation and subsequent privatisation (Hart, 1984). Thus one of the first actions of the 1979 Thatcher government was the deregulation of coach services (by the Transport Act 1980). Although this did not in itself mean increased competition but, rather, new quality controls and safety standards, and the removal of quantity controls for all scheduled services, the monopoly strength of the Scottish Bus Group and the National Bus Company ensured that further legislation privatising these companies followed. The subsequent deregulation of buses in 1985 saw a great deal of controversy and debate, in contrast to the acceptance of regulation in 1930 (Hibbs, 1991).

The Transport Act 1985 abolished road service licences (replacing them with registration of services with the TC), non-commercial services were to be put out to competitive tender by local authorities, and TCs no longer had any influence over levels of fares charged by operators. This was to be left to the market. Instead the TCs were now to try to ensure that maintenance and health and safety standards were met in the industry, accept registration of services, deal with complaints concerning particular services, and in general try to uphold competition in the bus industry.

The 1985 Act was intended, according to the White Paper, to increase consumer choice, increase supply, reduce fares, eliminate cross-subsidisation, expose subsidies, reduce government revenue support, maintain safety, encourage innovation and maintain services in areas of social need (Farrington and Mackay, 1987). It attempted to do so by a mixture of deregulation, competitive tendering (for subsidised services), privatisation and reduction of government subsidy (Gwilliam, 1990).

The consequences of the Act, however, are less clear. For example, there are difficulties in identifying any change in performance due to the legislation because of the long-run decline in bus use. Although cost savings of 31% have been calculated, due largely to increased productivity (19%) and wage reductions (7.5%), with the remainder due to fuel costs (3%) and savings from deferred investment (2%) (Heseltine and Silcock, 1990), one author has suggested that it will not be clear what the impact has been until the industry settles down (after some consolidation of operators), when we might better estimate the impact of the power of the new private monopoly suppliers (Evans, 1990). The continued expansion of several of the largest operators in Scotland through takeovers, particularly Strathclyde Buses, Stagecoach and GRT, suggests that we have not yet reached that period of stability.

In addition, controversies surrounding the privatisation continue, with the 'cheap' disposal of assets, the removal of £150 million from the Scottish Bus Group (SBG) pension fund and the more recent bonus payment to former directors of SBG for the loss of private health insurance. Although these may be thought to have relatively little to do with accounting, the 'cheap' disposal in particular has raised questions concerning creative accounting, the undervaluation of assets and the understatement of profits, and has clear implications for measurement of subsequent performance.

ACCOUNTING INFORMATION AND THE BUS INDUSTRY

Prior to the 1985 Act it appears that a great deal of accounting information was collected by the TCs in order to assess the reasonableness of proposed fare increases (Harte, 1993). Accountants were involved as expert witnesses in deliberations on fares, and on some occasions when matters went to a public inquiry. Prior to the 1985 Act, however, there was no requirement for bus companies to supply the TCs regularly with reports on their performance. Whether TCs consulted data at the Companies Registry is not known.

Since the introduction of the 1985 Act it appears that the main reporting of accounting information to the TCs arises when applicants for new routes must satisfy the need to be of 'appropriate financial standing . . . having available sufficient financial resources to ensure the establishment and proper administration of the business carried on or proposed' (Transport Act 1985). Financial standing requires a banker's or accountant's reference (the guidance notes issued by the TCs). The Department of Transport's application for public service vehicle operator's licence (PSV 421) requests evidence of financial standing in the form of audited accounts, or a statement of income and expenditure or a bank reference (although this is not necessary for applicants who held a PSV operator's licence before 1 January 1978). In a letter intended for general circulation to applicants, from one TC's office, it is suggested that bank statements or a corroborative statement of assets and liabilities may suffice.

Although the TCs are now concerned largely with issues related to competition, and other matters such as service reliability, maintenance and safety (bus companies may have the renewal of their licence refused due to maintenance problems – for example see *Bus Business*, 20 April 1988 and 9 March 1991), rather than price, it appears that they may connect the financial performance of bus companies to their non-financial performance, by using information on non-financial issues such as maintenance and safety as a basis for investigating the financial affairs of a bus company and vice versa (Harte, 1993) (see, for example, the case of Amberley Travel, an English company, in *Bus Business*, 9 March 1991). However, Harte's study revealed no evidence of systematic collection of accounting data, other than concerning applications.

Despite the indications that prior to the 1985 Act the TCs did not systematically collect annual reports and accounts, and that subsequently there was even less need to do so, previous research suggested the possibility that the Act may well have affected the nature of external reporting (Harte, 1993). This study revealed a narrowing of focus in reporting after 1985, where a few years earlier the undertaking involved in the study had reported financial information and various non-financial statistical details of performance in its accounts and statistics. The 1990 annual report and accounts were typical of the financial statements produced by large private companies, with sections on company information (e.g. bankers and auditors), directors' report, profit and loss account, balance sheet, fund statement, accounting policies, notes to the accounts and auditors' report (the only point of note was the company's use of replacement cost accounting for public service vehicles, a common practice in the industry at the time). In contrast, the 1981 accounts and statistics detail the membership of the transportation committee of the local authority, management, income and expenditure (including figures expressed per mile), the balance sheet (with public service vehicles at depreciated historical cost), analysis of income, analysis of expenditure, capital account items, season ticket sales, tickets sold data, traffic revenue and passenger analysis, passengers carried and mileage run (including graphs), statistics (including population served and route mileage), ratios (26, including passengers per bus mile, staff per bus, variable cost per mile), staffing, passenger and mileage statistics per route and bus fleet. Yet there are no details of accounting policies, no 'directors'' report and no auditor's report. In general what is revealed is a wider accounting of the performance of the bus company. Although not covering matters such as environmental impact, energy consumption, customer satisfaction, exploitation and alienation, such reporting indicates an apparent concern with more than simply the financial performance of the company.

Although governed by legislation and professional accounting regulation, as well as the stock market where relevant, annual reports and accounts offer the scope for managerial selection in reporting. Of particular interest is the extent to which managers focus on certain issues and not others, and so contribute to (and reflect) thinking in society (setting the agenda). For example, research by Tinker and Neimark (1988, p. 59) on the struggle over meaning in accounting research 'rejects the view of annual reports, either as neutral reflection of reality, or a downright falsification intended to manipulate a passive audience'. Tinker and Neimark attempt to 'delineate the active part that reports play in social conflict, by showing how these documents may down play, reinterpret and reconstruct a history of social and economic events' (ibid.). Clearly, this concern is not only with what is reported and how, but also with what is excluded. In addition, White (1988) suggests that disclosure of information by bus companies after deregulation has declined despite the development of managerial information, although he concludes that this is not surprising in a competitive market.

PERFORMANCE MEASUREMENT

Before turning our attention to the content of the annual reports and accounts of the bus companies, we should consider the general question of performance measurement and in particular the role of traditional accounting reports. Although accounting discourse draws on the ideas of neo-classical economics, there are substantial differences between the neo-classical economist's definition of profit and the accountant's (e.g. Whittington, 1984, who refers, among other things, to the difference in terms of the backward-looking accountant and the forward-looking economist). The influence of neo-classical economics should not be directly equated with accounting practice but, rather, seen as a dominant influence, which leads to a focus in accounting on objective market transactions expressed in financial terms (the money measurement concept) and restricted largely to those transactions and events which have an impact on the organisation's bank balance (the entity concept). Accounting practice appears to be constrained by 'an overarching metaphor encouraging a numerical view of reality' (Morgan, 1988, p. 480), though only some financial numbers enter the equation. Such numerical views are seen as objective, rather than as an interpretation of a complex reality which relies for its focus on what accounting is able to measure and chooses to measure (Morgan, 1988).

Traditional accounting is also often criticised for its subjectivity and flexibility, particularly in cost allocation (e.g. Thomas, 1969; Griffiths, 1986), its failure to reflect changing prices (Myddleton, 1984) or be based on an acceptable capital maintenance concept (Baxter, 1975), and its related failure to reflect future consequences in full (McMonnies, 1988). There are also many unresolved debates, e.g. regarding intangible assets such as brands and goodwill (Accounting Standards Board, 1993).

Yet accounting information, in its selective portrayal of performance, appears to play an important part in the functioning of society, perhaps as a result of it apparent simplicity, often involving a bottom-line or single-figure answer (Miller, 1992). Accounting information is also associated with characteristics of objectivity, verifiability and independence, and is expressed in a manner that is financial, consistent with the language of the profit system. Yet this pretension to objectivity and precision is challenged by Hines's (1991) account of the impasse which was reached with the attempted development of a conceptual framework (CF), in particular of the Financial Accounting Standards Board's (FASB) last Statement of Financial Accounting Concept (SFAC) 5 on recognition and valuation. Whereas the FASB's CF project originally set out to identify and prescribe the nature and purpose of external reporting, SFAC 5 fails to select a single value system to be used in external reporting. While the FASB's project assumes that financial accounting can reflect economic reality, and that economic reality exists independently of accounting, Hines shows how CFs tend, in the last resort, to appear to the informed reader (e.g. the investment analyst) when exploring the desirable characteristics of accounting information, and that ultimately, despite the lengthy discussions of desirable characteristics, the form of financial accounting is more likely to be determined by such users' views and appeals to professional judgement.

Thus accounting, as a social construction and a representation of economic reality and a basis for performance measurement, can be seen to contribute to the setting of the agenda, not only for regulation but also for wide debate and discussion of economic and social policy. The real power of accounting may be its ability to exclude, rather than its decision-making potential, since once you define something as 'real/the truth' it can have real consequences (Handel, 1982, quoted in Hines, 1989, p. 56). In this respect traditional financial accounting reports can be said to be partial, favouring the interests of owners of capital rather than other interest groups (Cooper and Sherer, 1984). The focus of traditional financial accounting reports on the financial performance (rather than the impact) of the reporting entity (its revenues and expenses, its assets and liabilities) precludes reporting on the wider impact, and gives priority to a particular view of what constitutes performance. Thus in the case of profit-maximising firms accounting reports on performance provide us with details such as turnover, costs, profits and assets, but not much detail of the wider economic (including financial), social and environmental impact and performance. Thus while Morgan (1988) suggests that accountants create partial and one-sided accounts of the world, financial accounting can also be seen as not merely a passive representation of reality but an agent in changing or perpetuating reality (Tinker, 1985). In our case there would seem to be the potential for accounting to reflect the new-found status of the bus undertakings and companies, as well as to contribute to debates surrounding their performance.

In contrast to the traditional model, there have been numerous attempts to develop a social accounting of entity performance, or accountings which are not based solely on the money-measurement concept, and are not restricted to traditional accounting's entity concept (see Gray, Owen and Maunders (1987) for an excellent review of literature and practice). Most recently, contemporary concerns with the environmental impact of business appear to be relevant here (see Owen, 1992, and Gray, Bebbington and Walters, 1993). Transport, in general, and buses as an example, is a matter of great concern to both industry and the public, and can be seen to raise various economic, social and environmental issues which are unlikely to be reflected by traditional accounting reports. In the case of the bus industry recent concerns have included the financial and environmental consequences of traffic congestion, energy consumption, the performance of old fleets compared to new 'green' buses, and wider social questions of access for disabled and disadvantaged people and women (particularly regarding design of buses and night travel), as well as a range of employment issues raised after privatisation. Although these additional matters rarely enter the debates concerning the nature of accounting and its attempts to report on performance or capture economic reality, there seems little doubt that to particular groups in society matters such as safety, quality, employment impact and environmental impact are as much a part of reality as is the performance portrayed by financial accounting. Certainly if we take the view that transport is, or instance, of central importance to people's lives, that everyone depends on public transport, and that travellers 'live with it, they love it, they hate it' (Campbell, 1989, p. 17) then these broader concerns could inform our discussion of the reporting of performance.

RESEARCH CONDUCTED

Using the annual *Road Passenger Transport Directory* (the *Little Red Book*), the development of the major Scottish municipal bus undertakings and the companies comprising the Scottish Bus Group was traced from 1979 to date. Table 15.1 lists the companies as included in the 1993/94 edition, with details of previous names, date of incorporation and years for which the annual report and accounts could be obtained. (The major Scottish companies in the period can be seen to belong to two groups, one the municipal bus companies of

Table 15.1   *Bus companies*

Company	Date of incorporation	Reports reviewed
The municipal companies		
Strathclyde Buses (formerly Greater		
Glasgow PTE and Strathclyde PTE)	13/2/86	1986, 1988–93
Grampian Regional Transport	20/2/86	1986, 1988–93
Lothian Region Transport	17/1/86	1987–93
Tayside Public Transport	28/2/86	1987–93
The former SBG companies		
Fife Scottish Omnibuses		
(W. Alexander and Sons Fife)	26/2/48	1979–93
Midland Bluebird (W. Alexander and		
Sons Midland, Midland Scottish		
Omnibuses)	3/8/42	1979–93
Bluebird Buses (W. Alexander and		
Sons Northern, Northern Scottish		
Omnibuses, Bluebird Northern)	3/4/36	1979–93
KCB (Central SMT, Central Scottish		
Omnibuses, Kelvin Central Buses)	23/6/26	1979–93
Highland Scottish Omnibuses		
(Highland Omnibuses)	8/4/30	1979–93
Eastern Scottish Omnibuses		
(Scottish Omnibuses)	4/4/49	1979–93
SMT Omnibuses	18/12/89	1989–93
Western Scottish Buses (Western SMT,		
Western Scottish Omnibuses)	24/9/13	1979–93
Clydeside 2000	15/11/90	1991–93
Western Engineering		
(Clydeside Scottish Omnibuses)	1/3/85	1985–93
Kelvin Scottish Omnibuses	1/3/85	1985–93
Lowland Omnibuses		
(Lowland Scottish Omnibuses)	1/3/85	1985–93
Strathtay Scottish Omnibuses	1/3/85	1985–93

Glasgow, Edinburgh, Aberdeen and Dundee, and the second, across-country and rural operations, formerly comprising much of the Scottish Bus Group at the beginning of the period.)

The first approach to obtain the annual reports and accounts was made to the Scottish Transport Group, parent company of the SBG. This proved fruitless, with the response received indicating that the reports had been disposed of following the privatisation of the SBG subsidiaries. Next, a standard letter was sent to the company secretary of each company listed, requesting copies of the past accounts. The response to this request was almost as poor. No company could supply the accounts for the full period. Most did not reply, and in the case of some which did they could offer only the current and previous years'. In the circumstances, following the issue of a reminder letter and further poor response, it was necessary to consult the relevant company files at Companies House. As a result, particularly in the case of the municipal undertakings, this meant that accounts were not available for the period before company forma-tion (prior to 1986 these bus operations were effectively local council depart-ments). This was particularly disappointing as the interesting case study report discussed in Harte (1993) had been seen in a municipal organisation.

The annual reports and accounts were obtained on microfiche from the Register of Companies, and analysed by a form of content analysis. Content analysis is a research technique which allows systematic investigation and eval-uation of the content of recorded communications (Kolbe and Burnett, 1991). Analysis can be conducted at various levels, for example of individual words or sentences. In this case analysis has been conducted at a more general level, largely in terms of sections of the annual report and accounts (e.g. the directors' report, the notes to the accounts, etc.). At this stage of the study content analysis was used to explore the reporting practices of the bus companies, rather than to test any specific hypothesis. Although it is essentially a counting exercise (Barratt, 1990) it should be seen less for its precision and apparent objectivity (Berelson, 1952) than – as in this case – an empirical starting point to generate new research evidence. Clearly its categories are theory-dependent, and rely on subjective clas-sification, and so to that extent lack objectivity.

Although in excess of 2,415 pages of 171 annual reports and accounts for the 17 companies were reviewed, the findings are disappointing. Throughout the period virtually all of the annual reports and accounts comprise the following structure:

Directors' report
Auditors' report
Profit and loss account
Balance sheet
Source and application of funds statement (with a cash flow statement in later
    years following the introduction of FRS 1)
Notes to the accounts

Such will be seen by most readers as following the standard approach of corpo-rate reporting. The main variations saw the inclusion of a chairman's statement (usually in the municipal company reports if at all, and less in later years), with more recent developments following legal and professional pronouncements, such as in respect of the statement on directors' responsibilities, reconciliation of the movement in shareholders' funds and a statement of the total recognised gains and losses. Other occasional disclosures included details of officers and professional advisers.

Probably the most interesting additional statement was that contained in the earlier years' reports of three SBG companies. In the annual report and accounts of Central SMT (1979–81), Highland Omnibuses (1979–81) and Scottish Omnibuses (1979–84 and 1986–7) a more detailed profit and loss account was presented, with greater detail of expenses in particular. However, in short, there was no evidence of the sort of reporting revealed in the 1981 account and statistics described in Harte (1993), and commented on above.

DISCUSSION

Whilst the findings presented above may not be entirely surprising, particularly given the limited information available on the municipal companies, the increasingly competitive environment, the fact that the companies could all be seen as subsidiaries of one kind or another up to 1986 and the need to use the reports filed with the Registrar of Companies, the results do suggest that annual reports and accounts are, and have been throughout the period, viewed as documents which comply with requirements. Despite the period of public ownership, by local authority control or public corporation, there is little evidence of variation in reporting throughout the period, other than due to the influence of the law and professional accounting pronouncements.

Clearly, a more detailed study may be more revealing, particularly of the few chairman's statements and reviews of business operations contained in the director's reports (these normally ran to only a few lines). However, *prima facie*, it appears that neither contain anything in the way of performance-related data – rather, a more general discussion of business performance and plans – or about the wider economic environment.

Yet despite these limited findings there are numerous suggestions of relevant performance indicators in the literature. For example, Dodgson and Topham (1988) specify indicators which are said to be often used in the industry, including distance per unit cost, vehicle hours per employee and distance per peak vehicle, although Henscher (1988) is critical of such indicators for their failure fully to explain productivity changes. This absence may be explained by the use of performance indicators in internal management rather than for external reporting. In the circumstances, with increased sensitivity to competition and takeover, it may be that there is little incentive to report to external parties on matters such as productivity. In the final section we take up the question of developing performance indicators for the bus sector, with particular emphasis on their use in external reporting.

CONCLUDING COMMENTS

Although this research study specifically set out to report on examples of any wider corporate reporting of performance, including the use of performance indicators, it did not do so with the intention of accepting such disclosure in an uncritical manner. Much of what has been levelled at traditional accounting can as easily be applied to performance measurement in general (particularly the apparent objectivity). As a consequence the proposals of Mackie and Nash (1982), albeit produced at a time when the sector was largely in the public sector, are not without fault. In their critique of the work of the Monopolies and Mergers Commission they suggest that performance indicators for the bus industry can be developed, but should be related to corporate objectives, be unambiguous, adequately distinguish between what a firm can and cannot control, and must be related to overall performance. In their critique of the Commission's primary, secondary and tertiary measures of social and commercial efficiency they discuss measurement difficulties, question the meaning of proposed indicators and are concerned with external influences over others. They are particularly critical of comparisons made between undertakings with different backgrounds. Yet, as Stewart and Walsh (1994) suggest, performance indicators are not likely to be complete in themselves, measures can be disputed, and indicators seen in isolation will fail to capture interactions. Stewart and Walsh also draw our attention to the problems of use, appearing to parallel Lukes's (1981) theory of underdeterminism, namely that the same 'facts' can be used to support different theories. Clearly, the choice of appropriate indicators is not a simple technical matter, and will involve political judgement.

Whilst the focus in the literature may continue to be on the measurement of performance for managerial purpose and capital markets, it does appear that a case can be made for a fuller accounting of the performance of the privatised bus companies. Although recent economic and social change has emphasised the efficient and effective use of resources, some would say to the neglect of alternative perspectives on the economy and a neglect of public accountability, in the case of buses this has been accentuated by the replacement of public monopolies with what are increasingly appearing to be private equivalents. That this has resulted in benefits to the taxpayer and shareholders in the privatised bus companies at the expense of labour does not seem to be in dispute (e.g. Smith, 1989).

In addition, the central importance of public transport to the mass of the population is not matched by collective rights over the use of resources and policy-making in general (Campbell, 1989). This study also reveals similarly limited forms of accountability. Morgan (1988) suggests that accountants need to be sensitive to the many dimensions of the realities which they are attempting to account for. In the case of the Scottish bus industry we have seen a consistently narrow focus in the reporting of performance during a period where most companies began as part of the public sector, but proceeded to become private firms during it. The indication of a wide variety of financial and non-financial reporting revealed in an earlier study (Harte, 1993) has not been confirmed here. It may well be the case that such reporting is contained in the annual reports and accounts which could not be obtained, and may in fact be the very reason for non-response.

References

Accounting Standards Board (1993) *Goodwill and Intangible Assets*. Discussion Paper, ASB, London.

Bagwell, P. (1974; 1988 reprint) *The Transport Revolution*, Routledge, London.

Barratt, D. (1990) *Media Sociology*, Routledge, London.

Baxter, W. T.(1975) *Accounting Values and Inflation*, McGraw-Hill, Maidenhead.

Berelson, B. (1952) *Content Analysis in Communication Research*, Free Press, Glencoe, Ill.

Button, K. (1988) Contestability in the UK bus industry, experience goods and economies of experience, in Dodgson and Topham (1988).

Campbell, B. (1989) Summer of discontent, *Marxism Today* (August), pp. 16–17.

Cooper, D. and Sherer, M. (1984) The value of corporate accounting reports: arguments for a political economy of accounting, *Accounting Organizations and Society*, Vol. 9, no. 3/4, pp. 207–32.

Dodgson, J. S. and Topham, N. (eds.) (1988) *Bus Deregulation and Privatisation*, Gower, Aldershot.

Evans, A. (1990) Competition and the structure of local bus markets, *Journal of Transport Economics and Policy*, Vol. 24, no. 3, pp. 255–82.

Farrington, J. and Mackay, T. (1987) Bus deregulation in Scotland – a review of the first six months, *Fraser of Allander Quarterly Economic Commentary* (August), pp. 64–70.

Gray, R., with Bebbington J. and Walters, D. (1993) *Accounting for the Environment*, Paul Chapman, London.

Gray, R., Owen, D. and Maunders, K. (1987) *Corporate Social Reporting*, Prentice-Hall, London.

Griffiths, I. (1986) *Creative Accounting*, Unwin Hyman, London.

Gwilliam, K. (1989) Setting the market free: deregulation of the bus industry, *Journal of Transport Economics and Policy*, Vol. 23, no. 1, pp. 29–43.

Gwilliam, K. (1990) Bus deregulation, *Journal of Transport Economics and Policy* (editorial), Vol. 24, no. 3, pp. 237–8.

Handel, W. (1982) *Ethnomethodology: How People Make Sense*, Prentice-Hall, Englewood Cliffs, NJ.

Hart, T. (1984) Scottish bus services and the 'buses' White Paper, *Fraser of Allander Quarterly Economic Commentary* (August), pp. 77–81.

Harte, G. (1993) Regulators' need for quality information and the provision of bus services in Scotland, in R. Sugden (ed.), *Industrial Economic Regulation*, Routledge, London.

Henscher, D. (1988) Productivity in privately owned and operated bus firms in Australia, in Dodgson and Topham (1988).

Heseltine, P. and Silcock, D. (1990) The effects of bus deregulation on costs, *Journal of Transport Economics and Policy*, Vol. 24, no. 3, pp. 239–54.

Hibbs, J. (1991) Tendered bus services, *Public Money and Management* (Spring), pp. 57–9.

Hines, R. (1989) The sociopolitical paradigm in financial accounting research, *Accounting, Auditing and Accountability Journal*, Vol. 2, no. 1, pp. 52–76.

Hines, R. (1991) The FASB's conceptual framework, financial accounting and the maintenance of the social world, *Accounting, Organizations and Society*, Vol. 16, no. 4, pp. 313–31.

Hopwood, A. (1986) Economics and the regime of the calculative, in S. Boddington, M. George and J. Michaelson (eds.), *Developing the Socially Useful Economy*, Macmillan, London.

Hunter, D. (1987) *From SMT to Eastern Scottish*, John Donald, Edinburgh.

Kolbe, R. and Burnett, M. (1991) Content analysis research: an examination of applications with directives for improving research reliability and objectivity, *Journal of Consumer Research*, Vol. 18, no. 2, pp. 243–50.

Lukes, S. (1981) Fact and theory in the social sciences, in D. Potter (ed.), *Society and the Social Sciences*, Routledge and Kegan Paul, London.

Mackie, P. and Nash, C. (1982) Efficiency and performance indicators: the case of the bus industry, *Public Money* (December), pp. 41–4.

McMonnies, P. (1988) *Making Corporate Reports Valuable*, ICAS/Kogan Page, London.

Midwinter, A. (1994) Developing performance indicators for local government: the Scottish experience, *Public Money and Management* (April–June), pp. 37–43.

Miller, P. (1992) Accounting and objectivity: the invention of calculating selves and calculable spaces, *Annals of Scholarship*, Vol. 9, pp. 1–21.

Morgan, G. (1988) Accounting as reality construction: towards a new epistemology for accounting practice, *Accounting, Organizations and Society*, Vol. 13, no. 5, pp. 477–85.

Mulley, C. (1983) The background to bus regulation in the 1930 Road Traffic Act: economics, politics and personalities in the 1920s, *Journal of Transport History*, Vol. 4, no. 2, pp. 1–19.

Myddleton, D. (1984) *On a Cloth Untrue*, Woodhead Faulkner, Cambridge.

Nash, C. (1985) Competition on an urban bus route – a comment, *Journal of Transport Economics and Policy*, Vol. 19, no. 3, pp. 313–16.

Owen, D. (ed.) (1992) *Green Reporting: Accountancy and the Challenge of the Nineties*, Chapman and Hall, London.

Road Passenger Transport Directory (various years) Ian Allan, Addlestone.

Savage, I. (1985) *The Deregulation of Bus Services*, Gower, Aldershot.

Sleeman, J. (1953) *British Public Utilities*, Pitman, London.

Smith, T. (1989) A US-eye view of bus deregulation, *Public Finance and Accountancy* (5 May), p. 12.

Stewart, J. and Walsh, K. (1994) Performance measurement: when performance can never be finally defined, *Public Money and Management* (April–June), pp. 45–9.

Thomas, A. (1969) *The Allocation Problem in Financial Accounting Theory*, American Accounting Association, Sarasota, Florida.

Thomson, P. (1992) Public sector management in a period of radical change: 1979–1992, *Public Money and Management* (July–September), pp. 33–41.

Tinker, T. (1985) *Paper Prophets: A Social Critique of Accounting*, Holt, Rinehart and Winston, Eastbourne.

Tinker, T. and Neimark, M. (1988) The struggle over meaning in accounting and corporate reporting: a comparative evaluation of conservative and critical historiography, *Accounting, Auditing and Accountability Journal*, Vol. 1, no. 1, pp. 55–74.

White, P. R. (1988) British experience with deregulation of local bus services, in Dodgson and Topham (1988).

Whittington, G. (1984) Accounting and economics, in B. Carsberg and T. Hope (eds.), *Current Issues in Accounting* (2nd edn), Philip Allan, Deddington.

16

The Rise and Fall of Value for Money Auditing

MARY BOWERMAN

INTRODUCTION

It has been claimed that value for money (VFM) auditing has been with us since the fifth century BC (Dewar, 1989). However, it has become widespread only during the last two decades. Normanton (1966, p. 103) argued that VFM auditing was a response to 'big government' in the twentieth century; and that it 'make[s] a growing contribution to the development of public administration and government as a whole – a contribution which no other organ of the state could possibly make'. But just when VFM auditing has firmly established itself in the public sector, the world it inhabits has changed and the need for and the role of VFM auditing are in dispute. Power (1994) suggests two extremes of the need for audit in general: on the one hand it can be argued that audit is a central part of the 'reinvention of government'; on the other, VFM audit can appear intrusive and out of step with a culture where managers are encouraged to be responsible for their own performance. Power asks (1994, p. 1) 'whether audits . . . in fact fuel the problems which they address by, for example, exacerbating distrust' and he cites the National Audit Office and its 'intensive scrutiny' as one aspect of the audit explosion.

Part of the confusion lies in the fact that the objectives, methodology and audit standards for VFM auditing vary between and within the audit bodies, and there are further differences between different client groups and national contexts. Looking back over the last few decades, it is possible to identify different approaches to VFM auditing and to some extent to match these to certain sets of circumstances. This review suggests an evolution of VFM audit from a 'hands-on' approach where auditors confronted managers and public with examples of waste and inefficiency to a more refined form where by the VFM ethos has empowered managers and the auditors are consigned to their familiar role of checking management's account of VFM achievements.

THE ORIGINS OF VALUE FOR MONEY AUDITING

Normanton (1966, p. 104) writes 'In England, it is doubtful whether the idea of an audit going beyond consideration of regularity was ever even considered in the early days of parliamentary control of accounts.' He gives an interesting insight into some of the early VFM auditing in the UK. One example, from an 1887 audit report, involved the purchase of ribbon for army medals for 20 shillings when it could have been purchased from another supplier for 14 shillings. This case pushed the boundary of auditing beyond regularity. The military department initially refused to reply to the report, thus provoking a landmark declaration from the Committee of Public Accounts (PAC): 'If in the course of his audit, the C&AG becomes aware of facts which appear to him to indicate an improper expenditure or waste of public money it is his duty to call the attention of parliament to this' (ibid., p. 105).

Despite occasional investigations of this type, audit remained mainly of the regularity variety until the late 1940s when the growth in expenditure following the Second World War was matched by a similar extension of the volume and range of VFM reports. Pallot (1991) associates the increased emphasis on VFM auditing with increasing concerns about government expenditure in the 1960s and 1970s which caused government auditors to take a wider perspective and to reorientate the audit approach towards 'comprehensive' or 'integrated' audits.

In England and Wales the statutory authority to conduct VFM studies was granted in 1982 for local government and 1983 for central government. The main public sector external auditors in Britain are the National Audit Office, the Audit Commission for England and Wales and the Accounts Commission for Scotland. VFM audits are also undertaken by the internal audit function (which is statutory for most UK public sector organisations) and also by management as part of its performance review function; however, there is little doubt that the external audit bodies have been the main catalyst. This chapter is confined to a consideration of external audit.

DEFINITION OF VALUE FOR MONEY AUDITING

There is no general agreement on what the term value for money audit actually means. INTOSAI's notion of an 'expanded scope' audit introduces the concept of auditing management activities: 'There is another type of audit which is oriented towards performance, effectiveness, economy and efficiency of public administration. This audit includes not only specific aspects of management, but comprehensive management activities, including organisation and administrative systems' (INTOSAI, 1977).

In the USA the General Accounting Office (GAO, 1988, para. 2.8) audit standards take this a step further and discuss performance auditing as including 'the extent to which desired results or benefits . . . are being achieved

. . . whether the objectives of a proposed, new or ongoing programme are proper, suitable or relevant'.

It is generally acknowledged that, as a minimum, VFM audit includes an examination of economy, efficiency and effectiveness. Sharkansky (1991, p. 2) discusses the different labels given to the activity (e.g. the three Es, value for money, operational auditing, effectiveness auditing, performance auditing, programme results auditing) and comments that 'While some may emphasise the nuances that distinguish these labels and what they signify, their communality lies in their concern with judging the quality of governmental activities as opposed to the auditor's classic concern with financial records.' The term 'value for money' will, therefore, be used in this chapter as a convenient expression and embracing VFM in its widest possible sense – include everything from economy to policy.

When the definition of VFM audit is so broad-based and difficult to pin down it is unsurprising that different audit bodies in different countries use a variety of approaches to audit VFM. In discussing VFM audit it may be helpful to distinguish between these different approaches. It is possible to identify six different types.

(1) *Review of management systems, arrangements and procedures* – auditor identifies poor value for money, makes recommendations for improvement and gives advice on management arrangements to improve value for money.
(2) *The value for money procedures audit* – auditor checks that an organisation has established objectives, and has a system for measuring performance and for ensuring that objectives have been achieved.
(3) *Policy audit* – auditor assesses whether a policy or programme has been effective as well as economical and efficient.
(4) *Audit of management representations of value for money* – auditor verifies information prepared by management on the achievement of value for money.
(5) *Comparative performance audit* – auditor compiles a database to compare cost/performance between similar organisations, and identifies and recommends best practice to improve value for money.
(6) *Quality audit* – auditor uses customer satisfaction surveys to evaluate successful performance; may also verify management's quality assurance information.

This list is not intended to be exhaustive nor does it imply that the auditor must select just one approach. Different types of audit may be selected for different projects and an individual audit may even feature aspects of several approaches. With the possible exception of 'comparative audit', the different approaches can be seen as representing the evolutionary development of VFM auditing. It would seem that the involvement of the auditor has an interactive effect with management systems and that as these systems improved the auditor has been able to move on to the next, possibly more efficient, audit approach.

The main determining features which influence the approach selected for a particular project include:

(1) the extent to which the auditor may question policy;
(2) the extent to which an issue is policy-sensitive;
(3) how much management information is available.

Review of management systems, arrangements and procedures

There are two possible stages of this approach, the first being to identify examples of bad VFM and the second to examine if management arrangements are adequate to secure good VFM.

In the first stage an individual study which brings to light examples of waste and inefficiency, usually within a fairly narrow area of management activity such as property, control of capital projects, purchasing, stores and energy conservation, or particular services within a department which are intended to lead to savings or improvements in the areas studied. This was the style of most 'early' VFM audits and remains a good standby for impact and media attention. The approach to such work is typified by advice from Butt and Plamer (1985) and Price Waterhouse (1990). Normanton (1966) gives many examples of this type of audit and the NAO issues a number of reports of this style each year. For example, it was suggested that the Ministry of Defence could save £7 million on unused or redundant telephone lines (NAO, 1994a). NAO (1988, p. 7) defines this type of audit as 'selective investigations of signs of possible serious waste, extravagance, inefficiency, ineffectiveness or weaknesses in control'.

The approach is sometimes extended into the second stage: to include an examination of the arrangements or systems which would normally be expected to be present in order to secure VFM. During the 1980s audit organisations began to undertake this type of audit to provide assurance and without necessarily uncovering a particular problem. This approach shares features of a (financial) internal controls review. The auditors may review planning and budgeting systems, decision-making processes, stores procurement, maintenance of buildings and regulations for planning, tendering, etc. This type of audit is typified by what NAO describes as 'good housekeeping', which means 'Major reviews of standard managerial operations which tend to follow common patterns or procedures or established good practice' (NAO, 1988, p. 7). The approach is also used in Canada: for example, the Auditor General found (1992, p. 61) that the Department of National Health and Welfare's policy and procedures 'do not ensure that disability benefits are paid only to those who continue to be eligible due to severe and prolonged disability'. The Audit Commission also takes this approach to some of its work, and has produced a series of reports on 'management arrangements' in local authorities, e.g. the preparedness of authorities for change such as compulsory competitive tendering (AC, 1988) and the role of the chief executive (AC, 1989a).

It is arguable that this type of audit has largely fulfilled its purpose; that, over the years, the advice given, and the embarrassment caused by adverse audit reports, have served to encourage management to puts its own house in order. As management assumes responsibility for their organisation's performance, this type of audit is likely to be seen as intrusive and as second-guessing management. The auditors themselves may appear guilty of ineffectiveness. NAO's (1993b, 1993c) reports on the Gulf War drew criticisms of lack of understanding of the difficulties facing the army in a war situation. The prospect of a Public Accounts Committee hearing exacerbates the problem; the VFM process can come to be seen as providing ammunition for the auditor and as a damage-limitation exercise by the audited body, rather than being a genuine search for improved VFM. The approach has also been accused of causing managers to view VFM audit as an adversarial process rather than something which requires mutual respect and co-operation. The auditors' reluctance to let go of this area may be due to their viewing the 'holding to account' as an important aspect of VFM audit. And if they do not uncover waste which later comes to light they could be accused of not doing their job properly. Studies of waste inefficiency do, however, hit the headlines and are a way in which audit bodies can demonstrate their success. This dilemma between VFM helping to improve management and VFM being used to hold managers accountable is discussed later in the chapter.

The value for money procedures audit

Again, there are potentially two stages to this approach. The first concentrates on the way the department measures its own VFM, the second extends the audit examination to arrive at a judgement as to whether or not VFM has been achieved.

This approach to VFM auditing may be seen a a response to the absence of reliable and meaningful performance data on public bodies (Brown, Gallagher and Williams, 1991, p. 189). This is at the heart of the NAO's approach to its 'major broad based investigations of a whole audited body, activity, project or programme investigating implementation and results' (NAO, 1988, p. 7). The approach is 'to examine how well . . . systems and controls operate, and whether they provide management with the necessary information to monitor performance satisfactorily . . . [and to] assess, against predetermined criteria, whether VFM is being achieved . . . [and to] make recommendations for improvements and to work with the body to improve financial control and VFM' (NAO, 1991a, p. 5). Many NAO reports are of this style, for example questioning the effectiveness of cervical and breast screening (NAO, 1992a) by reference to established objectives and systems for measuring performance. A review of sickness absence at the Inland Revenue (NAO, 1993a) found that although appropriate management arrangements were in place it was 'difficult to judge their impact on productivity and sickness absence levels' as there was no mechanism to monitor the outcome of these activities. The Auditor General of Canada (1992, p. 25) also takes this approach, for example to address the question: 'Is the government making progress in environmental protection?' He concludes (ibid.):

> The government and its partners will have to continue to work at developing indicators against which progress can be measured . . . there are gaps in environmental data . . . it is sometimes difficult to define acceptable standards of environmental quality . . . There must be complete, clear, concise, honest and accurate reporting of results against proposed targets, if Canadians are to be able to judge the success or failure of efforts to protect the environment.

The emphasis of such studies is to check that management has established such systems; to provide assurance, not necessarily to highlight waste.

An extension of the role (the second stage) is for the auditor to evaluate whether or not VFM has been achieved. This depends partly on whether objectives have been defined and whether the data are available. In some cases, studies do reveal that waste or loss has occurred, e.g. underpricing the electricity companies when they were privatised may have resulted in the taxpayer losing as much as £600 million (NAO, 1992b). If adequate management arrangements and procedures for measuring VFM were in place, however, the report implies that there is no blame to be apportioned, only lessons to be learnt.

The willingness of the auditor to judge achievement of VFM also depends on the political sensitivity of the potential conclusions: for example, neither the National Audit Office nor the Audit Commission has undertaken an investigation of the success of the internal market in the NHS despite many requests to do so. In general the auditors tend to stop short of giving an opinion on the overall ineffectiveness of a programme in these types of study.

This approach to VFM has its origins in systems theory and programme planning and budgeting systems (PPBS) and consequently shares similar problems. As Berggren (1981, p. 228) comments: 'The chief difficulty is that parliament and the government do not and cannot be expected to provide such specific and clear cut goals . . . the auditors often lack an unequivocal frame of reference for their own examination.' The approach can run into difficulty if politicians do not set clear policy objectives and in the real world there may not always be a neat, rational and systematic statement of objective for every area. Auditors who press for such a statement to be provided may be accused of interfering in policy and they may be tempted to confine their investigation to clear-cut cases where the facts speak for themselves rather than seeking to establish a link between ministerial policy objectives and results. Furthermore, in the contract culture it may appear outmoded to place emphasis on procedures, systems and central guidance rather than on the results achieved. Under new public management, responsibility for results lies down the line with management not up the line with politicians.

Policy audit

A policy audit questions whether a policy or programme has been effective as well as economical and efficient. The extent to which the auditor can question policy is the most fraught issue in VFM auditing. In most countries policy is the responsibility of elected representatives and the legislature and, while the auditors can examine how policy has been implemented, they may not question the merits of policy. Radford (1991, p. 929) contends that this is 'a distinction without a difference, for to comment on the outcome of a particular policy can be tantamount to passing an opinion on the merits of the policy itself'. Therefore there is as yet no distinguishable approach to the audit of policy, but there is increasing evidence that auditors are involved in the questioning and even in the creation of policy.

Geist (1991, p. 105) sums up the auditor's dilemma: 'on the one hand it is still unthinkable that state audit concern itself with matters of war and peace, or the fundamentals of the social and economic policy of a state – except in a marginal way . . . On the other hand it is becoming just as unthinkable that state audit concern itself, at a point historically removed, with matters that were never very important.'

Geist (ibid.) goes on to distinguish between 'Policy with a big P and policy with a small p. Policy with a big 'P' is grand policy, national policy which without a doubt continues to remain outside the purview of state audit', but small 'p' policy also involves important and sensitive activities and the auditors do need to be concerned with these. He contends that public life is concerned with policy decisions and their implementation mostly at a lower level such as where, how and when to allocate scarce resources.

Sharkansky (1991, p. 75) suggests that auditors are content to operate within these restrictions and to push the boundaries when it suits them. In his words: 'Auditors want an objective-sounding excuse to leave certain hot potatoes on someone else's plate.' Sharkansky suggests that on occasions the auditor goes beyond examining policy and becomes a policy-maker, citing the Israeli Comptroller of Audit's criticism of the government for not enacting certain policies and for not pursuing policies with sufficient vigour. The Auditor General of Canada has occasionally been quite closely involved in policy issues; in his 1992 report (p. 28) he reprimands the government for a three-year delay in implementing staffing policies: 'legislative change is needed and is long overdue – the status quo is unacceptable'.

In the UK the Audit Commission has on occasion criticised central govern-ment – for its lack of progress on community care (AC, 1986a) – and described government support for urban regeneration as 'a patchwork quilt of complexity and idiosyncracy' (AC, 1989b, p. 3) and expressed the view that there were serious drawbacks to the [community] charge in terms of economy, efficiency and effectiveness (AC, 1991a).[1] Radford (1991) contends that the Audit Commission has used its position to influence the way in which local government develops. In the case of Westminster City Council, the District Auditor (appointed by the Audit Commission) went beyond merely questioning policy and actually declared the council's housing policy 'illegal': 'My provisional view is that the council was engaged in gerrymandering, which I am minded to find is a disgraceful and improper purpose' (Magill, 1994, p. 7).

The NAO also has influenced policy through its studies. For example, its 1993 annual report (NAO, 1993d, p. 12) states: '[a] report on support for lone parent families noted that the number of lone parents receiving benefit had increased while the numbers receiving maintenance payments from liable relatives has fallen'. We are told that the Secretary of State subsequently announced new measures which included the establishment of the controversial Child Support Agency. The NAO came much closer to policy issues in its report on the Pergau dam (NAO, 1993e). The report acknowledges that it is not for the National Audit Office to question the merits of the policy decision and so does not explicitly criticise the decision to fund the project (White, Harden and Donnelly, 1994); nevertheless, the report did open up the issue – which led to a legal challenge and a subsequent ruling that ministers had knowingly breached the terms of the 1980 Overseas Development Act.

The occasional foray into the territory of 'policy' appears to be welcomed by the public and media. This can cause disappointment when the same approach is not followed on other issues tackled by the auditors (e.g. *Guardian*, 1994). The issue of the auditor's remit regarding policy is unlikely to be clarified through legislation but could usefully be tested more frequently by engaging in studies which confront questions of whether a particular policy has (or even will) result in VFM for the taxpayer. To ignore such questions reduces considerably the value of the audit.

Audit of management representations of value for money

The approaches described above are unfamiliar territory to the traditional financial auditor, the topics are more diffuse, the methodology is less clear and the final result more complex to interpret. The emphasis which new public management places on results rather than the systems by which results are achieved may have created a demand for the auditor to focus on those results as presented in the audited body's annual report. As reporting has improved Pallot (1991, p. 224) contends that the balance of work of government auditors can now shift 'from reporting on a wide range of unspecified issues to giving opinions on the integrity of information presented in department reports'.

Canada was one of the first countries to involve the auditor in evaluating the procedures established by auditees to measure and report on the effectiveness of their programmes. The Canadian Comprehensive Auditing Foundation (1987) recommended the audit of 'management representations'; that is, the information provided by managements to their governing bodies to demonstrate their accountability. The Foundation explains (1987, p. 67): 'The concept of management representations supported by audit opinions is already established for reporting and auditing financial information through periodic financial statements . . . [it] provides an opportunity for managers to explain effectiveness in a context that they and their governing bodies agree is appropriate.'

A type of management representation audit has also been in place in New Zealand since 1989 (Dalton, 1993). Statements of objectives and service performance are included in the annual report; these measure actual outputs and compare them with outputs agreed at the start of the year. The information is intended to enable the public to learn whether organisations have provided outputs agreed to at the beginning of the year. The New Zealand Audit Office suggests that measures should include quantity, quality, timeliness, location and cost. Initially, virtually all the authorities received qualified audits (Pallot, 1992), typically because many objectives and goals adopted were not readily measurable; however, some 'good' performance indicators were developed (e.g. to inspect 600 properties and investigate 70% of faults within a specified time scale, performance being reported against this target and giving an explanation for low success rates).

In 1988 legislation was passed in Sweden requiring government agencies to submit output and performance data in support of their annual budget requests. Such data are subject to audit by the National Audit Bureau. Agencies are required to present results of activity broken down by operational area and to set measurable goals (Swedish Ministry of Finance, 1995). The Swedish performance audit involves:

(1) critical evaluation of source of disclosure;
(2) computational verification;
(3) evaluation of methods for data collection;
(4) checking whether any essential disclosures have been omitted;
(5) an analytical review of income trends;
(6) review of cost accounting systems;
(7) review of quality assurance systems;
(8) evaluation of the reasonableness of management's conclusions;
(9) for the whole performance report looking to see whether:
    (a) it is relevant;
    (b) it reconciles with stipulated requirements;
    (c) it is possible to judge whether the activity has been conducted effectively.

In the UK in 1992 the Audit Commission was given the responsibility to specify performance indicators for local government and to publish comparative information. Significantly, the Commission must also specify information to be reported; this inevitably makes the indicators less sensitive to local circumstances and implicitly involves the auditor in deciding what constitutes 'good' performance (Bowerman, 1995). The local authority auditors are required to certify the information as genuine by examining the reliability of the systems used for collecting the data.

While audit of management representations of performance appears to be a cost-efficient approach to effectiveness auditing there are several inherent difficulties in reporting performance in this way. The first question is whether it can capture all aspects of performance. This is difficult to achieve because concepts of quality can be defined from different perspectives and because complex activities cannot usually be measured solely in terms of final performance, and may have to be supplemented by organisational and process-related criteria in order to obtain some indication of quality.

The second reservation concerns whether this type of audit provides useful information. For example, in the Swedish case (Swedish Ministry of Finance, 1995, p. 22) a 'clear' opinion states: 'the National Audit Office cannot for reasons of principle apply the expression "true and fair" to the performance report. However, the disclosures provided in X's performance report do not conflict with any conditions known to the National Audit Office.'

A qualified opinion may be of more use both as an indication of and a deterrent to inadequate performance and reporting. Overall, the management representations approach is based on the premise that the information will be used by Parliament and the public. There is, however, very little evidence that annual reports are read or used for decision-making so, ironically, the approach may make the results of VFM audit less visible. If taken to its logical conclusion it could return audit to a type of 'tick and check' function. VFM reports which report directly on an organisation's performance, for all their limitations, have enjoyed a much higher reputation than private sector audit reports.

Comparative performance audit

This approach involves the auditor in compiling a database to compare cost/performance between similar organisations. It can be used to assist the auditor in the selection of organisations or topics for investigation, to identify and recommend best practice to improve VFM and to monitor the success of the audit firms.

A main feature of the Audit Commission's work at local and national level is its use of comparative statistical data which provide a quantitative framework for inter-authority comparisons of performance. The Commission explains (1991b, p. 12) that

> the distinctive feature of all this [VFM] work is that it is based on well informed comparisons between one authority and another, and on comparisons between local performance and best practice. Locally, the aim is to adapt the lessons to the circumstances of each individual local authority. The approach is based on advice and persuasion, since auditors have no power in the VFM area to impose their views. They must work with the grain of local management.

The approach has been utilised by the Commission since it was first formed and, according to Henkel (1991), originated in part from comments in the 1976 Layfield Report, which drew attention to the need for comparative studies to promote economy, efficiency and effectiveness. The work was initially undertaken by the Local Government Management Services and Computer Committee (LAMSAC) but the auditors were instrumental in obtaining co-operation with the scheme and in using the information to assist them in their work. The approach exhibits some features of 'benchmarking' such as 'best in class' authorities and benchmark clubs in the form of data and quality exchanges. The Commission collects information on all major council and health service activities and their demographic background. This attempts to bring together all publicly available information on clients' unit costs, levels of service, staff numbers and demographic circumstances. The Commission has estimated that the task involves collecting and collating some 300,000 statistics from 30 different sources.[2] The central elements are statistical profiles for each council, comparing unit cost and levels of provision with the average for similar councils ('family group'), and highlighting areas which might be worth examining in more detail. (AC, undated.) The Commission has encouraged authorities to undertake their own performance review and has provided benchmark performance statistics supported by papers on setting up performance review mechanisms. The establishment of a quality exchange by the Audit Commission broadens performance review to include service quality and to describe quality assurance and control techniques. The Commission undertakes and publishes a number of comparative national VFM reviews each year for both health and local government, known as 'special studies'. These consist of detailed investigations of a number of authorities and seek to identify good management practice.

The Audit Commission has been instrumental in causing change in the way local government and, latterly, the NHS use their resources. It uses the comparative approach to identify best practice, which forms the basis of its recommendations to all authorities; for example a report (AC, 1993b) showed that £15 million could be saved if hospitals mended leaking pipes and used water more efficiently. A report on education for over-16-year-olds (AC, 1993c) proposed a model which could reduce the number of A-level failures and save up to £500 million per year. The Audit Commission also uses its database to monitor success of audit firms in different regions in identifying VFM opportunities. Radford (1991, p. 928) reports that between 1983 and 1989 the Audit Commission claimed to have identified potential annual savings of £1,328 million of which £662 million had been achieved. Radford claims that these savings were taken into account by the Department of the Environment when deciding funding levels for local authorities. He also comments that it is unclear how some of the levels of savings are arrived at and that the extrapolation of results sometimes appears to be over-optimistic.

The main criticism of the comparative approach is that it gives too much emphasis to cost cutting – through its ability to single out authorities spending over the 'family average'. It emphasises economy and efficiency rather than effectiveness. There are also problems concerning the comparability of the data; of ensuring that they reflect local circumstances and the quality of services provided. A further difficulty is that the approach can be interpreted as encroaching on policy: for example, high spending may be the result of a policy decision, say, to subsidise school meals.

Despite these limitations the benchmarking approach does offer benefits which could usefully be extended to other organisations, such as benefit offices, which are currently audited by the NAO but which do not appear subject to comparative analysis. It is, however, debatable whether this is a role for the auditor; ideally management should now take over quality exchange clubs and thereby take responsibility for its own performance.

Quality audit

During the 1990s customer satisfaction has become central to management philosophy in the public sector. The quality approach focuses on results and on controlling the quality of output in place of bureaucratic controls which prescribe how things are done (Coote, 1994). Customer choice is encouraged through enhanced competition – customers reject shoddy goods and shop elsewhere, so providers must either mend their ways or go out of business. Consumers are empowered by giving them a right to information, a complaints system and means of redress.

Concern with the customer perspective has affected audit in two ways: first, by using customer satisfaction levels to evaluate successful performance – for example, the National Audit Office explains in its 1993 annual report (1993d, p. 22) that 'Our studies have to develop particular methods for measuring the quality of service achieved . . . Frequently we have carried out our own surveys to find out what users think of the services they receive and how these might be improved.' The NAO used this approach to examine the quality of service offered by national museums and art galleries (NAO, 1993f) and the quality of NHS catering services (NAO, 1994b). The latter study undertook a survey of patient opinions and commissioned food experts to assess aspects of nutrition, presentation and health and safety. These reports appear similar to a *Which?* guide but are less useful to the 'consumer'. In the case of the museum report they illustrate that 'quality' and 'customer satisfaction' are transient – popular is frequently equated with good value and quality. The Audit Commission (1991c) developed a questionnaire to allow hospitals to measure quality for day surgery. However, it concentrates on the superficial aspects of the patients' experience, such as the availability of information about treatment, rather than the overall success of the treatment.

The second potential effect would be to involve the auditor in verifying information which is provided on quality assurance. The approach is well illustrated in the Commission's discussion document (1992) on its role in quality assurance in health care. The Commission proposed a variety of ways in which it could help in the quality assurance process. The proposals included the prioritising of the patient perspective and developing tools (such as questionnaires and analysis software) for use by NHS practitioners in assessing quality. The second set of proposals was more ambitious: it was suggested that the Commission could set itself up as a quality assurance accreditation agency. The proposal was ruled out 'at this stage' as it was acknowledged that to do so might compromise independence. A further proposal was that the Commission should 'publish performance league tables' for clinical and non-clinical areas – similar to its role in relation to the local authorities – but in the event the NHS indicators were defined by the Department of Health with advice from the Commission.

The use of a customer-focused approach to quality in the public sector has been criticised because it has been argued that as services are often free and choice is restricted there is often no straightforward causal link between customer satisfaction and organisational success. Indeed, if customer satisfaction leads to increased demand, rather than adding to the success of the providing organisation by boosting business and profits it can merely add to its troubles, because all the extra demand must be met with the same finite resources (Coote, 1994).

Furthermore, the quality approach has tended, so far, to involve consumerism and to relate to consumers in their capacity as service users. The relationships are actually more complex; for example, 'customers' are not the only ones who matter in schools – children, parents and employers must all be considered. As well as being interested in quality at the point of service, as citizens, they are also interested in impact on the wider community in the longer term. The narrow, individualistic concept is particularly inappropriate for human welfare services. In addition, the boundary between producer and user is not absolute: for example, education requires participation by the consumer and some consumers, such as prisoners or the mentally ill, may be reluctant to receive service (Black, 1994). Choice can also be illusory, as with hospitals in cases of accident or emergency; therefore the information provided by the auditor may be of little value if no choice is available or if customers are reluctant or unable to shop around. The audit approach to quality is still evolving, and auditors need to consider whether they can add to the information already produced by management and by consumer organisations or whether their role is best fulfilled by continuing to act as watchdogs for consumers/citizens/taxpayers through their other VFM approaches.

DISCUSSION

The differences in the six approaches discussed above can be explained, in part, by the need to adjust to a variety of circumstances. They may, however, also be due to the absence of general agreement about the purpose of VFM audit. If this is the case then VFM auditing fails its own first principle of clarifying objectives. The analysis of the variety of approaches reveals that there is no consensus as to why VFM audits are undertaken, who they are for or the methodology which should be employed.

Purpose

Objectives of the audit range from providing information for public accountability through to helping management. In the USA the General

Accounting Office (1988) sees VFM auditing as providing information which is wanted and needed to hold government agencies accountable. In the UK also, the NAO (1988, p. 8) carries out VFM audits predominantly for accountability purposes, 'to provide parliament with independent information, assurance and advice about economy, efficiency and effectiveness', although it has a secondary objective (NAO, 1992c, Section C1.9) helping audited bodies to improve their performance. By contrast, the Audit Commission (1993d, p. 15) interprets its main role as being to help management – 'to identify scope for improvements in economy, efficiency, and effectiveness and to use good practice as a lever to the not so good'.

For whom?

The question of purpose is linked to whom the report is aimed at. The NAO reports to Parliament via the Public Accounts Committee (PAC); by contrast, the Audit Commission national reports are for multiple audiences: central government, local authority members, local authority chief officers, professional bodies, the media and the general public. However, the VFM reports on individual local authorities are not available to the general public and are targeted primarily at chief officers and committee members. The target audience must influence the type of approach taken: if there is no mechanism for reinforcing the auditor's recommendations he or she must rely on persuading management. Linked to the constitutional tradition of reporting to the PAC is the practice of the NAO 'clearing' its findings with the government departments referred to in the reports. The rationale for this is that when the departmental accounting officer gives evidence at the subsequent PAC meeting the facts are not in dispute. Audit Commission reports are generally not evidential in nature, and although it consults various groups in preparing the reports it does not have to agree its findings with those bodies.

Methodology

There are further differences in the way the VFM audit is undertaken, the main distinguishing feature being whether or not the activity is an 'audit' and therefore conducted in accordance with auditing standards. In most cases the legislation does not use the word 'audit'; the terms 'study', 'review', 'investigation' or 'examination' tend to be used in its place. In practice many VFM investigations are conducted as audits. The US General Accounting Office first issued standards for VFM audits in 1972, INTOSAI has agreed international standards and, in Canada, the Public Sector Accounting and Auditing Committee issued standards in 1988. In the UK the NAO issued standards in 1988, and an Assistant Auditor General (Dewar, 1989, p. 4) claims: 'All examinations, however wide ranging, remain audit based. This requires the information obtained and evidence gathered to be verified for accuracy, sufficiency, reliability and relevance and in support of reported findings and conclusions.'

Sources of evidence are typically interviews, questionnaires, management information and expert studies. The need for an audit-based approach bears some relation to the reason the VFM review is undertaken – if it is to hold people accountable reliable evidence is required; if it is to identify good practice to improve management the same standards need not apply. The Audit Commission, therefore, does not conduct its national reviews as audits. A further dimension concerns how the results of investigations are reported. A direct report or attestation which serves the accountability relationship may merit the title 'audit' but those activities which assist management, for example advice on management information systems, may be better classed as consultancy.

THE FUTURE OF VALUE FOR MONEY AUDITING

The future of VFM auditing is at a crossroads. The environment within which public sector audit is operating is undergoing significant changes and the precise role of audit in the changing public sector is far from clear. The recent changes increase the need for government auditors to address the questions raised above and pose additional questions such as whether VFM auditing should be increased or reduced, whether it requires better planning and co-ordination, whether more VFM audit should be contracted out and whether VFM audit can be undertaken only if it demonstrably 'adds value'.

More of less?

The contracting out of many public services to the private sector and the growth of non-departmental public bodies, to which audit access may be limited, have reinforced doubts about the adequacy of the arrangements for the scope and power of audit and have led to suggestions that it should be increased. However, developments such as the audit of management representations give auditors a more 'arm's length' role in VFM. Perhaps the auditors have completed their task of enabling managers to take responsibility for VFM – can they now withdraw from VFM audit? Do changes in public sector management require less 'invasive' audit approaches?

At the same time, the aspects of public accountability which have attracted most public concern are those of probity and financial control rather than VFM. A recent Public Accounts Committee report (1994, p. v) warned: 'In recent years we have seen and reported on a number of serious failures in administrative and financial systems and controls within departments and other public bodies, which have led to money being wasted or otherwise improperly spent.' These failings were first identified through the work of the National Audit Office and they underline the importance of the need for traditional forms of public audit, including VFM audits like those described above under 'Review of management systems, arrangements and procedures'.

More co-ordination?

Where a programme is dependent on the performance of a number of agencies is the audit coverage sufficiently integrated? It is questionable how well the auditors work together to assess the impact of policies (Bowerman, 1994). For example, the national curriculum was developed by central government but implemented by local government and grant-maintained schools – the 'whole picture' has not been the subject of a VFM audit. More co-ordination would therefore seem essential in order to allow auditors successfully to undertake an audit of the success of the project, such as discussed above in 'The value for money procedures audit' and 'Policy audit'.

More contracting out?

While the need for accountability has increased, the monitoring of some publicly funded bodies has reduced. Schools, the former polytechnics, colleges of further education, and training and enterprise councils have all been removed from regular scrutiny by public sector auditors. They have been replaced by private sector auditors, often with no mandatory remit to review VFM and working to different expectations of accountability. Their reports are to appointed boards or supervisory departments and not to Parliament or the public. While there is still limited scope for public sector auditors to undertake VFM work, it is made difficult as they are not in routine contact with such bodies – there is a danger that an accountability gap may emerge. The Audit Commission's 1993 annual report (1993a) highlights the risk of reduced monitoring and warns of 'enormous' potential for waste in schools opted out of local authority control. Increasingly too, the audit bodies are required to compete for government audits; for example, in New Zealand almost 40% of government audit work is competitively tendered. Cameron (1995, p. 14) explains the rationale for this as being to improve the 'demonstrated efficiency and value for money in the conduct of audits' and to 'provide a clear business focus and a customer orientated approach'. The risk here is that the auditor is encouraged to regard the audited body, rather than the citizen, as the customer. As has happened in the private sector, this could lead to an unwillingness to upset the 'customer' for fear of losing the audit.

Adding value?

The emergence of competitive tendering for government audits and events such as the elimination of the Auditor General's Office in California (Thompson, 1993) have encouraged scrutiny of the costs and benefits of VFM auditing. This has resulted in the audit bodies seeking to demonstrate 'added value', for example by showing that the resultant savings will outweigh the cost of the audit. The NAO points out in its 1994 annual report (1994c) that its investigations during the year led to £229 million in VFM savings, £7 for every £1 of cost. It also reminds readers that it adds value by making positive, constructive recommendations for improvement. Producing reports which are useful to management is therefore also an important dimension of value added.

If auditors concentrate solely on detecting savings and being helpful to managers, there is a danger that they may lose sight of some of their other functions and their independence could be impaired. The NAO has been under pressure to abandon complex studies, particularly those on effectiveness, which are less likely to have a direct practical impact and are therefore difficult to demonstrate that they 'add value'. Radford (1991, p. 918) points to the curious relationship which the Audit Commission has with local authorities, 'acting both as an independent watchdog, with all the powers of inspection and enforcement which that entails, and at the same time as professional advisors, seeking to assist and serve their "clients" who pay for their services'. Day and Klein (1990, p. 113) describe the Audit Commission as 'a policeman constantly tempted to turn consultant'.

CONCLUSION

The discussion above suggests that VFM auditing may be in decline in the UK. The 'policy' audits of the late 1980s have been largely abandoned in favour of 'management arrangements', 'representations' or 'quality' audits. This movement corresponds with what Power (1995, p. 10) describes as the 'drift away from inspection to certification'. He contends (ibid.): 'In general, certification is a dependent, systems orientated, generalist practice which produces comfort certificates at acceptable cost. In contrast, inspection centred audit practices are independent, output orientated, specialist practices which are, potentially, adversarial but which are relatively costly.' As Power suggests, cost could be a major influence in the move towards a more certification-style VFM audit; other possible influences are the 'urge' to standardise audit approaches, to avoid provoking political controversy and to appear as 'client orientated' in the increasingly competitive public sector audit market.

The fundamental question which government auditors need to consider is whether VFM audit primarily for management or for the public. Most public sector external audit organisations have a tradition of reporting to the public and so to do otherwise will undermine their function and independence and could create a public sector expectations gap. If public accountability is the primary objective of VFM auditing the process may benefit from being adversarial as opposed to 'adding value'. This also requires auditors to report directly on their evaluation of an organisation's performance rather than a bland opinion resulting from the management representations audit. To forgo a consulting role need not mean that public bodies are deprived of the auditor's valuable advice; this can be given in a more arm's length manner than as a direct service to management.

VFM audit has lost its way; it needs to rediscover its accountability roots. It needs to be clear that its first duty is to the public and that added value to the public comes from knowing that the auditors are doing their job as watchdogs and not as consultants.

Notes

1. Examples quoted in Radford (1991).
2. Audit Commission Report and Accounts for year ending 31 March 1989, quoted in Radford (1991, p. 926).

References

Audit Commission (undated) *Auditing Local Government – A Guide to the Work of the Audit Commission*, Audit Commission, London.
Audit Commission (1986) *Making a Reality of Community Care*, HMSO, London.
Audit Commission (1988) *The Competitive Council*, HMSO, London.
Audit Commission (1989a) *More Equal than Others: The Chief Executive in Local Government*, HMSO, London.
Audit Commission (1989b) *Urban Regeneration and Economic Development – The Local Government Dimension*, HMSO, London.
Audit Commission (1991a) *The Administration of Community Charge: Some Longer Term Considerations*, Audit Commission, London.
Audit Commission (1991b) *How Effective Is the Audit Commission?*, Audit Commission, London.
Audit Commission (1991c) *Measuring Quality: The Patient's View of Day Surgery*, NHS Occasional Paper No. 3, HMSO, London.
Audit Commission (1992) *Minding the Quality: A Consultation Document on the Role of the Audit Commission in Quality Assurance in Health Care*, Audit Commission, London.
Audit Commission (1993a) *Annual Report 1993*, Audit Commission, London.
Audit Commission (1993b) *Untapped Savings: Water Services in the NHS*, NHS Occasional Paper No. 5, HMSO, London.
Audit Commission (1993c) *Unfinished Business: Full-Time Educational Courses for 16–19 Year Olds*, HMSO, London.
Audit Commission (1993d) *Adding Value – Strategy*, Audit Commission, London.
Auditor General of Canada (1992) *Report of the Auditor General of Canada to the House of Commons 1992*, Ottawa.
Berggren, G. R. (1981) Effectiveness auditing in Sweden, in B. Geist (ed.), *State Audit: Developments in Public Accountability*, Macmillan, London.
Black, S. (1994) What does the Citizens' Charter mean?, in A. Conner and S. Black (eds.), *Performance Review and Quality in Social Care*, Jessica Kingsley, London, pp. 215–28.
Bowerman, M. (1994) The National Audit Office and the Audit Commission: co-operation in areas where their VFM responsibilities interface, *Financial Accountability and Management*, Vol. 10, no. 1, pp. 47–64.
Bowerman M. (1995) Auditing performance indicators: the role of the Audit Commission in the Citizens' Charter initiative, *Financial Accountability and Management*, Vol. 11, no. 2, pp. 171–84.
Brown, R. E., Gallagher, T. P. and Williams, M. C. (1991) Auditing performance in government, in Frieberg *et al.* (1991), pp. 185–95.
Butt, H. A. and Plamer, D. R. (1985) *Value for Money in the Public Sector*, Basil Blackwell, London.

Cameron, J. W. (1995) Public service reform: the auditor's perspective, *International Journal of Government Auditing*, Vol. 22, no. 1, pp. 14–17.

Canadian Comprehensive Auditing Foundation (1987) *Effectiveness Reporting and Auditing in the Public Sector*, CCAF, Ottawa.

Coote, A. (1994) Performance and quality in public services, in A. Conner and S. Black (eds.), *Performance Review and Quality in Social Care*, Jessica Kingsley, London, pp. 200–14.

Dalton, N. (1993) Non-financial performance measures – a challenge in local government, *Accountants Journal of The New Zealand Society of Accountants*, Vol. 72, no. 3, pp. 64–7.

Day, P. and Klein, R. (1990) *Inspecting the Inspectorates*, Joseph Rowntree Memorial Trust, London.

Dewar, D. (1989) Value for money audit in the National Audit Office, *Internal Auditing* (October), pp. 2–5.

Frieberg, A., Geist, B., Mizrah, N. and Sharkansky, I. (eds.) (1991) *State Audit and Accountability: A Book of Readings*, Israel State Comptroller's Office, Jerusalem.

Geist, B. (1991) Auditing government policies, in Freiberg *et al.* (1991), pp. 101–9.

Geist, B. and Mizrahi, N. (1991) State audit: principles and concepts, in Frieberg *et al.* (1991). *Government Auditing Standards*, pp. 16–41.

General Accounting Office (1988) *Standards for Audit Programs, Activities and Functions*, US General Accounting Office, Washington.

The *Guardian* (1994) Terminological in-exactitude? (14 December), p. 22.

Henkel, M. (1991) *Government, Evaluation and Change*, Jessica Kingsley, London.

INTOSAI/United Nations (1977) *Public Sector Audit Standards*, United Nations Secretariat, New York.

Magill, J. (1994) *Statement by Mr John Magill the Appointed Auditor for Westminster City Council*, Touche Ross & Co., London.

National Audit Office (1988) *A Framework for Value for Money Audits*, NAO, London.

National Audit Office (1991a) *Helping the Nation Spend Wisely*, NAO, London.

National Audit Office (1991b) *Annual Report, National Audit Office 1991*, NAO, London.

National Audit Office (1992a) *Cervical and Breast Screening in England*, HC236 (1992/3), HMSO, London.

National Audit Office (1992b) *The Sale of the Twelve Regional Electricity Companies*, HC10 (1992/3), HMSO, London.

National Audit Office (1992c) *Audit Manual*, NAO, London.

National Audit Office (1993a) *The Management of Sickness Absence in the Inland Revenue*, HC676 (1992/3), HMSO, London.

National Audit Office (1993b) *Ministry of Defence: The Costs and Receipts Arising from the Gulf Conflict*, HC299 (1992/3), HMSO, London.

National Audit Office (1993c) *Ministry of Defence: Movements of Personnel, Equipment and Stores to and from the Gulf*, HC693 (1992/3), HMSO, London.

National Audit Office (1993d) *Annual Report 1993*, NAO, London.

National Audit Office (1993e) *Pergau Hydro-Electric Project*, HC908 (1993/4), HMSO, London.

National Audit Office (1993f) *Department of National Heritage, National Museums and Galleries: Quality of Service to the Public*, HC841 (1992/3), HMSO, London.

National Audit Office (1994a) *Ministry of Defence: Management of Telephones*, HC637 (1993/4), HMSO, London.

National Audit Office (1994b) *National Health Service: Hospital Catering in England*, HC329 (1993/4), HMSO, London.

National Audit Office (1994c) *Annual Report, National Audit Office 1994*, NAO, London.

Normanton, E. L. (1966) *The Accountability and Audit of Governments,* Manchester University Press, Manchester.

Pallot, J. (1991) Accounting, auditing and accountability, in J. Boston *et al.* (eds.), *Reshaping the State,* Oxford University Press, pp. 198–232.

Pallot, J. (1992) Local authority reporting – major advances made, *Accountants' Journal of the New Zealand Society of Accountants* (August), pp. 46–9.

Power, M. (1994) *The Audit Explosion,* DEMOS Paper No. 7, London.

Power, M. (1995) Audit and the decline of inspection. Paper given at the CIPFA Annual Conference, 14 June.

Price Waterhouse (1990) *Value for Money Auditing – The Investigation of Economy, Efficiency and Effectiveness,* Gee and Co., London.

Public Accounts Committee (1994) *The Proper Conduct of Public Business,* Eighth Report 1993/4, HMSO, London.

Radford, M. (1991) Auditing for change: local government and the Audit Commission, *Modern Law Review,* Vol. 54 (6 November), pp. 912–32.

Sharkansky, I. (1991) The auditor as policy maker, in Frieberg *et al.* (1991), pp. 74–94.

Sharkansky, I. (1991) The development of state audit, in Frieberg *et al.* (1991), pp. 1–13.

Swedish Ministry of Finance – Budget Department (1995) *Annual Performance Accounting and Auditing in Sweden,* Swedish Ministry of Finance, Stockholm.

Thompson, K. (1993) Elimination of the Auditor General's Office in California: are there national implications?, *Government Accountants Journal,* Vol. XLII, no. 1, pp. 37–40.

White, F., Harden, I. and Donnelly, K. (1994) Audit, accounting officers and accountability: the Pergau dam affair, *Public Law* (Winter), pp. 526–34.

Index

accountability, 171–2, 176–7, 190–1, 200, 205, 207–9
accountability (Stewart's ladder of), 171
Accounting Standards, 19–33
Accounting Standards Board (ASB), 4, 8–9, 11, 14, 16, 21–33, 184
Accounting Standards Steering Committee, 7, 21
Accounts Commission, 5, 195
activity-based costing (ABC), 5, 87–93, 104
activity-based cost management (ABCM), 87–93
aggregation, 13, 15, 26, 40, 50, 122
ailing firms, 36–9
ambiguity, 167–9
Amtrak, 121
arbitrariness, 154, 159, 164
assets, 20, 22–33, 35–9, 40–50, 55–6, 103, 114, 139–41, 146, 183, 185–6
Association of British Insurers (ABI), 52
audit, 77–85, 133–6, 194–211
Audit Commission, 5, 166, 194, 196, 198–9, 201–4, 206–10
audit policy, 4, 6
Auditing Practices Board (APB), 20, 77, 79–80, 85
Auditing Practices Committee, 80
Auditor General of Canada, 197–9

Baiman, S., 139–41
balance sheet, 4, 8–12, 14–15, 19, 23–8, 32–3, 184, 189
Baxter, W. T., 28, 185
BCCI, 77
Beattie, V., 78–9, 81
Beckers, S., 74, 169
benchmarking, 203–4
Black, F., 53, 56, 61–2, 74
bottlenecks, 96, 98–102, 104

Bourn, M., 117, 142
Bowerman, M., 201, 208
British Rail, 120–2, 127
bus companies, 6, 180–91

Cadbury Report, 52, 74, 77
Campbell, B., 187, 190
Canadian Comprehensive Auditing Foundation, 200
capacity, 96–9, 102
cash flow, 14–15, 25
CCAB, 79
central government, 110, 172, 181–2, 195–6, 198–200, 206–8
change, 18, 147, 168
checklist management, 115–18
choice, 205–6, 209
Citizens' Charter, 5, 110, 121, 125, 129, 172
clan control, 137, 141–2, 146, 150
Clarke, J., 166–7
commercialisation, 117–18, 180
community, 8, 205
Companies Acts, 24
comprehensive income, 11
conceptual framework, 185–6
conceptual statements, 18–33
Confederation of British Industry (CBI), 73, 87
consumerism, 177, 205
consumption, 167
contacts, 8, 138–4, 149–51
Cooper, R., 87–8
Coote, A., 204–5
Copeland, T. E., 56, 61, 74
The Corporate Report, 7–8
cost drivers, 5, 88–9, 92, 104
cost effectiveness, 70–1, 78
cost layering, 88
cost pools, 88, 90, 92

Cox, J., 95–6
culture, 110, 117, 137, 141, 144–5, 154
current value, 35–6

Darlington, J., 96, 98
Dearing Committee, 21
deferral, 28–9
departmental boundaries, 90–3
depoliticisation, 172, 176
depreciation, 37
deprival value (DV), 36–9
deregulation, 180–2, 185
Dewar, D., 193, 206
DHSS, 122–4, 141, 150, 205
directors, 52–74
discounted cash flow (DCF), 36–7
Dreyfus, S., 42, 48–9

economic calculation, 181
economic order quantities (EOQs), 97
economic value, 36, 38–9
economy, efficiency and effrectiveness
    (the three Es), 6, 111–15, 129,
    131–4, 166, 175, 177, 180, 194–5,
    199, 202–3, 206
Edwards, J. S. S., 12–13
effectiveness, 25, 129–36, 166, 173,
    175–6, 190, 201, 209
efficiency, 6, 97–100, 102, 110–15,
    126–7, 166, 170, 173, 175–7, 190
Egginton, D. A., 8, 73–4
environment, 8, 184, 186–7, 198
Ernst and Young, 15
ethics, 18, 80–1
executive share options (ESO), 4, 52–74
expense, 20, 24
external auditing, 194, 209
external reporting, 180, 184–5, 190
Ezzamel, M., 117, 138, 140, 142–6,
    150–1

failure, company, 77
Fearnley, S., 78–9, 81
Fédération des Experts Comptables
    Européens (FEE), 111, 113
Finance Acts, 73–4
Financial Accounting Standards Board
    (FASB), 20–2, 24–5, 28–9, 52, 69,
    185
financial statements, 4, 7–16
    elements of, 22
    summary measures of performance,
        10–14
    and time, 8–10
    users and uses, 7–8

Forker, J. J., 8, 73–4
Foster, T. W., 56–7, 61
'free form' audits, 77, 82–3, 85

Galloway, D., 96–7, 99–100
Garrett Automotive, 96
gearing, 14
General Accounting Office (GAO), 194,
    205–6
global performance measures, 11,
    113–14, 126, 175
Goldratt, E., 95–7, 104
'good housekeeping', 196
goodwill, 12, 185
governance
    corporate, 52, 69, 83
    in the NHS, 137–51
    participative, 176
Green Paper 1978, 8

Harte, G. 180, 183–4, 187, 189, 190
Hemmer, T., 56, 61, 65
Hines, R., 185–6
Hoel, P., 41, 46
Hong Kong and Shanghai Bank, 74
Hopwood, A., 180–1

IBM, 12
ICAI, 80
ICAS, 77, 80
illiquidity, 56–7, 65, 69, 71, 74
image-building, 78–9
incentives, 61, 69, 74, 84
'indignation factor', 135–6
inflation, 27
Innes, J., 82, 87–8, 96, 101
innovation, 137–8, 146–50
'inside information', 64
instantaneous expected returns, 40–1,
    44–6
Institute of Chartered Accountants in
    England and Wales, 21, 80, 83
Institute of Directors, 74
intention, 30
International Accounting Standards
    Committee, 21
INTOSAI, 194, 206
inventory, 95–104
Issitt, M., 169–70, 177

Jackson, P., 115–16, 118, 175
Jennergren, L. P., 56, 61
joint costs, 153–64
Joint Monitoring Unit (JMU), 80–1. 85
jointness, 38

Jones, T. C., 98, 176
just in time (JIT), 104

Kay, J. A., 12–13
Keat, R., 144–5
Koogler, P. R., 56–7, 61

Langan, M., 166–7
Lapsley, I., 120–1, 137–8, 140–3, 145–6, 149–50, 171
Layfield Report, 202
Law, A., 42
Lazonick, W., 138, 146–9
Lev, B., 44–6
liabilities, 20, 22–33, 183, 186
Likierman, A., 115–16, 118
litigation, 78, 81, 84
Littleton, A. C., 19, 32
Livingstone, J. L., 74
Llewellyn, S., 171, 174
local government, 5, 172, 175, 182, 184, 187, 189, 194, 196, 199, 201–3, 205–6, 208–9
London Transport, 120
long term(ism), 52–3
loss, 29–30

Main, B. G. M., 56, 76
management, 6, 8, 91, 109–11, 115–22, 124–7, 129–30, 135, 146, 155–64, 171, 175, 181, 184, 193–9, 200–2, 205–9
manufacturing, 87–93, 95–104, 153–64
market reforms, 137
markets and hierarchies (M&H), 143–5
matching, 24–32, 173
material distortion, 29
Matsunaga, S., 56, 61, 65
Mayer, C. P., 12–13
Mayston, D. J., 11, 113–15
Merton, R., 40, 42
Midland Bank, 74
Midwinter, A., 174, 180
Mitchell, F., 87–8, 96, 101, 171
models, microeconomic, 40–50
Moizer, P., 77–9, 81
monitoring, 80–1, 85, 139, 141, 171–2, 180, 208
Monopolies and Mergers Commission, 190
Morgan, G., 185–6, 190
motivation, 53, 60, 70–1, 74, 97, 146, 149

Naslund, B., 56, 61

National Association of Pension Funds (NAPF), 52
National Audit Office, 111–13, 193–4, 196–8, 200, 204, 206–9
nationlisation, 110, 118–22
Neimark, M., 181, 184
net realisable value (NRV), 36, 38
'new institutional economics', 139
New Zealand Audit Office, 201
NHS, 5–6, 117–18, 122–7, 133, 137–51, 153–64, 198, 203–5
'noise', 114
non-financial measures, 89, 91–3, 127, 183–4, 190
non-monetary assets, 19
Normanton, E. L., 193–4, 197

operating expenses/costs, 95–6, 99, 101–3
opportunity cost, 37, 155
option pricing model (OPM), 56–7, 61–2, 65–9, 71, 74
O'Reilley, C. A. III, 56
organisational design, 138, 148
overheads, 87–90, 93, 104, 114

Pallot, J., 194, 200–1
Paterson, R., 15, 19, 28
Paton, W. A., 19, 32–3
Peasnell, K. V., 9
performance audit, 194–5
performance indicators, 109–27, 175, 180, 189–90, 201
Perkin, H., 167–8
Plamer, D. A., 196
policy audit, 133–4, 195, 199–200, 209
Port, S., 41, 46
Power, M., 193, 209
presentation, 23
Price Waterhouse, 196
private sector, 1–104
privatisation, 6, 13, 111, 127, 130, 142, 181–3, 186–7, 190–1, 199
productivity, 138, 146, 148, 150, 167, 182, 190, 197
professionalism, 168–70, 177–8
profit (as a measure of effectiveness), 10–11, 130–1
profit and loss account, 8–11, 15, 20, 23–4, 27, 30, 32, 184, 189
Public Accounts Committee, 122, 194, 197, 206–7
public sector, 3–7, 107–210

quality audit, 195–6, 204–5, 209

quality control, 181–2
quality of service, 174, 202, 204–5

Radford, M., 199, 203, 209
railways, 5, 120–2, 127
rates of return, 12–13
ratios, 4, 7, 9, 11–14, 40–50, 99–101,
    103, 113, 119, 174
rebalancing, 44–7
recognition, 23
regularity, 194
regulation, 13, 119–20, 138, 180–2,
    186
relevance, 22
replacement cost (RC), 36–9
return on investment (ROI), 103
revaluation, 35–6
revenue, 20, 24
reward, 153–4
risk, 40–50, 54, 56, 143, 148, 167
Royal Mail Steam Packet, 24

sales value, 155, 157, 159–62
Sandilands Report, 11
Scholes, M., 53, 56, 61–2, 74
Securities Exchange Commission (SEC),
    52, 74
Seebohm Report, 168–9
self-assurance, 29–31
Sharkansky, I., 195, 199
Shevlin, T., 56, 61, 65
short term(ism), 4, 9–10, 52, 54, 70, 101,
    103, 130
Sibeon, R., 169–70
Simunic, D. A., 78, 82
Sleeman, J., 181–2
social services, 5, 166–78
Solomons, D., 11, 21
Sprouse, R. T., 28, 33
stability, 183
standardisation, 4, 171–3, 209
standard-setting, 18–33, 78–80, 84–5
Stevenson, O., 170, 178
stewardship, 22
Stewart, H., 153–4
Stewart, J. D., 167–8, 170–1, 175, 177,
    190
    ladder of accountability, 171
Stock Exchange, 16

Stone, C., 41, 46
Storey, R. K., 19, 20
Swedish Ministry of Finance, 201–2

tableaux de bord, 5, 90–3
tax, 54, 65–9, 71, 73
technical change, 47, 138, 147–8, 161
Tehranian, H., 53
tenure, 55–8, 70–1
theory of constraints (TOC), 5, 95–104
theory of the firm, 40–3
Thomas, A. L., 154–5, 157, 185
throughput, 95–6, 98–103, 123, 148, 173
time, 40, 43–5, 47, 54–55, 96, 99
Tinker, T., 181, 184, 186
Tippett, M. J., 8, 40–1, 44–7, 50, 74
Titmuss, R. M., 153, 168
total quality management (TQM), 104
Touche Ross, 82, 84
transaction cost economics (TCE),
    137–41, 150
Transport Act 1985, 180, 182–5
Travlos, N. G., 53
The Treasury, 110, 120
Trueblood Report, 7

undeterminism, 190
users, 22–3, 26–7, 31, 78, 81, 83, 135,
    186, 207
utilities, 13, 127, 199

value added, 89, 92, 174, 208–9
value for money (VFM), 111–13, 121–2,
    129–36, 166, 170, 180, 193–210
verification, 141, 185, 201
Vickrey, D., 56–7, 61
voluntary lapsing, 54–5

Waldron, D., 96–7, 99–100
Walsh, K., 167, 175, 190
Weston, J. F., 56, 61, 74
White, P. R., 181, 184
Whittington, G., 13, 40, 79, 185
Williams, A., 125–6
Williamson, O. E., 57, 139, 141, 148
Willmott, H., 138, 140, 143–6, 150–1
Wilson, G., 167, 174
Woodward, M., 169–70, 177
writing down, 35–9